A SKETCH

OF

ANCIENT PHILOSOPHY

FROM THALES TO CICERO.

CAMBRIDGE
UNIVERSITY PRESS

University Printing House, Cambridge CB2 8BS, United Kingdom

Cambridge University Press is part of the University of Cambridge.

It furthers the University's mission by disseminating knowledge in the pursuit of
education, learning and research at the highest international levels of excellence.

www.cambridge.org
Information on this title: www.cambridge.org/9781316626061

© Cambridge University Press 1881

First published 1881
First paperback edition 2016

A catalogue record for this publication is available from the British Library

ISBN 978-1-316-62606-1 Paperback

Pitt Press Series.

A SKETCH

OF

ANCIENT PHILOSOPHY

FROM THALES TO CICERO

BY

JOSEPH B. MAYOR, M.A.

PROFESSOR OF MORAL PHILOSOPHY AT KING'S COLLEGE,
FORMERLY FELLOW AND TUTOR OF ST JOHN'S
COLLEGE, CAMBRIDGE.

EDITED FOR THE SYNDICS OF THE UNIVERSITY PRESS.

Cambridge:
AT THE UNIVERSITY PRESS.

London: CAMBRIDGE WAREHOUSE, 17, Paternoster Row.
Cambridge: DEIGHTON, BELL AND CO.
Leipzig: F. A. BROCKHAUS.
1881

TABLE OF CONTENTS.

---

[1] Ritter in his *History of Ancient Philosophy* employs the terms Dynamical and Mechanical to distinguish the view which regards the universe as one great organism with an inherent power of movement and change, from that which regards it as a result of forces acting upon a number of independent elements.

B. SOCRATES TO ARISTOTLE.

PHILOSOPHY OF NATURE AND MAN.

[1] This is not a recognized title, but merely used here for the sake of convenience.

[2] Diogenes, as explained in the body of the work, is re-actionary, approaching more nearly to the earlier Ionic philosophers.

PREFACE.

THE readers whom I have chiefly had in my mind, in writing the following sketch of Ancient Philosophy, are Undergraduates at the University or others who are commencing the study of the philosophical works of Cicero or Plato or Aristotle in the original language. It has been my wish to supply to them, what I remember vainly seeking when I was in their position, something which may help them to find their bearings in the new world into which they are plunged on first making acquaintance with such books as Cicero's *De Finibus* or the *Republic* of Plato. The only helps which I had in similar circumstances some thirty years ago were a translation of Schleiermacher's *Introduction to the Dialogues of Plato*, of which I could make nothing, and Lewes' small *Biographical History of Philosophy*, of which the aim, as far as I could judge, was to show that, as philosophy was moonshine, it was mere waste of time to read what the philosophers had written. Things have changed since then. The noblest defence of ancient philosophy which has ever appeared, is contained in the chapters on the

Sophists and Socrates written by one, who might have
been supposed to be himself more or less a sympathizer
with Lewes, and in the elaborate examination of the speculations of the Ancients contained in the same Author's
Plato and *Aristotle.* During the same interval the charm
and the wit and the irony of Plato have for the first time
been made intelligible to English readers by Mr Jowett's
admirable translations; and the excellent German his-
tories of philosophy by Zeller, Ueberweg and Schwegler
have been translated into English. None of these
however, nor any others which might be named, seem to
me exactly to meet the wants of the case. They are too
long, too full, too hard, too abstract, or too vague, for a
first sketch. What is wanted is something to combine
conciseness with accuracy and clearness, something
which will be easy and interesting to readers of ordinary
intelligence, and will leave no doubt in their minds as to
the author's meaning. It is for others to judge how far
this object has been accomplished in the present book,
which is the outcome of various courses of lectures
delivered on the same subject during the last quarter
of a century.

But, though I write in the first instance for Classical
scholars, and have therefore thought myself at liberty to
quote the original Greek and Latin, wherever it seemed
expedient to do so; I am not without hopes that what I
have written may be found interesting and useful by
educated readers generally, not merely as an introduction
to the formal history of philosophy, but as supplying a

key to our present ways of thinking and judging in regard to matters of the highest importance. For Greece is in everything the starting-point of modern civilization. Homer is not more the fountain-head of Western poetry, than Socrates of Western philosophy. Allowing as much as we will to Semitic and Teutonic influences, it remains true that for Art and Science and Law, for the Philosophy of thought and of action, nay even for Theology itself, as far as the form is concerned, we are mainly indebted to Greece, and to Rome as the interpreter of Greece. Even that which we call 'common sense' consists of little more than the worn fragments of older systems of thought, just as the common soil of our gardens is composed, in great part, of the detritus of primeval rocks.

As we trace backwards the march of civilization, we find extraordinary contrasts in the degrees of progress made in its different departments. In some departments, as for instance in the inductive sciences and in mechanical inventions, the early stages have only a historical value: in others, as in geometry, we still use text-books written two thousand years ago. So in the arts: while in sculpture we despair of approaching Greece, in music we have far surpassed her, and in poetry we may claim equality at least, if not superiority. How stands it with regard to philosophy? Here too we find the same variety. While the fanciful speculations of the ancients as to the constitution and laws of the external universe, have for the most part vanished away before the touch of reality, and given place to the solid edifice of modern physical science; while the loose induction of Socrates and of Aristotle has been reduced in our own day into a definite system of Inductive Logic; while immense additions have thus been made to our knowledge of the external universe and of man as a part of the universe, that is, of the anatomy, the physiology and the habits of the human animal, there has been far less advance in the knowledge of man as a moral and intellectual being. Thus, Deductive Logic remains in its essentials the same as when it was first given to the world by Aristotle, and neither in Psychology nor in Ethics can it be said that the ancient systems have been finally superseded by any generally accepted system of modern times. No doubt many new facts have been observed and new explanations have been offered in reference to such subjects as comparative psychology, the association of ideas, the influence of heredity, the influence of nature on man, the laws of human progress, and so on. Above all, Christianity has imparted a far deeper feeling of the complexity of life, a sense of moral responsibility, of man's weakness and sinfulness, and of the regenerating powers of faith and love, such as was never dreamt of by the ancients. And yet, in spite of all this, is there any modern work of systematic morality which could be compared with Aristotle's *Ethics* for its power of stimulating moral thought? Most moderns appear to write under the consciousness that they are uttering truisms; or, if they escape from this, it is by running off from the main highway of morality into by-paths of psychology or physiology or sociology. Again, they are hampered by the suspicion that whatever concerns moral practice is more impressively and effectively treated of by religion; or else they consign, what, supposing it to be true, is the most important part of morality, to the region of the unknown and unknowable. The ancient moralists knew no such restrictions. Aristotle's, and still more Plato's, theory of conduct was no stale repetition of other men's thoughts; it was the full expression of their own highest aspirations and discoveries in regard to the duty, the hopes, and the destiny of man. And thus there is a freshness and a completeness about the ethics of the Ancients which we seek in vain in the Moderns. Even if it were otherwise, the comparison between pre-Christian and post-Christian systems of morality must always be full of interest and importance in reference to our view of Christianity itself.

One word more as to the general use of the history of philosophy. It was a saying of Democritus that a fool has to be taught everything by his own personal experience, while a wise man draws lessons from the experience of others. History of whatever kind supplies us with the means of thus gaining experience by proxy, and in the history of philosophy above all we have the concentrated essence of all human experience. For the philosopher is, no more than the poet, an isolated phenomenon. As the latter expresses the feeling, so the former expresses in its purest form the thought of his time, summing up the past, interpreting the present, and foreshadowing the future. We might be spared much of crudeness and violence and one-sidedness, if people were aware that what they hold to be the last result of modern enlightenment was perhaps the common-place of 2000 years ago; or, on the other hand, that doctrines or practices which they regard as too sacred for examination are to be traced back, it may be, to a Pagan origin. It is possible to be provincial in regard to time as well as in regard to space; and there is no more mischievous provincialism than that of the man who accepts blindly the fashionable belief, or no-belief, of his particular time, without caring to inquire what were the ideas of the countless generations which preceded, or what are likely to be the ideas of the generations which will follow. However firm may be our persuasion of the Divinely guided progress of our race, the fact of a general forward movement in the stream of history is not inconsistent with all sorts of eddies and retardations at particular points; and before we can be sure that such points are not to be found in our own age, we must have some knowledge of the past development of thought, and have taken the trouble to compare our own ways of thinking and acting with those that have prevailed in other epochs of humanity.

Had space permitted, I should have been glad to have followed the example set by Sir Alexander Grant in his Essays on Aristotle, and shown how the half-conscious morality of the Epic and Gnomic and Lyric poets, and of the early historians, provided the raw material which was afterwards worked up by the philosophers; and again how the results of philosophic thought became in their turn the common property of the educated class, and were transformed into household words by Euripides and the writers of the New Comedy, and still more by the Roman Satirists. But to do this would have swollen the volume to twice its present size, and perhaps it may suffice here to throw out a hint which any Classical scholar may put into practice for himself.

In conclusion I have to return my best thanks to the friends who have helped me by looking over portions of my proof-sheets, especially to my colleague Prof. Warr, to whose suggestion indeed it is mainly owing that a part of the Introduction to my edition of Cicero's *De Natura Deorum* has thus been expanded into a separate work on the History of Ancient Philosophy.

N.B. The references to Zeller are, except when otherwise stated, to the latest German edition, which is denoted by the small numeral following the number of the page. To the books recommended under Aristotle's *Ethics*, p. 100, add a new translation by Mr F. H. Peters, and the Essays V. and VI. contained in Grote's *Fragments on Ethical Subjects.*

May 20, 1881.

Ὅταν γὰρ ἔθνη τὰ μὴ νόμον ἔχοντα φύσει τὰ
τοῦ νόμου ποιῶσιν, οὗτοι νόμον μὴ ἔχοντες ἑαυτοῖς
εἰσὶν νόμος, οἵτινες ἐνδείκνυνται τὸ ἔργον τοῦ νόμου
γραπτὸν ἐν ταῖς καρδίαις αὐτῶν, συμμαρτυρούσης αὐτῶν
τῆς συνειδήσεως καὶ μεταξὺ ἀλλήλων τῶν λογισμῶν
κατηγορούντων ἢ καὶ ἀπολογουμένων.

S. PAUL. *ad Rom.* II. 14, 15.

Διότι τὸ γνωστὸν τοῦ θεοῦ φανερόν ἐστιν ἐν
αὐτοῖς· ὁ θεὸς γὰρ αὐτοῖς ἐφανέρωσεν. τὰ γὰρ ἀόρατα
αὐτοῦ ἀπὸ κτίσεως κόσμου τοῖς ποιήμασιν νοούμενα
καθορᾶται, ἥ τε ἀΐδιος αὐτοῦ δύναμις καὶ θειότης.

Ibid. I. 19, 20.

Ἦν μὲν οὖν πρὸ τῆς τοῦ Κυρίου παρουσίας εἰς
δικαιοσύνην Ἕλλησιν ἀναγκαία φιλοσοφία, νυνὶ δὲ χρησίμη
πρός θεοσεβείαν γίνεται, προπαιδεία τις οὖσα τοῖς τὴν
πίστιν δι' ἀποδείξεως καρπουμένοις.

CLEM. AL. *Strom.* I. c. 5 § 28.

ANCIENT PHILOSOPHY

FROM THALES TO CICERO[1].

GREEK philosophy had its origin not in the mother country, but in the colonies of Asia Minor and Magna Graecia. This is owing partly to the reflectiveness belonging to a more advanced civilization, and partly to the fact that the colonists were brought in contact with the customs and ideas of foreign nations. The philoso-

---

[1] The following works will be found useful by the student. They are arranged in what I consider to be their order of importance. Full references will be found in the two which stand at the head of the list and also in Ueberweg.

Ritter and Preller, *Historia Philosophiae Graecae et Romanae ex fontium locis contexta* (referred to as R. and P. below).

Zeller, *History of Greek Philosophy* (in German. Translations of portions have been published by Longmans).

Grote, *History of Greece*, together with his *Plato* and *Aristotle*.

Grant, *Ethics of Aristotle*, Vol. I. ed. 3.

Ueberweg, *History of Philosophy*, Vol. I. tr. by Morris.

Schwegler, *Hist. of Philosophy*, tr. by Sterling.

Döllinger, *The Gentile and the Jew*, translated by Darnell.

A. Butler, *Lectures on Ancient Philosophy*.

Mullach's *Fragmenta Philosophorum* in Didot's series ought to have been more useful than any of these, but its value is much lessened by the want of discrimination shown in the selection and arrangement of the writers quoted.

phers of the earliest, or Pre-Socratic period, are broadly
divided into the Ionic and the Italic Schools.　Both had
the same object of interest, to ascertain the nature, the
origin, the laws, the destiny of the visible world.　But
while the former, with the Ionic sensitiveness to all outward influences, dwelt more upon the material element itself, and the life which manifested itself in its ever-chang-
ing developments, the latter (who, if not themselves
Dorian, were yet surrounded by Dorian settlers, with
their Doric ideal of discipline, order, stability, superiority
to sense, as opposed to the Ionic ideal of free growth,
of ease, beauty and nature,) turned their thoughts more
to the laws by which the world was governed, or the one
unchanging substance which they believed to underlie its
shifting phenomena.

　　The first name in Greek philosophy is the so-called
founder of the Ionic or physical school, **Thales** of Miletus, a contemporary of Solon (B.C. 640—550), said to be
of Phenician descent.　With him begins the transition
from the mythological to the scientific interpretation of
nature, the transition, as Grote puts it, from the question
Who sends rain, or thunder, or earthquakes, and why
does he send it? to the question What are the antecedent conditions of rain, thunder, or earthquakes? The
old cosmogonies and theogonies suggested the idea of
development under the form of a personal history of
a number of supernatural beings variously related to each
other.　The first parent of all, according to Homer, was
Oceanus (*Il.* XIV. 201, 240), perhaps a nature-myth to be
interpreted of the sun rising and setting in the sea.
Thales stripped him of his personality, and laid down
the proposition that water is the one original substance

out of which all things are produced. Aristotle conjectures that he was led to this belief by observing that moisture is essential to animal and vegetable life: probably it was also from the fact that water supplies the most obvious example of the transmutation of matter under its three forms, solid, fluid and gaseous. Thales further held that the universe is a living creature; which he expressed by saying that 'all things are full of God.' and in agreement with this he is reported to have said that 'the magnet had a soul.'

The second of the Ionic philosophers was **Anaximander**, also an inhabitant of Miletus (B.C. 610—540). He followed Thales in seeking for an original substance to which he gave the name of ἀρχή, but he found this not in Water, but in the ἄπειρον, matter indeterminate (*i. e.* not yet developed into any one of the forms familiar to us) and infinite, which we may regard as bearing the same relation to Hesiod's primaeval Chaos, as Water did to the Homeric Oceanus. The elementary contraries, hot, cold, moist, dry, are separated from this first matter by virtue of the eternal movement belonging to it; thus are produced the four elements; the earth was in the form of a cylinder, self-poised, in the centre of the universe; round it was air, and round that again a fiery sphere which was broken up so as to form the heavenly bodies. As all substances are produced out of the Infinite so they are resolved into it, thus 'atoning for their injustice[1]' in arrogating to themselves a separate individual existence. The Infinite is divine, containing and directing all things: divine too are the innumerable

---

[1] Διδόναι γὰρ αὐτὰ τίσιν καὶ δίκην τῆς ἀδικίας. R. and P. § 18.

worlds which it is ever generating and re-absorbing into its own bosom.

After Anaximander comes **Anaximenes**, also of Miletus, who is supposed to have flourished about 520 B.C. While his doctrine approaches in many respects to that of Anaximander, he nevertheless returned to the principle of Thales in so far that he assumed, as the ἀρχή, a definite substance, Air, in contradistinction to the indefinite ἄπειρον of his immediate predecessor. Air is infinite in extent and eternal in duration. It is in continual motion, and produces all things out of itself by condensation and rarefaction, passing through successive stages from fire downwards to wind, cloud, water, earth and stone. As man's life is supported by breathing, so the universe subsists by the air which encompasses it. We are told that Anaximenes gave the name of God both to his first principle Air, and to certain of its products, probably the stars.

The greatest of the Pre-Socratic philosophers, **Heraclitus** of Ephesus, known among the ancients as the obscure and the weeping philosopher, was a little junior to Anaximenes. Following in the steps of his predecessor, he held that it was one and the self-same substance which by processes of condensation and rarefaction changed itself into all the elements known by us, but he preferred to name this from its highest potency *fire*, rather than to stop at the intermediate stage of *air*. But the point of main interest with him was not the original substance, but the process, the everlasting movement upwards and downwards, fire (including air), water, earth; earth, water, fire. All death is birth into a new form, all birth the death of the previous form. There is properly no existence but only 'becoming,' *i.e.* a continual passing from one existence into another. Each moment is the union of opposites, *being* and *not-being*: the life of the world is maintained by conflict, πόλεμος πατὴρ πάντων. Every particle of matter is in continual movement. All things are in flux like the waters of a river. One thing alone is permanent, the universal law which reveals itself in this movement. This is Zeus, the all-pervading reason of the world. It is only the illusion of the senses which makes us fancy that there are such things as permanent substances. Fire exhibits most clearly the incessant movement and activity of the world: confined in the body it constitutes the human soul, in the universe at large it is God (the substance and the process being thus identified).

The fragmentary remains of Heraclitus abound in those pregnant oracular sayings for which he was so famous among the ancients. Such are the following, in which the law of man and the law of nature are connected with the Will and Word of God. Fr. 91[1], 'Understanding is common to all. When we speak with reason we must hold fast to that which is common, even as a city holds fast to the law, yea, and far more strongly: for all human laws are fed by one law, that of God, which prevails wherever it will, and suffices for all and surpasses[2].' Fr. 100, 'The law is the rampart of the city[3].' Fr. 92,

---

[1] I give the numbering of Mr Bywater's edition.

[2] Ξυνόν ἐστι πᾶσι τὸ φρονέειν· ξὺν νόῳ λέγοντας ἰσχυρίζεσθαι χρὴ τῷ ξυνῷ πάντων, ὅκωσπερ νόμῳ πόλις καὶ πολὺ ἰσχυροτέρως. τρέφονται γὰρ πάντες οἱ ἀνθρώπειοι νόμοι ὑπὸ ἑνὸς τοῦ θείου· κρατέει γὰρ τοσοῦτον ὅκοσον ἐθέλει καὶ ἐξαρκέει πᾶσι καὶ περιγίνεται.

[3] Μάχεσθαι χρὴ τὸν δῆμον ὑπὲρ τοῦ νόμου ὅκως ὑπὲρ τείχεος.

'Reason is common to all, but most live as though under-standing were their own[1].'　Fr. 29, 'The sun shall not overpass his measure, else the Erinyes, the ministers of justice, will find him out[2].'　Fr. 19, 'Wisdom consists in one thing, to know the mind by which all through all is guided[3].'　Fr. 65, 'One thing alone wisdom willeth and willeth not to be spoken, the name of Zeus[4].'　I add a few apophthegms of a more miscellaneous character.　Fr. 46, 'Out of discord proceeds the fairest harmony[5].'　Fr. 47, 'The hidden harmony is better than that which is mani-fest[6].'　Fr. 11, 'The king to whom belongs the shrine at Delphi neither publishes nor conceals but shadows forth the truth[7].'　Fr. 12, 'The Sibyl, uttering with frenzied mouth words unmirthful, unadorned, untricked, reaches with her voice through a thousand years by the help of God[8].'　Fr. 122, 'After death there await men such things

---

[1] Τοῦ λόγου δ' ἐόντος ξυνοῦ, ζώουσι οἱ πολλοὶ ὡς ἰδίην ἔχοντες φρόνησιν.

[2] Ἥλιος οὐχ ὑπερβήσεται μέτρα· εἰ δὲ μή, Ἐρινύες μιν δίκης ἐπί-κουροι ἐξευρήσουσι.

[3] Ἓν τὸ σοφόν, ἐπίστασθαι γνώμην ᾗ κυβερνᾶται πάντα διὰ πάντων.

[4] Ἓν τὸ σοφὸν μοῦνον λέγεσθαι οὐκ ἐθέλει καὶ ἐθέλει, Ζηνὸς οὔνομα.

[5] Ἐκ τῶν διαφερόντων καλλίστη ἁρμονία.

[6] Ἁρμονία ἀφανὴς φανερῆς κρείσσων.

[7] Ὁ ἄναξ οὗ τὸ μαντεῖόν ἐστι τὸ ἐν Δελφοῖς, οὔτε λέγει οὔτε κρύπτει, ἀλλὰ σημαίνει.

[8] Σίβυλλα δὲ μαινομένῳ στόματι ἀγέλαστα καὶ ἀκαλλώπιστα καὶ ἀμύριστα φθεγγομένη χιλίων ἐτέων ἐξικνέεται τῇ φωνῇ διὰ τὸν θεόν, which Coleridge has thus translated (*Lit. Rem.* III. p. 419)

　　　　　　　—not hers
　　To win the sense by words of rhetoric,
　　Lip-blossoms breathing perishable sweets;
　　But by the power of the informing Word
　　Roll sounding onward through a thousand years
　　Her deep prophetic bodements.

as they think not nor expect¹.' Fr. 4, 'Eyes and ears are bad witnesses when the soul is barbarous².' Fr. 7, 'To him that hopes not, the unhoped will never come³.' Fr. 8, 'They that search for gold, dig much ground and find little⁴.' Fr. 16, 'Great learning does not teach wisdom⁵.' Fr. 75, 'The dry light is the wisest soul⁶.'

Heraclitus is the first philosopher of whom we read that he referred to the doctrines of other philosophers. He is said to have spoken highly of some of the seven Wise Men, but condemned severely Pythagoras and Xenophanes as well as the poets Hesiod, Homer and Archilochus. Though I agree with Ueberweg in classing him with the older Ionics, yet his philosophy was no doubt largely developed with a reference to the rival schools of Italy. Thus there is something of a Pythagorean colour in fragments 46 and 47 quoted above.

We must now cross the water with **Pythagoras** of

---

¹ Ἀνθρώπους μένει τελευτήσαντας ἄσσα οὐκ ἔλπονται οὐδὲ δοκέουσι.

² Κακοὶ μάρτυρες ἀνθρώποισι ὀφθαλμοὶ καὶ ὦτα, βαρβάρους ψυχὰς ἐχόντων.

³ Ἐὰν μὴ ἔλπηαι, ἀνέλπιστον οὐκ ἐξευρήσει.

⁴ Χρυσὸν οἱ διζήμενοι γῆν πολλὴν ὀρύσσουσι καὶ εὑρίσκουσι ὀλίγον.

⁵ Πολυμαθίη νόον ἔχειν οὐ διδάσκει.

⁶ This has reference to the doctrine that fire is the essence of spirit. It was illustrated by the obscuration of the faculties in drunkenness, and by the supposed ill effect of a foggy district on the intelligence of the inhabitants. The *siccum lumen* of the *Novum Organum* is borrowed from it. There are three different forms of the original maxim, which may possibly be all due to Heraclitus, as we see from other fragments (e.g. 66) that he was fond of playing on words. In Fr. 74 it runs αὔη ψυχὴ σοφωτάτη καὶ ἀρίστη, in Fr. 75 αὐγὴ ξηρὴ ψυχὴ σοφωτάτη καὶ ἀρίστη, in Fr. 76 οὗ γῆ ξηρή, ψυχὴ σοφωτάτη καὶ ἀρίστη.

Samos, born about 580 B.C., who settled at Crotona in Italy, 529 B.C., and there founded what is known as the Italic school[1]. He seems to have found in the mysteries and in the Orphic hymns the starting point which Thales had discovered in Homer; and there can be little doubt that his doctrine and system were also in part suggested by his travels in Egypt. He established a sort of religious brotherhood with strict rules and a severe initiation[2], insisted on training in gymnastics, mathematics and music,

---

[1] There is no one of the early philosophers about whose history and doctrines it is more difficult to ascertain the exact truth than Pythagoras. This is owing in part to the fact that neither Pythagoras himself nor any of his immediate disciples committed their teaching to writing, and also that the earliest Pythagorean treatise, composed by Philolaus a contemporary of Socrates, is only known to us through fragments, the genuineness of which is disputed; but still more it is owing to the luxuriant growth of an apocryphal Pythagorean literature among later eclectic philosophers, who desired to claim the authority of Pythagoras for their own speculations. This was particularly the case with Neo-Pythagoreans and Neo-Platonists, such as Porphyry and Iamblichus, who selected him, as Philostratus had done Apollonius of Tyana, to be the champion of the old religion, and opposed his claims, as prophet and miracle-worker, to those put forward by the Christians in the name of their Master or His Apostles. In the account which I have given in the text I have mainly followed Zeller who has examined the evidence with extreme care, testing all later reports by the statements of Plato and Aristotle.

[2] It was said by later Pythagoreans that the noviciate lasted for five years, and that absolute silence had to be observed throughout that time. One rule strongly insisted on for all the brotherhood was daily self-examination, as we see by the following lines taken from the miscellaneous collection of Pythagorean precepts entitled the *Golden Verses*, which Mullach attributes to Lysis, the tutor of Epaminondas, but which, as a collection, are probably of much later date:

and taught the doctrines of immortality and of the transmigration of souls, and the duty of great abstemiousness, if not, as some report, of total abstinence from animal food[1]. Three points may be noticed about this society, (1) their high ideal of friendship, evinced in the maxims κοινὰ τὰ τῶν φίλων εἶναι, τὸν δὲ φίλον ἄλλον ἑαυτόν, and in the well-known story of the devotion of Damon and Phintias; (2) the admission into their body, as into the Epicurean society of later times, of female associates, of whom the most distinguished was Theano, the wife of

> Μηδ' ὕπνον μαλακοῖσιν ἐπ' ὄμμασι προσδέξασθαι,
> πρὶν τῶν ἡμερινῶν ἔργων τρὶς ἕκαστον ἐπελθεῖν·
> πῇ παρέβην; τί δ' ἔρεξα; τί μοι δέον οὐκ ἐτελέσθη;
> Ἀρξάμενος δ' ἀπὸ πρώτου ἐπέξιθι, καὶ μετέπειτα
> δειλὰ μὲν ἐκπρήξας ἐπιπλήσσεο, χρηστὰ δὲ τέρπου.

Plato (*Rep.* X. 600) bears witness to the marked character of the Pythagorean life (Πυθαγόρειος τρόπος τοῦ βίου); and Herodotus (II. 81) connects the religious rites practised by them with those of the Orphic sect and of the Egyptians, ὁμολογέουσι δὲ ταῦτα (the use of linen garments) τοῖσι Ὀρφικοῖσι καλεομένοισι καὶ Βακχικοῖσι, ἐοῦσι δὲ Αἰγυπτίοισι καὶ Πυθαγορείοισι. (I do not agree with Zeller in putting a comma after Αἰγυπτίοισι.)

[1] The earliest notice we have of Pythagoras is contained in some verses of Xenophanes in which allusion is made to his doctrine of metempsychosis. Pythagoras is there said to have interceded for a dog which was being beaten, professing that he recognized in his cries the voice of a friend.

> καὶ ποτέ μιν στυφελιζομένου σκύλακος παριόντα
> φασὶν ἐποικτεῖραι καὶ τόδε φάσθαι ἔπος·
> παῦσαι, μηδὲ ῥάπιζ', ἐπειὴ φίλου ἀνέρος ἐστὶ
> ψυχή, τὴν ἔγνων φθεγξαμένης ἀΐων.

It was believed that he retained the memory of his own former transmigrations, and that he had once recognized a shield hanging up in a temple, as one which he had himself carried at Troy under the name of Euphorbus, (see Hor. *Od.* I. XXVIII. 1. 10).

Pythagoras; (3) the unquestioning submission with which
the dicta of the master were received by his disciples, as
shown by the famous αὐτὸς ἔφα, *ipse dixit*, which was to
them an end of all controversy. The brotherhood, first
established at Crotona, soon gained great influence with
the wealthier class in that and the neighbouring cities;
but after some twenty years of prosperity they seem to
have provoked the opposition of the democratic party by
their arrogance and exclusiveness. Pythagoras himself is
said to have been banished from Crotona and taken
refuge at Metapontum. A worse fate overtook his followers about a hundred years later, when their church at
Crotona was burnt down, and they themselves massacred
with the exception of two. The school appears to have
died out altogether about the middle of the 4th century
B.C., but revived in the time of Cicero.

The new and startling feature in the Pythagorean
philosophy, as opposed to the Ionic systems, was that it
found its ἀρχή, its key of the universe, not in any known
substance, but in number and proportion. This might
naturally have occurred to one who had listened to the
teaching of Thales and Anaximander. After all it makes
no difference, he might say, what we take as our original
matter, it is the law of development, the measure of condensation, which determines the nature of each thing.
Number rules the harmonies of music, the proportions of
sculpture and architecture, the movements of the heavenly
bodies[1]. It is Number which makes the universe into a

----

[1] He believed that the intervals between the heavenly bodies
corresponded exactly to those of the octave, and that hence arose
the Harmony of the Spheres, which mortals were unable to hear,
either because it was too powerful for their organs of hearing or be-

κόσμος[1], and is the secret of a virtuous and orderly life. Then, by a confusion similar to that which led Heraclitus to identify the law of movement with Fire, the Pythagoreans went on to identify number with form, substance and quality. One, the Monad, evolved out of itself Limit (order), exhibited in the series of odd numbers, and the Unlimited (freedom, expansiveness), the Dyad, exhibited in the series of even numbers, especially of the powers of Two; out of the harmonious mixture of these contraries all particular substances were produced. Again, One was the point, Two the line, Three the plane, Four the concrete solid (but from another point of view, as being the first square number, equal into equal, it was conceived to be Justice). Yet once more, One was the central fire, the hearth of the universe, the throne of Zeus. Around this revolved in regular dance ten spheres; on the outside that of the fixed stars, within this the five planets in their order, then the Sun, the Moon, the Earth, between which and the central fire was interposed the imaginary Anti-Chthon or Counter-Earth, cutting off our view of the central fire and leaving us dependent on the reflection of its light by the Sun, which was not in itself luminous. The separation of the Earth into its two hemispheres was for the purpose of making up the Decad, the symbol of totality. As the Decad was the sum of the first four numbers ($1 + 2 + 3 + 4 = 10$), special sacredness attached to this group, known under the name Tetractys[2].

---

cause they had never experienced absolute silence. Arist. *Cael.* II. 9, Plin. *N. H.* II. 22.

[1] Pythagoras is said to have been the first who called the universe by this name.

[2] Compare the Pythagorean oath contained in the *Golden Verses,*

The number Ten was also the number of the Pythagorean categories, or list of contraries, thus given by Aristotle (*Met.* I. v. 986), Limit and Unlimited, Odd and Even, One and Many, Right and Left, Male and Female, Rest and Motion, Straight and Curved, Light and Darkness, Good and Bad, Square and Oblong.

These mystical extravagances appear to have been the necessary introduction to the sciences of Arithmetic and Geometry, just as Astrology and Alchemy were the introduction to Astronomy and Chemistry. Indeed we find that men like Copernicus and Kepler were to some extent influenced and guided in their investigations by the ideas of Pythagoras. Nor was he himself deficient in knowledge of a more exact kind, if it is true that he was the discoverer of the theorem which we know as the 47th in the first book of Euclid, and was also acquainted with such properties of numbers as are mentioned by Zeller (I. p. 322[4]).

The Pythagorean doctrine of the soul and of God is variously reported. If we may trust the oldest accounts, there does not seem to have been any close connexion between the religious and philosophical opinions of

οὐ μὰ τὸν ἀμετέρᾳ γενεᾷ παραδόντα τετρακτύν, παγὰν ἀενάου φύσιος ῥιζώματ᾽ ἔχουσαν. There was of course no end to the fancies which might be connected with numbers. Thus, One was reason, as being unchangeable; Two was opinion, and the earth as the region of opinion; Three was perfection, as comprising in itself beginning, middle, and end; Five was marriage, the union of odd and even. Later Pythagoreans made the Monad God, the Dyad Matter, the Triad the World. For other interpretations, see Zeller I. p. 359[4] foll. The five regular solids were supposed to be the ultimate forms of the five elements, the cube of earth, pyramid of fire, octahedron of air, icosahedron of water, dodecahedron of the etherial element which encompassed the universe on the outside.

Pythagoras. We are told that he believed in One God eternal, unchangeable, ruling and upholding all things, that the soul was a 'harmony[1],' that the body was its prison[2], in which it was punished for past sin and disciplined for a divine life after death, that those who failed to profit by this discipline would pass into lower forms of life, or suffer severer penalties in Hades.

Heraclides Ponticus reports (Diog. L. *Proem.* 12, Cic. *Tusc.* v. 3) that Pythagoras was the first to call himself φιλόσοφος, a lover of wisdom, saying that the name σοφός, used by the older sages, properly belonged to God alone. He compared human life to the gathering at the Olympic games, where some came to win glory, others to make gain, others to watch the spectacle: the philosopher, he said, resembled these last in despising honour and gain, and caring only for knowledge. Other sayings attributed to Pythagoras are the following: 'man is at his best when he visits the temples of the Gods[3].' 'Choose the best life; use will make it pleasant,' (Stob. *Flor.* I. 29). 'Do not speak few things in many words, but many things in few words,' (Stob. *Flor.* xxxv. 8). 'Either be silent, or speak words better than silence,' (Stob. *Flor.* xxxiv. 7). 'Be sleepless in the things of the

---

[1] The statement of Cicero and others that Pythagoras held the human soul to be a portion of the Divine soul (*Cato M.* 78) is not confirmed by the earlier authorities.

[2] So Philolaus (R. and P. § 124) διά τινας τιμωρίας ἁ ψυχὰ τῷ σώματι συνέζευκται καὶ καθάπερ ἐν σάματι τούτῳ τέθαπται. Plato adds that he condemned suicide as desertion of our post, ἔν τινι φρουρᾷ ἐσμεν οἱ ἄνθρωποι, καὶ οὐ δεῖ δὴ ἑαυτὸν ἐκ ταύτης λύειν οὐδ' ἀποδιδράσκειν.

[3] Βέλτιστοι ἑαυτῶν γίνονται ἄνθρωποι ὅταν πρὸς τοὺς θεοὺς βαδίζωσιν, Plut. *Def. Or.* 183, see Cic. *Leg.* II. 11.

spirit; for sleep in them is akin to death,' (Stob. *Flor.* 1. 19). 'It is hard to take many paths in life at the same time,' (Stob. *Flor.* 1. 27). 'It is the part of a fool to attend to every opinion of every man, above all to that of the mob,' (Iambl. *V. P.* 31).

The second of the Italic schools was the Eleatic, founded by **Xenophanes** of Colophon in Asia Minor (b. 569 B.C.), who migrated to Elea in Italy about 540 B.C. While the Pythagoreans strove to explain nature mathematically and symbolically, the Eleatics in their later developments did the same by their metaphysical abstractions. Xenophanes himself seems to have received his first philosophical impulse in the revulsion from the popular mythology. In his philosophical poem he condemns anthropomorphism and polytheism altogether, and charges Homer and Hesiod with attributing to the Gods conduct which would have been disgraceful in men. 'If animals had had hands they would have depicted Gods each in their own form, just as men have done[1]. God is one, all eye, all ear, all understanding; he is for ever unmoved, unchangeable, a vast all-embracing sphere.'

---

[1] Πάντα θεοῖς ἀνέθηκαν Ὅμηρος θ' Ἡσίοδός τε
ὅσσα παρ' ἀνθρώποισιν ὀνείδεα καὶ ψόγος ἐστίν,
οἳ πλεῖστ' ἐφθέγξαντο θεῶν ἀθεμίστια ἔργα,
κλέπτειν μοιχεύειν τε καὶ ἀλλήλους ἀπατεύειν.

Εἷς θεὸς ἔν τε θεοῖσι καὶ ἀνθρώποισι μέγιστος,
οὔτι δέμας θνητοῖσιν ὁμοίιος οὐδὲ νόημα.
Οὖλος ὁρᾷ, οὖλος δὲ νοεῖ, οὖλος δέ τ' ἀκούει.

Ἀλλ' εἴτοι χεῖράς γ' εἶχον βόες ἠὲ λέοντες,
ἢ γράψαι χείρεσσι καὶ ἔργα τελεῖν ἅπερ ἄνδρες,
ἵπποι μὲν θ' ἵπποισι βόες δέ τε βουσὶν ὁμοίας
καί κε θεῶν ἰδέας ἔγραφον καὶ σώματ' ἐποίουν,
τοιαῦθ' οἷόν περ καὐτοὶ δέμας εἶχον ἔμοιον.

It is disputed whether the last expression is to be taken literally, implying that the universe is God, or whether it is a metaphor to express God's perfection and omnipresence. With all his freedom of censure Xenophanes is far from claiming for himself that oracular authority which the Pythagoreans ascribed to the dicta of their master. 'It is not for man,' he says, 'to hope for certainty in these matters of high speculation. However well he speaks, he has not attained to knowledge, but only to probability at best[1].'

The chief representative of the Eleatic School is **Parmenides** (b. 515 B.C.). The fragments of his philosophical poem, collected by Mullach, amount to more than 150 hexameters. He disengaged the doctrine of Xenophanes from its theological form, and ascribed to Being what his predecessor had ascribed to God. His philosophy is the antithesis of that of Heraclitus. While Heraclitus said 'all is motion and change, the appearance of fixity is merely illusion of the senses;' Parmenides asserted, with distinct reference to him, that all that exists has existed and will exist the same for ever, that it is change and multiplicity which is illusory. It is only by thought we can become conscious of the really existent; being and thought are the same, sense can only give rise to uncertain opinion. In such language we see partly a protest against the vagueness of the conception of development or 'becoming,' by which the Ionic philosophers endeavoured to explain the origin of things, 'You say fire becomes water, but each thing *is* what it *is*, and can never be

---

[1] Καὶ τὸ μὲν οὖν σαφὲς οὔτις ἀνὴρ γένετ' οὐδέ τις ἔσται
εἰδὼς ἀμφὶ θεῶν τε καὶ ἄσσα λέγω περὶ πάντων·
εἰ γὰρ καὶ τὰ μάλιστα τύχοι τετελεσμένον εἰπών,
αὐτὸς ὁμῶς οὐκ οἶδε· δόκος δ' ἐπὶ πᾶσι τέτυκται.

otherwise;' partly an idea of the indestructibility of matter; partly an anticipation of the later distinction between necessary and contingent truth; thus one point dwelt upon by him was the impossibility of any separation of parts of space.

But though truth only belonged to the world of real existence, Parmenides condescended to give his romance of nature for the benefit of those who could not penetrate beyond the world of phenomena. He begins with two principles, light and darkness, also called fire and earth, or male and female; and supposes all things to proceed from their mixture. The existing universe consists of a central fire, the seat of the presiding Deity, and of several concentric rings of mingled light and darkness, bounded on the outside by a wall of flame. The first-born of Gods was Love, by whom the union of opposites is brought about. In this we may trace a reminiscence of the Hesiodic Ἔρως.

Zeno of Elea (b. 490 B.C.) is chiefly known from his arguments showing the absurd consequences of the ordinary belief in the phenomenal world. Parmenides must be right in denying motion and multiplicity, for their assertion leads to self-contradiction. Zeno was in consequence called the inventor of Dialectic. His arguments, especially the famous 'Achilles,' still find a place in treatises on Logic[1].

[1] It is thus given by Mill (*System of Logic* II. 385[2]), 'The argument is, let Achilles run ten times as fast as the tortoise, yet if the tortoise has the start, Achilles will never overtake him. For suppose them to be at first separated by an interval of a thousand feet: when Achilles has run those thousand feet, the tortoise will have got on a hundred: when Achilles has run those hundred, the tortoise will have run ten, and so on for ever: therefore Achilles may run for ever without overtaking the tortoise.'

The clearly marked opposition between the Ionic and the Eleatic views of nature, as shown in Heraclitus and Parmenides, had a powerful influence on the subsequent course of philosophy. Empedocles, Anaxagoras, and the Atomists agreed in accepting the Eleatic principle of the immutability of substance, while denying its absolute Oneness; and they explained the Ionic 'becoming' as the result of the mixture of a number of unchangeable substances. **Empedocles** of Agrigentum (b. 500 B.C.) 'than whom,' says Lucretius, 'Sicily has produced nothing holier, more marvellous or more dear,' held that there were four eternal, self-subsistent elements or 'roots of things,' which were being continually separated and combined under the influence of Love and Hatred. At times Love has the upper hand, at times Hate. When Love has the complete supremacy the elements are at rest, united in one all-including sphere (Σφαῖρος): when Hate prevails, the elements are entirely separate. The soul, like all other things, is formed by the mixture of the elements, and is thus capable of perception, for like can only be perceived by like[1]. In regard to the origin of living things, Empedocles imagined that the several parts or limbs were in the first instance produced separately in the bosom of the earth, eyes apart from brows, arms from shoulders, etc.; and that these were afterwards joined at haphazard, giving rise to all sorts of monsters, ox-headed men, men-headed oxen; and that it was only after successive trials that nature gave birth to perfect animals, fitted to survive and to propagate their

---

[1] γαίῃ μὲν γὰρ γαῖαν ὀπώπαμεν, ὕδατι δ' ὕδωρ,
αἰθέρι δ' αἰθέρα δῖαν, ἀτὰρ πυρὶ πῦρ ἀΐδηλον
στοργῇ δὲ Στοργήν, Νεῖκος δέ τε νείκεϊ λυγρῷ.

race[1]. In his opinions on the Gods and on religion, Empedocles was chiefly influenced by Pythagoras. He believed in the existence of Daemons intermediate between Gods and men, some of which had passed into mortal bodies as an atonement for former sins, and could only be restored to their original state after long ages of discipline. While at one time he speaks of God as one spirit pervading the world in swift thought, in other places he speaks of Gods produced like men from the mixture of the elements, but possessed of a longer existence, and then again we find divinity attributed to Sphaerus and the four elements and two moving powers.

Empedocles closes the series of those philosophers who used the medium of verse for their speculations. We have still nearly 500 verses remaining of his two great philosophical poems (the Περὶ φύσεως and Καθαρμοί) so highly praised by Lucretius in the well-known lines—

'Carmina quin etiam divini pectoris ejus
  vociferantur et exponunt praeclara reperta,
  ut vix humana videatur stirpe creatus.'

The claim to divinity seems to have been seriously put forward by Empedocles himself in the line χαίρετ᾽, ἐγὼ δ᾽ ὑμῖν θεὸς ἄμβροτος, οὐκέτι θνητός, and one of the stories told about his death was that he had been carried up to heaven in a chariot of fire; the more common belief however seems to have been that reported by Horace—

—deus immortalis haberi
  dum cupit Empedocles, ardentem frigidus Aetnam
  insiluit.

Returning now to Ionia, we see the effect of the Eleatic school in the speculations of **Anaxagoras** of

[1] See the lines quoted in R. and P. § 175.

Clazomenae (b. 500 B.C.), the friend and teacher of Pericles and Euripides, of whom Aristotle says that he appeared among the older philosophers like a sober man among drunkards. Instead of the four elements of Empedocles, which he declared to be themselves compounds, he assumed an indefinite number of 'seeds' of the different kinds of matter. To these seeds later philosophers gave the distinctive name of 'homœomeries,' denoting that the constituent particles of bodies were of the same nature as the bodies which they composed, while the unqualified atoms of Democritus gave rise to the different qualities of their compounds by the mode in which they were compounded. In the beginning these seeds were huddled together in a confused chaos, then came *Nous*, the pure self-moving intelligence, almighty and all-wise (this takes the place cf the half-conscious Love and Hate of Empedocles), and communicated a rotatory impulse to the inert mass, by means of which the cognate particles were gradually brought together and reduced to order. *Nous* is the soul of the world and dwells in all living things, even plants, as the principle of their life. Whether Anaxagoras called it by the name of God is doubtful. Plato and Aristotle complain that, having begun well, he failed to make full use of the right principle with which he started, and turned his attention to mechanical causes, only having recourse to *Nous* as a *deus ex machina* when the others failed.

Diogenes of Apollonia in Crete was a younger contemporary of Anaxagoras, against whom he took up a reactionary position and defended the older Ionic doctrine, assuming *Air* to be the one principle out of which all things were produced, and assigning to it all the attri-

butes of *Nous*. Both he and Anaxagoras taught at
Athens, but were compelled to leave it on a charge of
impiety.

Of far greater importance is **Democritus**, born at
the Ionic colony of Abdera in Thrace, B.C. 460, the chief
expositor of the Atomic theory, which was originated by
his elder contemporary and friend, Leucippus the Eleatic.
Briefly stated, their doctrine is that of Anaxagoras, minus
Nous and the qualitative diversity in the seeds or atoms.
They adopted the Eleatic view so far as relates to the
eternal sameness of Being, applying this to the indivisible,
unchangeable atoms, but they denied its unity, continuity
and immobility, and they asserted that 'Not-being' (the
Vacuum of their system) existed no less than 'Being,'
and was no less essential as an $\dot{a}\rho\chi\dot{\eta}$, since without it
motion would be impossible. The atoms are absolutely
solid and incompressible, they are without any secondary
qualities, and differ only in size (and therefore in weight),
in figure, position and arrangement. Though too small
to be seen or felt by us, they produce all things by their
combinations; and the compounds have various qualities
in accordance with the differences in the constituent
atoms, the mode of arrangement, and the larger or smaller
amount of vacuum separating the atoms. Thus Soul, the
divine element pervading the world, is a sort of fire
made up of small, round, smooth atoms in continual
motion, and largely mixed with vacuum. The account
given by Democritus of the origin of the existing universe
is that there were, to begin with, an infinite number of
atoms carried downwards by their own inherent gravity
at different rates in proportion to their magnitude, that
thus they impinged one upon another, and gave rise to

all sorts of oblique and contrary movements, out of which
was generated an all-absorbing rotatory motion or vortex.
Under these various movements corresponding atoms
found their fitting places and became entangled and
hooked together so as to form bodies. Thus the earthy
and watery particles were drawn to the centre where
they remained at rest, while the airy and fiery rebounded
from them and rose to the circumference, forming a sort
of shell between the organized world and the infinitude
of unorganized atoms on the outside. There was an
endless number of such worlds in various stages of
growth or decay under the influx or efflux of atoms; the
destruction of each world followed upon its collision with
another world.

The account given of the mind and its operations
was as follows:—Particles of mind or soul were distributed throughout the body, and were continually es-
caping owing to their subtle nature, but, as they escaped,
their place was taken by other particles inhaled in the
breath. When breathing ceased there was nothing to
recruit the living particles, and death speedily followed.
Every mental impression was of the nature of touch, and
was caused either by actual contact with atoms as in the
case of taste and hearing, or by images thrown off from
bodies external to us, and entering in through the pores.

These images were a kind of film consisting of the
surface atoms which were continually floating off from
all bodies without any disturbance of their mutual order,
and were, so to speak, a sample of the object from which
they were detached. Democritus used the same word
(εἴδωλα) for certain anthropomorphic combinations of
the finest soul-atoms, which he believed to exist in the

air and to be at times perceived by men. These were the Gods of the popular religion, not immortal, though longer lived than men: some were friendly, some malignant; he prayed that he might himself only meet with the former.

Democritus was contrasted with Heraclitus by the ancients, as the laughing with the weeping philosopher, see Juvenal x. 28 *foll.* In both we find the same lofty aristocratic spirit; both stand aloof from the herd, and scan with critical eyes the follies of men; but the wisdom of the younger is characterized by shrewd common-sense and good-humoured contentment, and has nothing of that mysterious gloom which pervades the utterances of the elder. The writings of Democritus seem to have rivalled those of Aristotle in extent and variety, and in beauty of style to have been scarcely inferior to Plato. I select a few aphorisms from the Fragments, which fill about forty pages in Mullach's collection. Fr. 11, 'Men have invented for themselves the phantom, fortune, to excuse their own want of prudence[1].' Fr. 17, 'The chiefest pleasures come from the contemplation of noble deeds[2].' Fr. 29, 'He is a man of sense who rejoices over what he has, instead of grieving over what he has not.' Fr. 30, 'The envious man is his own enemy.' Fr. 32, 'A life without a holiday is a long road without an inn. Fr. 92, 'He who would be happy must not be busy about many things, nor engage in business beyond his powers.' Fr. 94, 'It is better for a man to find fault with himself than with his neighbour.' Fr. 100, 'Reverence thyself no less than thy neighbours, and be equally on thy guard against wrong-

---

[1] Ἄνθρωποι τύχης εἴδωλον ἐπλάσαντο, πρόφασιν ἰδίης ἀβουλίης.

[2] Αἱ μεγάλαι τέρψιες ἀπὸ τοῦ θεᾶσθαι τὰ καλὰ τῶν ἔργων γίνονται.

doing, whether all or none shall know it.' Fr. 107,
'Those only are dear to God, who hate injustice.' Fr.
109, 'It is the motive, not the outward act, which proves
a man just[1].' Fr. 116, 'Sin is caused by ignorance of
the better course.' Fr. 132, 'Education is an ornament
in prosperity, a refuge in adversity.' Fr. 138, 'Adversity is the only teacher of fools.' Fr. 142, 'Do not
seek to know all things, or you will be ignorant of all
things.' Fr. 149, 'To bear injury meekly is the part
of magnanimity.' Fr. 161, 'He who loves none will be
loved by none.' Fr. 245, 'He whom all fear, fears all.'
Fr. 224, 'The doer of injustice is more miserable than
the sufferer.' Fr. 225, 'The whole world is the father-
land of the good.' Fr. 238, 'Different men have different
pleasures, but goodness and truth are reverenced alike
by all[2].' Fr. Phys. 1 and 5, 'The objects of sense are
not what they are supposed to be: Atoms and Void alone
have real existence. There are two kinds of judgment,
the genuine and the obscure: the obscure is that of
sight, hearing, feeling and the rest; the genuine is distinct (ἀποκεκριμένη) from all of these. Truth lies at the
bottom of a well (ἐν βυθῷ).'

Democritus closes the series of the pre-Socratic
dogmatists, men who devoted themselves to the investigation of Nature as a whole, believing that the
investigation would lead to the discovery of the truth.
Between these and Socrates, the great regenerator of
philosophy, is interposed the sceptical or Sophistic era.

---

[1] Ἀγαθὸν οὐ τὸ μὴ ἀδικέειν, ἀλλὰ τὸ μηδὲ ἐθέλειν.

[2] Ἀνθρώποισι πᾶσι σεβαστά ἐστι τὸ ἀγαθὸν καὶ ἀληθές· ἡδὺ δὲ
ἄλλο ἄλλῳ.

That the latter was a natural and necessary stage in the development of Greek thought will be apparent from the following considerations:—

What we are told about Pythagoras and his disciples must have been more or less true of all the early philosophers. The sage, no less than the poet, believed himself the organ of a special inspiration, which, in the case of the former, revealed to him the inner truth of nature; those who were worthy to receive the revelation listened with reverence to his teaching, and rested their faith implicitly on their master's authority. But when different schools sprang up, each asserting their own doctrines with equal positiveness; when the increase of intercommunication spread the knowledge of these contradictory systems throughout the Greek-speaking world; when philosophical questions began to be popularized by poets like Euripides, and discussed in the saloons of a Pericles or an Aspasia; when Zeno's criticisms had made clear to the public, what had been an esoteric truth to the hearers of Parmenides and Heraclitus, that not merely traditional beliefs, but even the evidence of the senses was incapable of standing against the reason of the philosophers,—the result of all this was a widespread scepticism either as to the existence of objective truth altogether (Protagoras), or as to the possibility of the attainment of physical truth by man (Socrates). If we remember at the same time the incredibly rapid development in every department of life which took place in Greece and especially in Athens during the 5th century B.C.; the sense, which must have forced itself on all the more thoughtful minds, of the incompetency of the old beliefs to explain the problems of the new age which was dawning upon them; and on the other hand the growing importance of oratory and the immense stimulus to ambition held out, in a state like Athens, to those who were of a more practical turn of mind,—we shall not be surprised if there was much curiosity to learn the opinions of the most advanced thinkers, and much eagerness to acquire the argumentative power by which a Zeno could make the worse cause appear the better. The enlightened men who came forward to supply this demand called themselves by the name of Sophists, or professors of wisdom. They were the first who made a profession of the higher education, and some of them amassed considerable fortunes by their lectures on rhetoric, the art of speaking, which was also made to include instruction in regard to political and social life. The speculative interest of the older philosophers was in them changed into a predominantly practical interest, 1st, as to how to acquire wealth and notoriety for themselves, and 2ndly, as a means to this, to attract by omniscient pretensions, by brilliant declamation and startling paradox, clever and ambitious young men of the richer classes; and then to secure their continued discipleship by careful training with a view to the attainment of political power[1].

Protagoras of Abdera (B.C. 490—415) and **Gorgias** of Leontini in Sicily (B.C. 480—375) are the earliest of the so-called Sophists. Protagoras taught in Sicily and at Athens, from which latter place he was banished on a

---

[1] The general features of the Sophistic period are photographed in the Clouds of Aristophanes, and in Thucydides' chapters on the Plague of Athens and the Corcyrean revolution, and his speeches generally.

charge of impiety in consequence of his treatise on Theology, in which he declared his inability to arrive at any
conclusion as to the nature or even the very existence of
the Gods[1]. His treatise on Truth began with the famous
sentence, 'Man is the measure of all things;' meaning
that truth is relative, not absolute, that what each man
holds to be true is true to him; and similarly in regard
to conduct, that it is impossible to pronounce universally
that one kind of conduct is right, another wrong: right
and wrong depend upon opinion; what is generally
thought right is right generally; what each thinks right
is right for him, just as each man's sensations are true
for him, though perhaps not for another; there is therefore no more reason for one general assertion than for
another, perhaps an opposite assertion. It is plain that
this was a sort of conciliation-theory naturally springing
from the fact of the opposition of philosophical schools:
'each of you are equally right relatively, equally wrong
absolutely; there is no need for quarrel.' Protagoras
also wrote on Grammar and Philology. Gorgias is said
to have first come to Athens in B.C. 427, and afterwards
to have travelled about giving lectures from town to town.
He devoted himself mainly to the cultivation of rhetoric,
but also wrote a treatise περὶ φύσεως, in which he maintained 1st 'that nothing exists' (i.e. doubtless 'in the
absolute Eleatic sense'); 2nd that, if anything did exist,
still it could not be known; 3rd that, even if it could be
known, the knowledge of it could not be communicated
to others. **Hippias** of Elis and **Prodicus** of Ceos

---

[1] περὶ μὲν θεῶν οὐκ ἔχω εἰδέναι, οὔθ' ὡς εἰσὶν οὔθ' ὡς οὐκ εἰσίν·
πολλὰ γὰρ τὰ κωλύοντα εἰδέναι, ἥ τε ἀδηλότης καὶ βραχὺς ὢν ὁ βίος
τοῦ ἀνθρώπου. Diog. L. IX. 51.

were some twenty years younger than Protagoras. The former was best known for his scientific attainments: he is said to have given utterance to the revolutionary sentiment of the age in the phrase, ‘Law is a tyrant over men, forcing them to do many things contrary to nature.’ Prodicus is famed for his moral apologue on the Choice of Hercules narrated by Xenophon. He is reported to have considered the Gods of the popular religion to be merely deified utilities, Bacchus wine, Ceres corn, &c.

But the extreme effects of the disintegration of established beliefs were not seen in the teachers, but in some of their pupils who were less dependent on public opinion, young aristocrats who fretted under democratic rule, and were eager to take advantage of the disorganized state of society in order to grasp at power for themselves. Such was the Callicles of the *Gorgias,* such Critias and Alcibiades, both disciples of Socrates, of whom we have now to speak.

Socrates was born at Athens 470 B.C.; he was the son of Sophroniscus a sculptor, and Phaenarete a midwife. While sharing the general scepticism as to the possibility of arriving at certainty in regard to the Natural Philosophy which had formed the almost exclusive subject of earlier speculation, he maintained, in opposition to most of the popular teachers of his time, the certainty of moral distinctions, and laid down a method for the discovery of error on the one side, and the establishment of objective truth on the other. The main lines of his philosophy are given in three famous sentences: (1) that of Cicero, that he brought down philosophy from heaven to earth[1]; (2) his own assertion that he practised in regard to the soul the art of midwifery (μαιευτική) which his mother had practised in regard to the body, bringing to birth and consciousness truths before held unconsciously[2]; (3) Aristotle's statement that Socrates was the first to introduce inductive reasoning and general definitions[3]. But more important than any innovation in regard to method was the immense personal influence of Socrates. His force of will, his indifference to conventionalities, his intense earnestness, both moral and intellectual, contrasting so strongly with the dilettanteism of ordinary teachers, and yet combined with such universal interest and sympathy in all varieties of life and character, his warm and genial nature, his humour, his irony, his extraordinary conversational powers, these formed a whole unique in the history of the world; and we can well believe that they acted like an electric shock on the more susceptible minds of his time. For we must remember that Socrates did not, like earlier philosophers, content himself with imparting the results of solitary meditation to a few favoured disciples: nor did he, like the Sophists, lecture to a paying audience on a set subject; but obeying, as he believed, a divine call, he mixed with men of every class wherever they were to be found, cross-questioning them as to the grounds of their beliefs, and endeavouring to awaken in them a consciousness of their ignorance and a desire for real knowledge. His own account of his call is as follows: one of his disciples was

---

[1] Cic. *Tusc.* v. 10.

[2] Plat. *Theaet.* p. 149 foll.

[3] Δύο γάρ ἐστιν ἅ τις ἂν ἀποδοίη Σωκράτει δικαίως, τούς τ᾽ ἐπακτικοὺς λόγους καὶ τὸ ὁρίζεσθαι καθόλου. Arist. *Met. M.* 4.

told by the Oracle at Delphi that Socrates was the wisest of men. Socrates could not conceive how this should be, as he was conscious only of ignorance; but he determined to question some of those who had the highest repute for wisdom; accordingly he went to statesmen and poets and orators, and last of all to craftsmen, but everywhere met with the same response: none really knew what were the true ends of life, but each one fancied that he knew, and most were angry when Socrates attempted to disturb their illusion of knowledge. Thus he arrived at the conclusion that what the oracle meant was that the first step to knowledge was the consciousness of ignorance, and he believed, in consequence of other divine warnings, that it was his special mission to bring men to this consciousness.

The next step on the way to knowledge was to get clear general notions, by comparing a number of specific cases in which the same general term was employed; or, according to the phraseology of ancient philosophy, to see the One (the kind or genus, the general principle, the law, the idea,) in the Many (the subordinate species or individuals, the particulars, the phenomena, the facts) and conversely to rise from the Many to the One. The process of doing this he called Dialectic, *i.e.* discourse, since it was by question and answer that he believed the proposed definition could be best tested, and the universal idea which was latent in each individual could be brought to light. Truth and right were the same for all: it was only ignorance, mistake, confusion which made them seem different to different men. And similarly it is ignorance which leads men to commit vicious actions: no one willingly does wrong, since to do right is the only way to happiness, and every man desires happiness[1]. Thus virtue is a knowledge of the way to happiness, and more generally, right action is reasonable action; in other words, virtue is wisdom, and each particular virtue wisdom in reference to particular circumstances or a particular class of objects. Thus he is brave who distinguishes between what is really dangerous and what is not so, and knows how to guard against danger, as the sailor in a storm at sea; he is just who knows what is right towards men; he is pious who knows what is right towards God; he is temperate who can always distinguish between real and apparent good. Training therefore and teaching are essential to virtue, and above all the training in self-knowledge, to know what are man's needs and capacities, and what are one's own weak points. No action can be really virtuous which is not based on this self-knowledge.

In regard to religion, Socrates, while often employing language suited to the popular polytheism, held that there was one supreme God who was to the universe what the soul of man was to his body, that all things were arranged and ordered by Him for good, and that man was the object of His special providence and might look for guidance from Him in oracles and otherwise. The soul was immortal, and had in it a divine element. Socrates believed that he was himself favoured beyond others in the warning sign (τὸ δαιμόνιον) which checked

---

[1] Compare Xen. *Mem.* IV. 8. § 6, 'He lives the best life who is always studying to improve himself, and he the pleasantest, who feels that he is really improving,' (ἄριστα ζῆν τοὺς ἄριστα ἐπιμελο-μένους τοῦ ὡς βελτίστους γίγνεσθαι, ἥδιστα δὲ τοὺς μάλιστα αἰσθανο-μένους ὅτι βελτίους γίγνονται).

him whenever he was about to take an ill-judged-step[1].

The personal enmity provoked by the use of the Socratic *elenchus*, and the more general dislike to the Socratic method as unsettling the grounds of belief and undermining authority, a dislike which showed itself in the Clouds of Aristophanes as early as 423 B.C., combined with the democratic reaction, after the overthrow of the Thirty, to bring about the execution of Socrates in the year 399 B.C. The charges on which he was condemned were that he did not believe in the Gods of the established religion, that he introduced new Gods, and that he corrupted the young: the last charge probably referring to the fact that Socrates freely pointed out the faults of the Athenian constitution, and that many of his disciples took the anti-popular side.

Our authorities for the life of Socrates are the writings of his two disciples, **Xenophon** and **Plato**, which are

[1] Much has been written on the exact nature of the δαιμόνιον. I take nearly the same view as Zeller (*Socrates* tr. p. 94), that it was a quick instinctive movement, analogous in its action to what we know as conscience and presentiment, but not identical with either, combining with a natural sensitiveness for whatever was right and fitting the practised tact acquired by large experience of life. To this sudden decisive mandate of the inward monitor, Socrates ascribed a supernatural origin, because he was unable to analyse the grounds on which it rested, attributing it, as he did all other good things, to the favour and goodness of God. We note here an element of mysticism, which showed itself also in the sort of brooding trance to which he was occasionally liable (cf. Plat. *Symp.* 220). It belonged to his wonderful personality to unite in himself, as perhaps none other but Luther has ever done, robust common-sense with deep religious mysticism, keen speculative interest with the widest human sympathies.

related to one another much as the Gospel of St Mark to that of St John. Xenophon (440—355 B.C.) was a soldier and country gentleman with a taste for literature, who endeavoured to clear his master's memory from the imputation of impiety and immorality by publishing the *Memorabilia*, a collection of his noteworthy sayings and discourses. Other discourses of Socrates are given in his *Apologia*, *Convivium*, and *Œconomicus*. What has been said above as to the method and the belief of Socrates may be illustrated by the following passages from the *Memorabilia*. In a conversation with Euthy-demus[1] the question arises as to the nature of jus-tice. To discover what injustice is, it is necessary to consider what kind of actions are unjust. 'It is unjust,' says Euthydemus, 'to lie, deceive, rob, &c.' On Socrates reminding him that such actions are not thought unjust in the case of enemies, Euthydemus amended his definition by adding 'if practised on a friend.' 'But,' says Socrates, 'it is not unjust in a general to encourage his soldiers by a lie, or in a father to im-pose upon his child by giving medicine in his food, or in a friend to rob his friend of the weapon with which he is about to kill himself.' Euthydemus has no answer to make, so Socrates turns to another point, and asks which is the more unjust, to tell a lie intentionally or unin-tentionally. The answer naturally is that it is worse to lie with intention to deceive. Socrates, arguing on his principle that all virtue is knowledge, asks whether a man must not be taught to be just, as he is taught to read and write, and whether the man who misspells in-

[1] *Mem.* IV. 2.

tentionally does not know his letters better than one who
misspells without intending it; whether therefore he who
intentionally commits an unjust action must not have a
better knowledge of what is just than he who commits it
unintentionally, and consequently be a juster man, since
justice consists in the knowledge of what is just. Socrates
then proceeds to show that Euthydemus' ideas of what
is really good are no less confused and self-contradictory
than his ideas about justice, and Euthydemus goes away
convinced that he knows nothing, and thinking himself
no better than a slave. 'Such,' adds Xenophon, 'was a
frequent result of conversing with Socrates; in many
cases those who had been thus humiliated kept out of
his way for the future; these he called cowards; but
Euthydemus on the contrary thought his only hope of
improving himself was to be continually in the society
of Socrates, and Socrates, finding him thus docile and
eager to improve, taught him simply and plainly what he
thought it most useful for him to know.'

I have selected this conversation for the sake of
comparison with a conversation on the same subject
which I have quoted below from Plato's *Republic.* It
is interesting to note that it ends with a negative
conclusion, as so many of the Platonic dialogues do,
its object being to destroy a false belief of knowledge and awaken interest, not to communicate any
definite doctrines. The paradox as to the superior
morality of intentional wrong-doing reappears in Plato.
And no doubt, if we are comparing the moral condition
of two persons guilty of the same act of treachery
or ingratitude, one of whom did wrong knowing it to
be wrong, while the other had no feeling of wrong in

the matter, we should agree with Socrates in considering
the latter more hopelessly immoral than the former[1]:
but it is plain, from many passages both in Xenophon
and Plato, that Socrates was really carried away by his
analogy between the art or science of life (which was his
view of virtue) and the particular arts and sciences; and
that he never gave due attention to the phenomena of
human weakness (ἀκράτεια) and moral choice (προαίρεσις)
which were afterwards so carefully analyzed by Aristotle.

One other passage from Xenophon may be cited here,
as the first appearance of the argument from Final Causes[2].
Socrates is endeavouring to prove to Aristodemus that
the world is the work of a benevolent Creator, not the
result of chance.   After laying down the principle that
the adaptation of means to ends is an evidence of intelligent activity, he proceeds to point out the adaptations
existing between the several parts of man's nature and
also between his nature and his environment.   Man is
endowed with instincts which lead him, independently of
reason, to perform those actions which are essential for
self-preservation and for the continuance of the species;
he has senses capable of receiving pleasure, and he finds
objects around him of such a nature as to give him
pleasure; he is favoured above all other animals in the
possession of hands and in the faculty of speech and the
power of thought, through which he is made capable of
higher pleasures and brought into communication with
higher objects.   His consciousness of his own reason is
a proof to him of a Reason outside of him, from which
that reason was derived.

[1] See Arist. *Eth*. III. i. 14.
[2] *Mem*. I. 4, cf. IV. 3.

Plato is distinguished from the other disciples of Socrates as the one who represents most truly the many-sidedness of his master, completing indeed and developing what was defective in him and incorporating all that was valuable in the earlier philosophers. Before treating of him it will be convenient to speak shortly of the 'imperfect' or one-sided Socraticists.

Euclides of Megara, the founder of the Megaric and so ultimately of the Sceptic school, was chiefly attracted by the negative teaching of Socrates, and his followers are noted as the inventors of various sophisms which served them as offensive weapons against their opponents. The main positive doctrine attributed to them is that they identified the Good, which Socrates called the highest object of knowledge, with the Absolute One of Parmenides, denying the existence of Evil.

Antisthenes, the founder of the Cynic and indirectly of the Stoic school, was the caricature of the ascetic and unconventional side of Socrates. Nothing is good but virtue, nothing evil but vice. Virtue is wisdom and the wise man is always perfectly happy because he is self-sufficient and has no wants, no ties and no weaknesses. The mass of men are fools and slaves, and the wise man is their appointed guide and physician. Acting on these principles the Cynics were the mendicant Friars of their time, abstaining from marriage and repudiating all civil claims, while they professed themselves to be citizens of a world-wide community. On the subject of religion Antisthenes stated explicitly, what was doubtless implied in the teaching of Socrates, that there was only one God, who is invisible and whose worship consists in a virtuous life.

The name 'Cynic' may have had a reference in the first instance to Cynosarges, the gymnasium in which Antisthenes taught; but it speedily received the connotation of dog-like, brutal, which seems to have been justified by the manners of some members of the school. Diogenes, the more famous disciple of Antisthenes, was fond of speaking of himself as ὁ κυών, and it seems to have been a usual thing with the Cynics, as with the other Socratics, to draw inferences as to the true and unsophisticated nature of man, from the habits of dogs and other animals[1]. The aim of the school being to return from a corrupt civilization to a state of nature, they put forward three main 'Counsels of Perfection,' as we may call them, by which this was to be attained, freedom (ἐλευθερία), frankness or outspokenness (παῤῥησία), and self-sufficingness or independence (αὐτάρκεια). The Cynics, and especially Diogenes, were famous for their pithy sayings and for their pungent biting wit. The following are taken from Mullach's collection. *Antisthenes* Fr. 65, 'Give me madness rather than pleasure[2].' Fr. 88, ' If you pursue pleasure, let it be that which follows toil, not that which precedes it.' Fr. 64, 'The only pleasure that is good is that which does not need to be repented of.' Fr. 55, 'To be in ill repute is good,

---

[1] Compare in Mullach's Collection of Fragments, *Diog.* § 33, 'other dogs bite their enemies, but I my friends for their good;' also § 122, § 145, § 190, § 210, &c. In § 286 men are said to be 'more miserable than beasts because of their luxury and effeminacy. If they would live the same simple lives, they would be equally free from diseases whether of mind or body.' Similarly Plato in the *Republic* makes the dog his pattern for the education and mode of life of the Guardians. See II 375 foll., and V 451 foll.

[2] μανείην μᾶλλον ἢ ἡσθείην.

as toil is good.' Fr. 105, 108, to the question 'what he had gained from philosophy?' he replied 'to be able to endure my own company;' 'what kind of learning was the most necessary?' 'to unlearn what is evil.' Fr. 44, discussing with Plato the nature of general conceptions, he said[1], 'I can see this horse, but not your ideal horse.' 'Yes,' said Plato, 'for you have the sight with which this horse can be seen, but you have not acquired the sight with which the ideal can be seen.' We read of similar encounters between Diogenes and Plato; thus, by way of ridiculing the latter's definition of man, a 'featherless biped,' Diogenes brought a plucked fowl into the lecture-room; upon which Plato is said to have amended his definition by adding πλατυώνυχος, 'with broad nails' (*Fr.* 124). On another occasion he is said to have come into Plato's house when he was entertaining some friends, and trampled on the beautiful carpets, saying, 'thus I trample on Plato's pride;' to which Plato replied, 'with no less pride, Diogenes[2].' The story of his interview with Alexander is familiar to every one. Among other characteristic sayings may be mentioned Fr. 281, 'It belongs to the Gods to want nothing, to godlike men to want as little as possible.' Fr. 113, 'Oppose to fortune courage, to law nature, to passion reason.' Fr. 295, 296, 'Nothing can be accomplished without training (ἄσκησις). Training of the soul is as necessary as that of the body. All things are possible by training.' We read that he crowned himself with the pine-wreath, claiming to have won a greater victory than that at the Isthmia, in his contest with

[1] Ἵππον μὲν ὁρῶ, ἱππότητα δὲ οὐχ ὁρῶ.
[2] Fr. 82, Πατῶ τὸν Πλάτωνος τῦφον. Ἑτέρῳ γε τύφῳ, Διόγενες.

poverty, disgrace, anger, grief, desire, fear, and, above all, pleasure (Fr. 294).

In spite of a good deal of exaggeration and something of charlatanry, it is probable that the influence of the early Cynics was not without its use in awaking men to a higher view of life; but it was not till the time of the Roman Empire that Cynicism became a real power, fostering freedom of thought and speech in the midst of the soul-crushing despotism of a Nero or a Domitian[1]. If at times the Cynic reminds us of the 'all-licensed fool' of the Middle Ages, at other times, as in the striking discourse in which Epictetus bids a friend pause before he assumes that name, he rises almost to the sublimity of a Hebrew prophet. Epictetus there reminds his friend that 'to be a Cynic is not merely to wear coarse clothing, to endure hard fare, to beg his bread, to rebuke luxury in others; it is to stand forward as a pattern of virtue to all men, to be to them the ambassador of Zeus, showing them how far they have strayed from what is right and true, how they have mistaken good for evil, and evil for good. It is the duty of the Cynic to shame men out of their peevish murmurings by himself maintaining a cheerful and contented disposition under whatever pressure of outward circumstances. If reviled and persecuted, it is his duty to love his persecutors and, far from appealing to the courts against ill-usage, to render thanks to God for giving him an opportunity of exercising his virtue and setting a brighter example to others. While fearless in reproving vice, he should avoid giving

[1] See Epict. *Diss.* III. 22, and Bernays' very interesting tract *Lucian und die Kyniker.*

unnecessary offence, and endeavour, as far as possible, to recommend his teaching, not only by persuasiveness of speech, but also by manner and personal appearance, never allowing hardness to degenerate into rudeness or coarseness. If the Cynic were living in a society of wise men, it might be his duty to marry and bring up children like himself; but as things are, he must look upon himself as a soldier in active service, and keep himself free from all ties which might interfere with his great work of delivering the Divine message to the blind and erring world.'

Aristippus of Cyrene the founder of the Cyrenaic school, resembled Antisthenes in dwelling exclusively upon the practical side of his master's teaching. Holding that we can never be conscious of anything beyond our own feelings, he held of course that it was impossible to attain objective knowledge. We each have feelings of what we call sweetness, whiteness, and so on, but what is the nature of the object which causes those feelings, and whether the feelings which others call by the same name are really the same as our feelings, on these points we know nothing. The only thing of which we can be sure, the only thing of importance is, whether our feelings are agreeable or disagreeable. A gentle movement of the mind is agreeable and we call it pleasure; a violent movement is disagreeable and we call it pain. Every pleasure is in itself equally desirable, but we may get a greater amount of pleasure by one sort of action than by another. Thus Aristippus interpreted the somewhat ambiguous language of Socrates about happiness in a purely eudaemonistic sense, and declared that the only rule of life was to enjoy the present moment. But for such enjoyment it is not enough simply to follow the passing impulse. The immediate pleasure obtained by gratifying an impulse may be more than balanced by a succeeding pain. The mind must be trained by philosophy to estimate and compare pleasures and pains, to master its impulses where their indulgence would lead to an overplus of pain, to be able promptly to discern and to act upon the possibilities offered by every situation of life, keeping itself ever calm and free, unfettered by the prejudices and superstitions of the vulgar. Accordingly it was the boast of Aristippus, no less than of Antisthenes, '*mihi res, non me rebus subjungere conor*[1].' His apophthegms and witticisms were scarcely less famous than those of Diogenes. The following may suffice as specimens.

(Mullach, Fr. 6,) asked what good he had gained from philosophy, he replied 'to converse freely ($\theta a \rho \rho a \lambda \dot{\epsilon} \omega s$) with all.' Fr. 8 and 15, asked why philosophers seek the rich and not the rich philosophers, he replied, 'because the former know what they need, the latter do not. The physician visits his patient, but no one would prefer to be the sick patient rather than the healthy physician.' Fr. 30, when reproached for his intimacy with Lais, he defended himself in the words $\dot{\epsilon} \chi \omega$ $\Lambda a \dot{\iota} \delta a$ $\dot{a} \lambda \lambda$' $o \dot{\upsilon} \kappa$ $\dot{\epsilon} \chi o \mu a \iota$. Fr. 53, 'He is the true conqueror of pleasure, who can make use of it without being carried away by it, not he who abstains from it altogether.' Fr. 50, Dionysius reminded him, on his begging for money, how he had once said that a philosopher could never be in want. 'Give the money,' said he, 'and we will discuss that point afterwards.'

---

[1] See Horace *Epp.* I. 17. 13—32.

The money being given, he said, 'You see it is true, I am not in want.' (Compare with this the manner in which he got his wants supplied in shipwreck, Fr. 61.)

Among the more prominent members of this school was Theodorus, surnamed the Atheist, who lived towards the close of the 4th century, B.C. Objecting to the doctrine of his predecessor on the ground that it did not leave sufficient scope to wisdom, since pleasure and pain are so much dependent on outward circumstances, he put forward as the chief good, not the enjoyment of passing pleasure, but the maintaining of a calm and cheerful frame of mind. The anecdotes related of him have quite a Stoic ring. Thus, when Lysimachus threatened to crucify him, he answers 'keep your threats for your courtiers: it matters not to Theodorus whether his body decays in the earth or above the earth.' Euhemerus, the rationalizing mythologist so much quoted by the Fathers, is said to have been a pupil of his. His contemporary, Hegesias, called πεισιθάνατος from his gloomy doctrine, considered that, as life has more of pain than pleasure, the aim of the wise man should be not to obtain pleasure, but to steel himself against pain. Thus in the end the Cyrenaic doctrine blends with the Cynic.

Plato[1], the '*deus philosophorum*' (Cic. N. D. II 32), was born of a noble family at Athens 428 B.C. and, like his brothers, Glaucon and Adimantus, and his relations Critias and Charmides, became a disciple of Socrates in 408 B.C. After the death of his master he left Athens and lived at Megara with Euclides. From thence he

[1] The best complete edition is Stallbaum's with Latin notes, the best English translation Jowett's in 5 vols. Oxford, 1875.

visited Cyrene, Egypt, Magna Graecia and Sicily. After nearly ten years of travelling he took up his residence again at Athens in 389 B.C. and began to lecture in the gymnasium of the Academia. At the request of Dion he revisited Sicily in 367 with a view of winning over Dionysius the Younger to the study of philosophy, and again in 361 in the hope of reconciling him to Dion; but he was unsuccessful in both attempts, and indeed seems to have been himself in considerable danger from the mercenaries of the tyrant. He died in his eightieth year, B.C. 347.

Building on the foundation of Socrates, he insists, no less than his master, on the importance of negative Dialectic, as a means of testing commonly received opinions; indeed most of his Dialogues come to no positive result, but merely serve to show the difficulties of the subject discussed and the unsatisfactory nature of the solutions hitherto proposed[1]. As he makes Socrates the spokesman in almost all the Dialogues, it is not always easy to determine precisely where the line is to be drawn between the purely Socratic and the Platonic doctrine, but the general relation of the one to the other may be stated as follows.

In his theory of knowledge Plato unites the Socratic definition with the Heraclitean Becoming and the Eleatic Being[2]. Agreeing with Heraclitus that all the objects of the senses are fleeting and unreal in themselves, he held

---

[1] These are classified by Thrasyllus as λόγοι ζητητικοί, dialogues of search, in opposition to the λόγοι ὑφηγητικοί, dialogues of exposition. Among the sub-classes of the former are the μαιευτικοί (obstetric), and πειραστικοί (testing).

[2] See Aristotle *Met.* A 6. 987, M 4. 1078.

that they are nevertheless participant of Being in so far
as they represent to us the general terms after which they
are named. Thus we can make no general assertion
with regard to this or that concrete triangular thing : it is
merely a passing sensation : but by abstraction we may
rise from the concrete to the contemplation of the Ideal
triangle, which is the object of science, and concerning
which we may make universal and absolutely true
predications. If we approach the Ideal from below,
from the concrete particulars, it takes the form of the
class, the common name, the definition, the concept,
the Idea; but this is an incomplete view of it. The
Ideal exists apart from, and prior to, all concrete
embodiment. It is the eternal archetype of which the
sensible objects are the copies. It is because the soul in
its pre-existent state is already familiar with this archetype,
that it is capable of being reminded of it when it sees its
shadow in the phenomenal existences which make up the
world of sense[1]. All learning is reminiscence[2]. What

[1] The reader will remember the magnificent ode in which
Wordsworth has embodied Plato's sublime conception. The fact
which underlies it was well illustrated by the late Prof. Sedgwick,
commenting on Locke's saying that "the mind previous to experience is a sheet of white paper" (the old *rasa tabula*), "Naked
he comes from his mother's womb, endowed with limbs and senses
indeed, well fitted to the material world, yet powerless from want of
use: and as for knowledge, his soul is one unvaried blank; yet has
this blank been already touched by a celestial hand, and when
plunged in the colours which surround it, it takes not its tinge from
accident, but design, and comes forth covered with a glorious
pattern." *Discourse*, p. 53. The Common-sense Philosophy of the
Scotch and the *à priori* judgments of Kant are other forms of the
same doctrine.

[2] Cf. *Meno*, p. 81, and Grote's *Plato* II. p. 7, 'Socrates illustrates

cannot be traced back to this intuitive consciousness in the soul itself is not knowledge, but mere opinion. Dialectic is the means by which the soul is enabled to recover the lost consciousness of the Ideal. The highest Ideal, which is the foundation of all existence and all knowledge, is the Ideal Good or Goodness (ἡ ἰδέα τοῦ ἀγαθοῦ), personified in God. He, as the Creator or Demiurgus, formed the universe by imprinting the ideas on formless chaotic Matter. The process of creation is described in the *Timaeus* under the form of a myth, Plato holding, like Parmenides, that it was not possible to arrive at more than a symbolical adumbration of physical truth. The cause and ground of creation is the goodness of God, who seeks to extend his own blessedness as widely as possible. He begins his work by constructing the soul of the world out of the two elements before him, the immutable harmonious Ideals and changing discordant Matter. This soul he infuses into the mass of matter, which thereupon crystallizes into the geometrical forms of the four elements, and assumes the shape of a perfect sphere rotating on its axis. The Kosmos thus created is divine, imperishable and infinitely beautiful. Further, each

the position, that in all our researches we are looking for what we have once known but have forgotten, by cross-examining Meno's slave; who, though wholly untaught, and never having heard any mention of geometry, is brought by a proper series of questions to give answers out of his own mind furnishing the solution of a geometrical problem. From the fact that the mind thus possesses the truth of things which it has not acquired in this life, Socrates infers that it must have gone through a pre-existence of indefinite duration.' The same argument is used in the *Phaedo* to prove the immortality of the soul.

element is to have living creatures belonging to it. Those belonging to the element of fire are the Gods, both the heavenly bodies and those of whom tradition tells us. All these were fashioned by the Demiurgus himself, but the creatures belonging to the other elements, including the mortal part of man, were the work of the created gods. The immortal part of man, the reason, is of like substance with the soul of the world, and was distributed by the Demiurgus amongst the stars till the time came for each several particle to enter the body prepared for it by the created gods, when it combined with two other ingredients, the appetitive (τὸ ἐπιθυμητικόν) and the spirited (τὸ θυμοειδές) which it had to bring into subjection. If it succeeded, it returned to its star on the death of the body ; if it failed, it was destined to undergo various transmigrations until its victory was complete. In all these physical speculations Plato was much influenced by the Pythagoreans.

We have now to speak of his ethical doctrines, which were based upon the psychological views mentioned above. The soul is on a small scale what the State, or city, is on a large scale : it is a constitution which is in its right condition when its parts work harmoniously together, when the governing reason is warmly supported by its auxiliary the heart, and promptly and loyally obeyed by the appetites. Thus perfect virtue arises when wisdom, courage and temperance are bound together by justice. The highest good is the being made like to God ; and this is effected by that yearning after the Ideal which we know by the name of Love.

Thirty-five Dialogues have come down to us under the name of Plato, the greater number of which are all but universally acknowledged to be genuine. Five of these are classified as 'logical' in the catalogue of Thrasyllus; one, the *Timaeus*, as 'physical;' in the remainder the ostensible purpose commonly is to define the meaning of some ethical term, as the *Laches* turns on the definition of Courage, the *Charmides* on the definition of Temperance, the *Republic* on that of Justice. But, in a writer so discursive, and so little systematic as Plato, it is impossible to carry out any strict system of classification: all that can be done is to group different dialogues together from one or another point of view; as we may call the *Apology*, *Crito*, *Euthyphro* and *Phaedo* Socratic in a special sense, because they give the substance of discourses really held by the historic Socrates. Or again we may trace a gradual progress from the simpler and narrower doctrines of the *Protagoras*, the *Lysis*, the *Charmides*, the *Laches*, which hardly pass beyond the Socratic point of view, to the *Phaedrus*, the *Gorgias*, the *Phaedo*, the *Symposium*, in which the Ideal theory is developed along with the doctrines of pre-existence and immortality: until at length we arrive at the culminating point of the Platonic philosophy in the *Republic*, that unsurpassable monument of genius, which stands on the same level in the world of speculation, as the Agamemnon or the Parthenon in the world of Art. We may observe the growth of Pythagorean mysticism in the *Timaeus;* and finally, in the deeply-interesting dialogue of the *Laws*, we may listen to the sadder and sterner tones in which the aged Plato, summing up his life's experience, confesses that he had been too sanguine in his hopes as to what could be effected by philosophy, and avows his belief that the deep-rooted evil in nature and in man must be traced back to an evil spirit counterworking the action of the divine spirit in the universe[1]; and that the lessons of philosophy must be supplemented and enforced by religion, if they are to have a real practical power over the mass of men.   In addition to the extant Dialogues, we find references to lectures of a more esoteric character upon the Chief Good, in which the theory of Ideas seems to have been mixed up with quasi-Pythagorean speculations on the symbolism of Number.

Perhaps the best way in which I can employ the brief space at my disposal, in order to give some notion of Plato's manner of treating a subject, will be to append here an abstract of the *Republic*[2], and then to illustrate, from that and from other dialogues, his three styles, dialectical, expository, and allegorical.

In the 1st Book of the *Republic* we have an excellent example of a dialectical discussion, which will be given more in detail below; upon the nature of Justice or Righteousness.   The conclusion arrived at is that Justice is in all respects superior to injustice, the opposite thesis having been maintained by Thrasymachus, and that the just man is happier than the unjust, not only because he is loved by the Gods and by all good men, but because Justice is that quality of the soul by which it is enabled to perform well its proper functions.   Socrates however allows that the discussion had been too rapid, and that they ought to have determined the exact nature of justice before arguing as to its effects.   Accordingly in the 2nd Book two of his disciples put forward the difficulties they

[1] Cf. x. 896.

[2] On the *Republic* see the interesting paper by Mr Nettleship in 'Hellenica,' and the translation by Davies and Vaughan.

feel on the subject, and beg of Socrates to prove, if he can, that justice is not only good in its results, but good and desirable in itself. Though men agree to commend justice, yet they generally do this in such a way as to imply that, if a man could practise injustice without fear of detection and retaliation or punishment, he would be happier than a just man who suffered under a false imputation of injustice, particularly if it be true that the favour of the Gods may be won by sacrifices and offerings, irrespectively of the moral character of the worshipper.

Socrates commences the expository portion of the dialogue by proposing to examine the nature of justice and injustice on a larger scale in the State. Tracing the rise of the State we shall be able to see how justice and injustice spring up within it. Society is founded in the wants of the individual : men enter into partnership because no one is sufficient to himself. Experience soon teaches the advantages of division of labour: thus one is a husbandman, another a builder, another a clothier; and with the growth of the community a whole class of distributors are needed in addition to the producers. If the State becomes wealthy and luxurious it will speedily be involved in war, and we shall need a standing army of thoroughly trained soldiers. Like good watch-dogs, they must be brave to resist the enemy, while at the same time they are gentle towards the citizens whom they guard. They must be carefully selected and trained up from their earliest years to be true Guardians of the State, trained in mind by music (including under this term literature), trained in body by gymnastics. The earliest training will be that by means of tales partly fictitious and partly true. Tales, such as those of Homer and Hesiod, which attribute wicked actions to the Gods, or represent the heroes as mastered by passion or bemoaning the approach of death, must be altogether excluded, and only such admitted as inculcate truth, courage, self-control, and trust in the unchanging goodness of God. God, being perfectly good, can never deceive, never be the cause of evil : when he sends what is apparently evil, it is really good in the form of chastisement. But not only the substance of these tales, but the form also must be under strict regulation. The style, the rhythm and the music must all be simple, grave and dignified, expressive of the feelings of a noble and virtuous man, never stooping to imitate folly or vice. Similarly in every branch of art, our youthful Guardians must be familiarized with all that is beautiful, graceful and harmonious, in order that they may learn instinctively to hate what is ugly, and thus may be fitted to receive the fuller teaching of reason, as they advance in years. The use of gymnastic is not only to train the body, but to develop the spirited element in the mind, and so supplement the use of music, which develops especially the philosophic element and by itself might induce too great softness and sensitiveness. For this second branch of education we need the same rules as for the first; it must be simple, sober, moderate. When our Guards have been thus trained, we shall select the ablest, the most prudent, the most public-spirited, to be governors or chief Guardians ; the rest we shall call the 'Auxiliaries.' To prevent jealousies we must instil into all the citizens the belief that the Guardians are born with a certain mixture of gold in their composition, the Auxiliaries with a like mixture of silver, and the inferior classes with brass and iron ; that it is the duty therefore of the rulers carefully to test the nature of each citizen, and not allow one of golden nature to remain in a lower class, or one of iron in the higher, since the city is fated to perish if ever brazen or iron men become its Guardians. Finally the Guardians and Auxiliaries are to live together in a camp, having no private property or home, but maintained by the contributions of the other citizens. Otherwise they will become tyrants rather than Guardians, wolves instead of watch-dogs.

Adeimantus here objects that the Guardians will be worse off than the other citizens. To which Socrates replies that the end of the true legislator is not to make any particular class happy, but to provide that each class and each citizen shall perform aright their proper function, and thus contribute to the general welfare of the city as a whole. One of the duties of the Guardians will be to take care that the citizens are not unfitted for their work or estranged from each other by the entering in either of poverty or riches. Another will be to prevent the city outgrowing its proper limits and losing its unity in that way: a third to guard against any innovation in the constitution, especially as regards the training of the Guardians themselves.

The State being thus fully organized, we have now to look for justice in it. If it is a perfect State, it must possess all virtue, *i.e.* it must be wise, brave, temperate and just. If we can discover the three former characteristics in our State, then the virtue which remains unaccounted for will be justice. Now the State is wise in the wisdom of its Guardians; it is brave in the bravery of its Auxiliaries, who have learnt in the

course of their training to form a true estimate of
what is, or is not, really formidable, and have acquired,
through the same training, sufficient strength of mind to
hold fast to these convictions in spite of all temptation.
Temperance is another name for self-mastery, by which
we understand the subordination of a lower self to
a higher self in the individual : in our State it will mean
the willing obedience of all the citizens to the Guardians
who form the smallest class. Finally justice is that
principle of conduct which lies at the root of all these,
and which we assumed in the very foundation of our
State, the principle, namely, that each citizen should
do his own work without meddling with others. Our
city will be just, as long as each class in it confines itself
to its own proper work; it will become unjust, when one
class usurps the position of another, especially if a lower
class usurps that of a higher.

We have now to apply this analogy to the individual.
As there are three classes in the State, so there are three
parts or elements existing in the individual mind. One
is Appetite (τὸ ἐπιθυμητικόν), such as we are conscious
of when we thirst; another Reason (τὸ λογιστικόν), which
at times forbids us to drink, though thirsty; the third
Spirit or the sense of honour, (τὸ θυμοειδές), which at
times assists the reason to keep under the appetites,
at times itself chafes and frets, like a wild horse, under
the control of reason. The virtues then of the individual
will be analogous to those of the State. He will be wise
through the wisdom of the rational element within him ;
brave, through the courage of the spirited or irascible
element; temperate, through the willing obedience of
the two inferior elements to the superior; just, when each

part of the soul performs its own proper function without encroaching upon the others. And this inward harmony will show itself outwardly in just deeds, while injustice is an unnatural discord and disease in the soul, and manifests its presence outwardly in all unjust and criminal actions. From this it must follow that justice in itself, apart from its consequences, must be always the greatest good, and injustice the greatest evil of the soul, as health is the greatest good and disease the greatest evil of the body.

In the 5th Book Socrates explains at length the community of women and children to which he had before alluded. The greatest evil to a State being separation of interests, and the greatest good being unity of interests and harmony of feeling, it must be our object to weld the whole city into one body, in which every part sympathizes with every other part, and the separate parts cease to talk of 'mine' and 'not mine,' but all together speak of 'ours.' But, as long as we have separate homes and separate families, we cannot hope for this complete blending of interests. It will be otherwise in our model State. Our women will go through the same training as the men; for the common opinion which restricts all women to a narrow circle of family duties is altogether contrary to nature : women have the same variety of aptitudes and ability as men; they only differ from men in being weaker. As we do not refuse to make use of female watch-dogs because they are weaker than the male, so we shall not forbid a woman to be a Guardian if she shows the requisite qualifications for the office. In regard to the rearing of children, it will be the duty of the rulers to follow the example of skilful breeders, and secure the best offspring by selecting the best parents. No union of Guardians or Auxiliaries will be allowed without the sanction of the rulers, and the children will be removed at once to a state-establishment, where they will be brought up under the charge of nurses, unknown to their parents; but every child will regard every man of mature age as a father; and all of the same age will be to each other brothers and sisters.

It is a question how far this ideal is capable of being put into practice. The only chance of it would be by the union of political power and philosophy in the same person. And here it becomes necessary to distinguish between the true philosopher and the pretender. The true philosopher, while he eagerly pursues every kind of wisdom and is enamoured of every kind of beauty, is never satisfied with the contemplation of isolated truths or of individual beautiful objects, but presses onwards till he sees the Ideal itself, which alone is always true, always beautiful, and is the cause of beauty and truth in other things by entering into them and irradiating them with some faint gleams of its own perfection. One who is thus familiar with the Ideal will be most likely to keep continually before his eyes the type of the perfect State, and to make laws in accordance with it. Having his mind occupied by such high thoughts, he will be in no danger from those temptations to voluptuousness, avarice and other weaknesses, which beset ordinary rulers. He will possess in fact those four characteristics which make up perfect virtue.

Adeimantus here objects that Socrates' picture of the philosopher is not in accordance with experience. Those who devote themselves to philosophy are generally thought useless, if not unprincipled. Socrates replies that this is owing to the corrupt state of public opinion, through which the qualities of mind which go to make a philosopher are perverted by adverse influences, while philosophy is left in the hands of pretenders who bring discredit upon it; or, if here and there a genuine philosopher is to be found, he is powerless to resist the stream, and is content if he can keep himself pure from the world, and retain the hope of a better life to come. In such a State as we are describing, the philosopher would not only reach a higher stage of growth himself, but he would secure his country's welfare as well as his own. The next point then is to show by what kind of education the Guardians may be raised into philosophers. Besides the tests previously mentioned, they must now be exercised in a variety of studies, terminating in the highest of all studies, that of the Ideal Good, the knowledge of which is needed, if they are to be perfect Guardians. What then is the Ideal Good? Socrates answers by an analogy. The Ideal Good is, in the invisible world, which is apprehended by the intellect and not by the senses, that which its offspring, the Sun, is in the visible world. As the Sun is the source of life and light to visible things, so the Ideal Good is the source of being and of knowledge in the intelligible world[1]. The use of education is to turn

---

[1] The analogy may be presented in a parallelism, as follows :

Sphere.	τὸ ὁρατόν the visible.	τὸ νοητόν the intelligible.
Supreme Cause.	ἥλιος.	ἰδέα τοῦ ἀγαθοῦ.
Effect		
(1) *Objective.*	γένεσις, 'becoming.'	οὐσία, 'being.'
(2) *Subjectivo-*		
objective.	φῶς, light.	ἀλήθεια, truth.

the mind from that which is visible and temporal, and to fix it upon the invisible and eternal. The preparatory studies are Arithmetic, Plain and Solid Geometry, Astronomy, Harmonics; he who has been duly trained in these will be fitted to enter on the crowning study of Dialectic, which does not start with assumed premisses, like the others, but examines and tests the premisses themselves, and will not rest till it has traced back each portion of knowledge to its fundamental idea, and further has seen how all ideas are connected with the Ideal Good.

The subject of education being thus completed, the argument proceeds to the consideration of the different kinds of constitution, and the corresponding varieties of character. Since all that has had a beginning is liable to decay, the time will come when the breed of Guardians will degenerate. The spirited or irascible element will

(3) *Subjective.* ὄψις, sight. ἐπιστήμη, knowledge.
Human Organ. ὄμμα, the eye. νοῦς, the reason.

A further parallelism will represent the action of the mind within the two spheres. Thus regarded, the visible world is the sphere of opinion (δοξαστόν), the other of knowledge (γνωστόν), and both are capable of subdivision, thus :

	δοξαστόν, world of opinion.		γνωστόν, world of knowledge.	
Object	images	things	mathematical abstractions	ideas
Mental operation.	εἰκασία, conjecture.	πίστις, faith.	διάνοια, discursive reasoning, starting from hypotheses.	νόησις, intuition, which tests hypotheses by the aid of dialectic.

overpower the rational element; and the two upper classes will enslave the third, and devote themselves to wars of conquest. Thus the aristocracy, or government of the best, will be changed into a 'timocracy' or government of honour, resembling that of Sparta; and corresponding to this we shall have the timocratical or ambitious man. The next stage in the downward progress will be the change from the love of honour and power to the love of wealth, giving rise to an oligarchical government or plutocracy, under which the old harmony will entirely disappear, and the city will be divided into two hostile communities, the few rich opposed to the many poor. Correspondingly to this, when the son of an ambitious father is taught by his father's calamities the danger of ambition, he becomes industrious, prudent and parsimonious, providing the means of enjoyment without the skill or the courage to use them. Democracy is the constitution which succeeds plutocracy, when those who have wasted their property by extravagance offer themselves as leaders to the discontented poor, and with their aid expel the rich and establish equality of rights. The democratical man is one who uses the money left by his father to gratify every impulse and indulge in every amusement, keeping himself however within certain limits of moderation. Lastly we have the passage from democracy to tyranny, when some popular leader has succeeded in putting down an insurrection of the rich, and having surrounded himself with a body-guard proceeds to establish his power by putting to death the bolder and more able citizens, and grinds down the rest by every kind of extortion and oppression. The tyrannical man is the son of the democratical man, but in him the father's various and comparatively innocent impulses are swallowed up by one over-mastering and lawless passion, which he gratifies at the expense of whatever violence or crime. If the tyrannical man is able to find a sufficient number of followers like himself, he makes himself an actual tyrant in his city and thus attains the summit of wickedness and injustice.

And now we have to answer the question which of these conditions is the happiest, which the most miserable. There can be no doubt as to which is the happiest, and which the unhappiest city, but some have maintained that, however unhappy may be the city which is under tyrannical rule, the tyrant himself is happy. But the facts are the same in both cases. As in the State, so in the tyrant, the better part is enslaved to the worse, the soul is for ever agitated by fierce and violent impulses; it is conscious that it is sinking deeper and deeper into wretchedness and crime, and is terror-stricken at the prospect of coming vengeance. The same conclusion follows from a consideration of the different kinds of pleasure. Each element of the soul has its appropriate pleasure. Thus he who is governed by reason enjoys the pleasures of wisdom, and extols these above the pleasures derived from honour or from wealth, while those in whom the irascible, or the appetitive element is strongest, magnify these latter pleasures above the former. Whose judgment are we to take? Manifestly that of him who both possesses the faculty of judgment and has had experience of all pleasures, that is, the philosopher; for he alone has the necessary mental qualifications, and has tasted both the pleasures of appetite and of honour; while the other two have never tasted the pleasures of knowledge. Again the pleasures which spring from philosophy are the only pure pleasures: other pleasures are for the most part merely negative, consisting in a momentary release from pain. He that drinks only escapes the pain of thirst for the moment, but he who has become conscious of mental emptiness and feels himself replenished by instruction, is nourished by a food more real and true. Further even the inferior pleasures cannot be fully enjoyed except by one in whose soul reason is supreme. Thus we conclude that it is best for every one to be governed by the divine principle of reason residing in his own soul; but if not, that this government must be imposed upon him from without; that the worst of all conditions is to be unjust, and then to evade the penalties by which injustice might be cured and the soul restored to health.

In the Tenth book Plato reverts to the subject of poetry and imitation, and lays down the rule that the only poetry allowed in the model State will be hymns in honour of the Gods and of virtuous men. He then introduces a consideration which, he says, adds tenfold force to all that has been urged in favour of justice, viz. the immortality of the soul, for which he gives the following as a new and additional proof. Whatever perishes, perishes in consequence of some particular vice or disease which belongs to it. If there be any thing which can withstand the corroding effect of its own special vice, that thing would be indissoluble and imperishable. The soul is liable to the disease of injustice, but we do not find that it ever dies of this disease. We must conclude therefore that it is imperishable. Thus, in considering the natural consequences of justice, we must not limit ourselves to this life, but must raise our eyes to the eternity beyond.

As we have proved that justice is in itself best, we need no longer fear that we shall be thought to base its claim on mere accessories, if we view the facts as they really are, and confess that the just man will always be seen in his true character by the Gods, and will be loved and favoured by them, however he may seem to be neglected with a view to his better training in virtue in this life. For it is impossible, we shall say, that he whose chief object it is to grow like to God, should ever be really neglected by him whom he resembles. And as for man, we shall say that, in the end at any rate, justice and injustice will be detected and will receive their due deserts of honour and dishonour. And yet these rewards are nothing in comparison with those which await the just in Hades, as we gather from the story of Er, who was permitted to return to earth after visiting the unseen world, and brought back with him the report of all that he had witnessed there.

In dealing with a book so pregnant and suggestive as the Republic, it is difficult to know where comment is likely to be most useful. The few remarks which I am able to make will have reference (1) to Plato's intention in writing the book; (2) to the circumstances which may have contributed to give it its special form and colouring; (3) to the anticipations of later thought and especially of Christian thought which may be found in it; (4) to the more striking examples of divergence between Plato and the prevalent views of his own or of later times.

(1) Some have held that the object of the writer is fully given in the name by which the book is commonly known, and that whatever travels beyond political philo-

sophy is to be regarded as a part of the scaffolding of the dialogue, or put to the account of Plato's incurable love of rambling. Others have been equally sure that the model State is a mere piece of machinery for the exhibition of Justice. Others have considered that its main object was to put forward a new theory of Education. The true view is given in a sentence of the *Laws*, 'our whole State is an imitation of the best and noblest life[1].' The root or foundation of this perfect life is righteousness, which is no spontaneous product of human nature, but must be fostered by careful training; and that life cannot be fully manifested except in a community.

Next follows the subordinate question, 'Did Plato mean his State to be a practical model, or did he mean it for an ideal, which might guide or suggest legislation, but could not be actually realized in practice?' His own language seems to waver; thus, while in VI. 502 it is stated that it is indeed difficult to carry out this ideal, but certainly not impossible, if the government were in the hands of philosophers; in IX. 592 Socrates, in reply to Glaucon's remark, that such a city is not to be found on earth, claims no more for it than that perhaps a pattern of it may exist in heaven for him who wishes to behold it, and beholding to organize himself accordingly; adding that it is of no importance whether it does now, or ever will, exist on earth. This double aspect of the State, in which it appears at one time as an improved Greek city, at another as the ideal society, the βασιλεία θεοῦ or *civitas dei*, reminds one of the double meaning of Jewish prophecy, by which the changing fortunes of the little

[1] *Leg.* VII. 817 πᾶσα ἡ πολιτεία ξυνέστηκε μίμησις τοῦ καλλίστου καὶ ἀρίστου βίου.

Israelite kingdoms are made to bring out fresh features of the great Messianic idea.

(2) The impulse which Plato received from the circumstances of his times is partly negative, from the state of affairs in Athens and in Sicily, partly positive, from Egypt, Sparta and the Pythagorean brotherhood. To the natural distaste of the philosophic student for the rule of the unthinking Demos, there was added a distinct reprobation of some of the existing customs or institutions of Athens, as for instance the seclusion of women,—a feeling which seems to have been widely spread among the Socratic School, perhaps owing in part to the influence of Aspasia,—and then, above all, in Plato's case, indignation at the ingratitude shown towards his master. If this dislike of the rule of the many led him at times to sigh for a paternal despotism, his experience in Syracuse taught him that there was one thing worse than an unprincipled democracy, and that was a selfish and unprincipled tyranny. In Egypt with its fixed system of castes and its long unbroken traditions, in Sparta with its Lycurgean discipline, he beheld the supremacy of Law, the sacrifice of the individual for the good of the whole[1]; in the brotherhood of Pythagoras he saw the same discipline joined to higher and wider aims, not merely the attainment of order and strength in the body politic, but the perfection of human nature as displayed in its best representatives.

(3) One of the most striking anticipations of later thought to be found in the book is the comparison between the constitution of the State and that of the soul, and the consequent building up of ethics upon the

[1] See Grote's chapter on the legislation of Lycurgus.

foundation of psychology. The State is a moral unit; the soul is a composite being, which is then only in a healthy condition when each constituent element is in due relation with the others, and performs its proper functions aright. Just so Bp. Butler in his Sermons insists that we do not fully explain the moral nature of man by giving a list of its various parts or elements, but that it involves also certain natural relations between these parts; that it is the function of reflexion or conscience to govern, and of the other elements or principles of man's nature to obey. Plato's psychological analysis is no doubt very defective. He entirely omits the benevolent affections, which form the instinctive basis of virtue, and limits the emotional part of man's nature to the appetites and the sense of honour, which last however he disguises as a quasi-malevolent affection, thus narrowing it down to one of its secondary developments. Still, here, as elsewhere, he supplied to Aristotle the starting-point for a more accurate analysis, and in giving prominence to spiritedness, or the sense of honour, as a main help to right actions, he has been truer to fact than the great majority of subsequent philosophers. The specification of the four so-called cardinal virtues makes its first appearance in Plato, who assumes it as a thing generally admitted, though he also endeavours, not very successfully, to show that it may be inferred from the nature of the State and of man. His conception of δικαιοσύνη, the will to do what is right, is too broad and general to justify its being placed on a level with the other more specific virtues. In this sense it really includes them all; for, if reason performs rightly its work of thinking and governing, the man will be wise and prudent; if the spirited element does its part, he will not only be courageous but will exhibit in all his actions a 'proud submission' to the voice of reason; if the appetites work rightly, they will supply all natural wants without overstepping the line of honour and of right. Proceeding to the consideration of the State itself, the idea of a community which is to realize before the eyes of men the pattern of heavenly perfection, to develop and strengthen all virtue in its citizens, and to guard them from the pernicious influences to which man's ordinary life is exposed[1]—such a conception has naturally been looked upon as an anticipation of the Church: and the principle so often insisted on, that the Guardians are not to think of their own happiness but to sacrifice themselves for their subjects, as the good shepherd sacrifices himself for his sheep[2]—this naturally recalls the words of the Gospel, contrasting the duties of the Christian governor with the claims made by those who exercise lordship among the Gentiles. Even the strange aberrations of the fifth book, describing the communism of the Guardians, might seem like broken visions of the future, when we think of the first disciples who had all things in common, and, in later days, of the celibate clergy, and the cloisteral life of the religious orders. Of social and political principles or institutions first enunciated or advocated by Plato, though in part suggested by the practice of Sparta, we may notice the division of labour, and, as a consequence of this, the establishment of a standing army, the recognition of the equality of the sexes, the duty of national education for the young, and of self-education

[1] *Rep.* VI. 491.
[2] I. 345, IV. 420.

continued through life for the philosopher, the limitation
of wealth and of population, the abolition of an idle
class. In the rules laid down for education the most
noticeable points are the importance attached to the
early training of the feelings and the imagination by
means of fictitious narratives, and the strict censorship
over religious and moral instruction. The great principle
is laid down that, God being perfectly good, all teaching
which represents him as doing wrong, or as the cause of
evil, or as capable of change, must be forbidden as false
and injurious. Similarly with regard to the use of Art : it
is only admissible where it tends to produce a high and
noble temper in the citizens : immoral or enfeebling
art, like immoral or enfeebling religion, is to be expelled
from the state. There is much that is interesting in the
details of the Platonic education, in regard to which
I would refer the reader to Mr Nettleship's excellent
paper contained in the volume entitled 'Hellenica.'
But beyond all special details, the great, the surpassing
merit of the Republic lies in its power to kindle a
love of the ideal, to make a man ashamed of preferring
lower pleasures to higher, or of living only for himself
or for his own pleasure, instead of living and working
for the general good. Plato gives him the spirit to
strive after this, because he encourages him to believe
in the existence of an unseen world of beauty and of
goodness, to which he of right belongs, however much he
may have fallen from it ; he tells him that he may be
converted from low and earthly thoughts and aims, and
be enabled to hold communion with the Divine essence
even here by the help of philosophy ; that life should be
a *commentatio mortis*, and that he who perseveres in the

practice of justice and the pursuit of wisdom will hereafter be readmitted to that august assembly, and dwell in
heaven with the Gods and with the wise and just of all
ages. It is not to be wondered at that, when they
met with teaching like this, some of the Christian
Fathers should have thought that Plato must have
learnt his wisdom from the Bible, or on the other
hand that Celsus should have charged the Evangelists
with borrowing from Plato[1].

(4) Our last point is what may be called the eccen-
tricity of Plato. Many of his doctrines were regarded as
paradoxes in his own day and have now become common-
places, such as, that it is better to suffer than to do
wrong, better for the wrong-doer to be detected and
suffer punishment than to escape. Other paradoxes we
are perhaps on the way to accept. But there are some
which are more shocking to the improved feeling of the
present day than they were when first uttered. A flagrant
example is the communism of the Guardians, of which
Mr Jowett writes 'the most important transaction of
social life, he who is the idealist philosopher converts
into the most brutal. The married pair are to have no
relation to each other except at the hymeneal festival:
their children are not theirs but the State's, nor is any tie
of affection to unite them. Yet here his own illustration
from the animal kingdom might have saved Plato from a
gigantic error. For the nobler sort of birds and beasts
nourish and protect their offspring and are faithful to one
another.' The explanation is that women in Athens

---

[1] See Ackermann, *Das Christliche im Plato*, p. 3 foll., and Havet
Le Christianisme et Les Origines, I. 203 foll. The view taken by
the latter is that of a modern Celsus.

at that time were much in the position of Turkish women
at the present day. Rome had still to teach the world
that the true nursery of patriotism is the Family; and
neither Plato nor any other Greek, unless perchance
Euripides, could form any conception of what marriage
was destined to become when the proud patriotism of
the Roman matron was softened and idealized under the
combined influence of Christianity and Teutonism. The
romance of affection, so far as it existed, was perverted
into an unnatural channel by that evil custom which had
run through Greek society like a plague; and the glamour
of this romance was powerful enough to blind even a
Plato in some degree to the foulness which it covered. It
is only in his last dialogue, the Laws, that he seems to
have discovered its true character and speaks with just
severity of its enormity[1]. Marriage in Athens was commonly arranged as a mere matter of business with a view
to private aggrandisement; Plato made it still more a
matter of business, but with him the gain sought was a
public one, the improvement of the breed of citizens. The
chief motive, however, which led him to abolish family life
was his fear of the unity of the State being dissolved by
separate interests; he thought that these interests would
disappear if none could speak of wife or child or property
as his own. Aristotle in his criticism has shown how little
such mechanical rules would answer the purpose intended[2].

[1] Compare the difference of tone in *Rep.* v. 468 and *Laws* VIII.
836—840.

[2] There can be no doubt that Plato's regulations in regard to
marriage, like those in regard to the bodily training of women, were
in part suggested by the customs of Sparta; where, as Grote says,
'the two sexes were perpetually intermingled in public, in a way
foreign to the habits, as well as repugnant to the feelings, of other

My space does not allow me to treat of the other stumbling-blocks of the Republic, the expulsion of poets, the principle that philosophers must reign: for all such I must refer the reader to the excellent discussion prefixed to Mr Jowett's translation.

I proceed now to give examples of Plato's different styles. An analysis of the argument of the first book of the Republic may suffice for his Dialectic.

This book serves as an introduction to the rest by raising the various difficulties which are to be solved afterwards, or by distinguishing various moral standpoints existing in Athens at the time. Thus the aged Cephalus represents the simple pre-scientific morality of old times; he has a sure instinct of what is right and wrong in action but has never attempted to theorize about them. His son Polemarchus has advanced a step further, he is ready with a definition of justice taken from Simonides, and is glad to discuss it with Socrates. Thrasymachus is the representative of the new lights to whom the old-fashioned morality and old-fashioned

Grecian states.' 'The age of marriage was deferred by law until the period supposed to be most consistent with the perfection of the offspring.' 'The bride seems to have continued to reside with her family, visiting her husband in his barrack in the disguise of male attire and on short and stolen occasions.' 'To bring together the finest couples was regarded by the citizens as desirable, and by the lawgiver as a duty: no personal feeling or jealousy on the part of the husband found sympathy from any one, and he permitted without difficulty, sometimes actively encouraged, compliances on the part of his wife consistent with this generally acknowledged object. So far was such toleration carried that there were some married women who were recognized mistresses of two houses and mothers of two distinct families.' *Hist. of Greece* II., p. 509 foll.

maxims are mere ridiculous prejudices: the fetters imposed by tradition have been broken by reason; man
should be guided by nature and not by law, and nature
bids him enjoy himself.   Lastly in the second book we
have the 'third thoughts' of the two Socratics, the doubt
whether reason and nature may not after all be nearer to
the old traditional, than to the new enlightened view;
and the remaining books, as we have seen, are employed
in proving that such is the case.

   The points raised in the remarks of Cephalus are (1)
in reference to the nature of happiness; it is not mere
sensual enjoyment, but rather the calmness which arises
from the subjection of the senses[1]; not the wealth which
enables a man to gratify his desires, but the peace which
arises from the harmony of the inner nature; (2) as to
the connexion of justice and happiness; the unjust are
filled with remorseful fears of judgment to come, the just
have hope in their end; (3) as to the definition of justice;
it is to speak the truth and repay what is owed.

   When the critical process is to begin, the representative of the unconscious morality leaves the stage,
and his place is taken by Polemarchus.   It having been
already shown that it is not always just to give back what
is owed (e. g. in the case of a madman's sword), the
definition is slightly modified and confirmed by the
authority of Simonides.   It now stands thus:

       'Justice is to restore to each man his due.'
   What then is due?

           'Good to friends, harm to enemies.'
   But if we try this definition by facts, we shall not find
that it is justice to which we attribute the rendering of

[1] p. 329.

good and evil, but now one art, now another, e. g. in disease the art of medicine. It seems therefore that the definition requires limitation. What due thing then is it which justice renders back, and to whom?

'Justice renders good to friends, harm to enemies, in war,' to which the following additions are made in course of the argument:

'and in peace also,'

'viz. in partnerships,'

'i. e. money-partnerships,'

'for keeping money safe.'

To which final definition Socrates replies that (1) it makes justice useless, (2) that it implies ingenuity in stealing (on the principle of 'set a thief to catch a thief') and is therefore unjust.

[To examine this piece of 'dialectic': it is evident that the definition of Simonides is too objective, not based upon the character or the intention of the just man, but on the thing performed. Polemarchus' mistake is that he conceives justice throughout in the early Socratic manner, as an art, not as a habit. He is willing to have it compared with cookery or medicine, and does not see that it is not parallel with these, but a habit of the mind which must show itself in every act. If it is assumed to be an art, it is easy to prove that there is really no place left for it, that every department of human action has its own special art, and that the kind of action singled out as most distinctively just will be either mere inactivity, something best performed by an infrangible iron safe, or a thorough acquaintance with the tricks of thieves, and quickwittedness in devising expedients to meet them; but such a science, as it fits a man for attack as much as for defence, has no more right to be called the science of justice than of injustice.[1]]

Returning to the original definition, Socrates asks

---

[1] Cf. Arist. *Eth.* v. 1. 4. δύναμις καὶ ἐπιστήμη δοκεῖ τῶν ἐναντίων ἡ αὐτὴ εἶναι, ἕξις δὲ ἡ ἐναντία τῶν ἐναντίων οὔ· οἷον ἀπὸ τῆς ὑγιείας οὐ πράττεται τὰ ἐναντία, ἀλλὰ τὰ ὑγιεινὰ μόνον.

what is to be understood by 'friends'. Does it mean 'those whom a man thinks honest and good'? Then, since we do not always think aright, it may be just to help the bad and injure the good. Does it mean 'those who are really just, whether we think so or not'? Then it may be just to injure those whom we call our friends and to benefit those whom we call our enemies, reversing the original definition. Thus we arrive at the amended definition ;

'Justice is to help friends, if good, injure enemies, if bad.'

Here Socrates lays hold of another point. Is it consistent with justice to injure, to do harm? Harm, in its true sense, means degrading a man in a moral point of view, making him less just, less righteous. Can it be the part of righteousness to make a man less righteous?

[This high view of what is beneficial and what is harmful recurs in p. 379, where it is shown that God harms none. He may punish and inflict pain, but it is only to bring out good in the end. Man has no right to harm for the sake of harming. This is the opposite of the old Greek view that the true manly character was shown in the power and will to favour friends and injure enemies.]

Polemarchus being silenced, Thrasymachus brings forward a new definition,

'Justice is the interest of the stronger ;
i. e. of the sovereign power in the state.'

' It is just for the subject to obey his ruler and to act for his ruler's interest.'

How then, if the ruler enjoins what is not for his own interest? Then the act will be just by one part of the definition, unjust by the other.

Amended definition (1) 'What the stronger imagines to be for his interest is just.'

Amended definition (2) 'Justice is obedience to the true governor who always enjoins what is for his interest.'

But the true governor is one who practises the art of government unmixed with other arts, who is in fact an impersonation of the art. Now, is the notion of self-interest involved in the art? Compare the pilot's art, the physician's art; they may be combined with other arts, but nothing is essential to them beyond the healing of the sick and the management of the vessel. The art simply exercises an oversight over that to which as an art it belongs; but the art is stronger than that which it oversees; therefore the art provides for the interest of the weaker, and the true governor, who personifies the art, will accordingly act not for his own interest, but for the interest of his subjects, who are the weaker[1].

Thrasymachus brings forward an instance on his side; 'why should the ruler, the ποιμὴν λαῶν, regard the interest of his people in any other light than the shepherd does that of his sheep?' and then lays down broadly the principle that

'Justice is one's own loss, another's gain; injustice one's own gain, another's loss.'

' This may be most clearly seen in the complete injustice of the tyrant, whom all count happy and enviable; though they profess to blame injustice on a small scale, because they are afraid of suffering it.'

Socrates begins by disputing Thrasymachus' illustration, and points out that Thrasymachus is here deserting

---

[1] This argument is used by Aristotle *Pol.* III. 6.

his former ground, describing not the true shepherd, but the banqueter or money-maker. If we confine our attention to the art of government, we shall see that it cannot be itself profitable to the governor, because no one will undertake it without a bribe. The bargaining for this bribe belongs to a special art, the art of wages; it is no more a function of government, than piloting is a function of medicine; yet a man may recover his health by acting as pilot, just as he might get wages by governing. The governor would not be less a governor if he chose to perform his work gratuitously. As regards the kind of wages offered to induce men to devote their time to study the interests of others in governing them, they are usually paid either in money or honour, or the motive appealed to may be the fear of being misgoverned by others. If it were not for the last motive the best men would prefer to remain subjects, and thus receive, instead of bestowing, benefit.

Thrasymachus reasserts that perfect injustice is more profitable than perfect justice, the former being good policy, the latter at best a weak good-nature. Socrates on the other hand proceeds to argue that justice is knowledge, injustice ignorance. For the just man is one who sets limits to his actions, who will never overstep the bounds of justice, or seek to get more than a just man should. On the other hand the unjust observes no limits, but seeks to gratify every impulse and to get as much as he can. Which of the two is the scientific character? In the case of the musician and physician it is shown that the scientific are distinguished from the ignorant by this very property of attending to rules, not overstepping the bounds laid down by the masters of the

science. In like manner the just man must be scientific
as compared with the unjust.

[The argument turns on the thoroughly Greek conception of the
superiority of the limited to the unlimited, the defined to the un-
defined, πέρας to ἄπειρον. Aristotle made limitation, or the avoidance
of extremes, a part of his definition of virtue.]

Socrates then proceeds to overthrow the assertion
that

'Injustice is stronger than justice'

by showing that if an unjust city is strong, it can only be
so on the principle of 'honour among thieves,' some
remnant of justice in its internal relations. If the citizens
are unjust to each other, if they illtreat and oppress one
another, there can be no unity and therefore no strength.
In like manner, if injustice exists in an individual, it must
destroy all inward concord, and so make him half-hearted
and irresolute in action; he becomes an enemy to
himself and to the Gods and all just men. The same
argument will overthrow the remaining assertion of
Thrasymachus, viz. that

'Injustice is happier than justice.'

But this is also shown to be false from a consideration
of the nature of virtue. The soul, like the eye or ear or
anything else, has a special work or function to perform,
and can only perform that work aright if possessed of the
fitting quality or virtue. The function of the soul is life
and thought, the virtue of the soul is justice; a just soul
will live well, an unjust soul will live ill. But living well
is happiness, living ill misery. Therefore justice is shown
to be more profitable than injustice, being wiser, stronger
and happier, as well as better.

Then follows in the second book the argument of

Glaucon, which we will give in Professor Jowett's abstract slightly altered, as an example of Plato's expository style.

'To do injustice is said to be a good; to suffer injustice an evil. As the evil is discovered by experience to be greater than the good, the sufferers make a compact that they will have neither, and this compact or mean is called justice, but is really the incapacity to do injustice. No one would observe such a compact if he were not obliged. Let us suppose that the just and unjust had two rings, like that of Gyges in the well-known story, which made them invisible; then no difference would appear in them, for every one does evil if he can, and he who abstained would be regarded by the world as a fool. Men may praise him in public out of fear for themselves, but they will laugh in their hearts. And now let us frame an ideal of the just and unjust. Imagine the unjust man to be master of his craft, seldom making mistakes and easily correcting them; having gifts of money, speech, strength—the greatest villain bearing the highest character : and at his side let us place the just in his nobleness and simplicity, being, not seeming, without name or reward, clothed in his justice only, the best of men, but thought to be the worst, and let him die as he has lived. The just man will then be scourged, racked, bound, and at last crucified ; and all this because he ought to have preferred seeming to being. How different is the case of the unjust, who clings to appearance as the true reality ! His high character makes him a ruler; he can marry where he likes, trade where he likes, help his friends and hurt his enemies ; having got rich by dishonesty, he can worship the Gods better, and will therefore be more loved by them than the just.'

Adeimantus adds further arguments to the same effect and concludes as follows:

'The origin of the evil is that all men from the beginning have always asserted the honours, profits, expediencies of justice. Had they been taught in early youth the power of justice and injustice inherent in the soul, and unseen by any human or divine eye, they would not have needed others to be their guardians, but every one would have been the guardian of himself. And this is what I want you to show, Socrates: other men use arguments which rather tend to strengthen the position of Thrasymachus that might is right; but from you I expect better things. And please to exclude reputation; let the just be thought unjust and the unjust just, and do you still prove to us the superiority of justice.'

I add four other specimens of Plato's expository style taken, the 1st from the *Symposium* p. 210, on the love of Ideal Beauty; the 2nd from the *Laws* v p. 731, on Selfishness; the 3rd also from the *Laws* x p. 887, on Atheism; the 4th from the *Phaedo* p. 85, on the need of a Revelation. The translations are borrowed with slight alterations from Professor Jowett.

The Love of Ideal Beauty.

'He who has been instructed thus far in the things of love and who has learned to see the beautiful in due order and succession, when he comes towards the end will suddenly perceive a nature of wondrous beauty;—a nature which in the first place is everlasting, not growing and decaying, or waxing and waning; in the next place, not fair in one point of view and foul in another, or fair to some and foul to others, or in the likeness of a face or hands or any other part of the bodily frame, or in any form of speech or knowledge, or existing in any other being; but beauty absolute and simple, which, without diminution and without increase or any change, is imparted to the ever growing and perishing beauties of all other things. He who under the influence of true love, rising upwards from these, begins to see that beauty, is not far from the end. And the true order of ascent is to use the beauties of earth as steps along which he mounts upwards for the sake of that other beauty; going from one to two, and from two to all beautiful forms, and from beautiful forms to beautiful exercises, and from the performance of beautiful exercises to the learning of beautiful ideas, until at last he arrives at the end of all learning, the Idea of Beauty itself and knows what the essence of Beauty really is. "This, my dear Socrates," said Diotima, "is the life which is truly worth living, when a man has attained to the contemplation of beauty absolute; a beauty which if you once beheld, you would see not to be after the measure of gold, and garments, and that youthful beauty, whose presence now entrances you so, that you and many a one would be content to live, seeing only and conversing with those whom they love, without meat and drink if that were possible; you want only to be with them and look at them. But what, if a man had eyes to behold the true beauty, the divine beauty, I mean, pure and clear and unalloyed, not clogged with the pollutions of mortality, and all the colours and vanities of human life? Do you not see that in that communion only, beholding beauty

with the eye of the mind, he will be enabled to bring
forth, not images of beauty, but realities (for he has hold
not of an image, but of a reality), and bringing forth and
nourishing true virtue to become the friend of God, and
be immortal, if mortal man may?"

Selfishness.

'The greatest evil to men generally is one which is
innate in their souls, and which a man is always excusing
in himself and never correcting; I mean what is expressed in the saying, that every man by nature is and
ought to be his own friend. Whereas the excessive love
of self is in reality the source to each man of all offences;
for the lover is blinded about the beloved, so that he
judges wrongly of the just, the good, and the honourable,
and thinks that he ought always to prefer his own interest to the truth. But he who would be a great man
ought to regard what is just, and not himself or his
interests, whether in his own actions or those of others.
Through a similar error men are induced to fancy that
their own ignorance is wisdom ; and thus we, who may be
truly said to know nothing, think that we know all things;
and because we will not let others act for us in what we do
not know, we are compelled to act amiss ourselves.
Wherefore let every man avoid excess of self-love, and
condescend to follow a better man than himself, not allowing any false shame to stand in the way.'

Atheism.

'Who can be calm when he is called upon to prove
the existence of the Gods? How can one help feeling
indignation at those who will not believe the words they
have heard as babes and sucklings from their mothers
and nurses, words repeated by them like charms both in

earnest and in jest; who have also heard and seen their
parents offering up sacrifices and prayers—sights and
sounds delightful to children,—sacrificing, I say, with all
earnestness on behalf of them and of themselves, and
communing with the Gods in vows and supplications as
though they were firmly convinced of their existence;
who likewise see and hear the genuflexions and pros-
trations which are made at the rising and setting of the
sun and moon both by Greeks and barbarians in all the
various turns of good and evil fortune, not as if they
thought that there were no Gods, but as if there could be
no doubt of their existence, and no suspicion of their
non-existence;—if men know all these things, and without reason disregard them, how is it possible in gentle
terms to remonstrate with them, when one has to begin
by proving to them the very existence of the Gods?
Yet the attempt must be made, for it would be unseemly
that one half of mankind should go mad in their lust of
pleasure, and the other half in righteous indignation at
them.   Our address to these lost and perverted natures
should not be spoken in passion; let us suppose ourselves to select some one of them, and gently to reason
with him, smothering our anger:—O my son, we will say
to him, you are young, and the advance of time will make
you reverse many of the opinions which you now hold.
Wait therefore, until the time comes, and do not attempt
to judge of high matters at present; and that is the
highest of all of which you now think nothing—to know
the Gods rightly and to live accordingly.   And in the
first place let me indicate to you one point which is of
great importance, and of the truth of which I am quite
certain:—you and your friends are not the first who have

held this opinion about the Gods. There have always been persons more or less numerous who have had the same disorder. I have known many of them, and can tell you, that no one who had taken up in youth this opinion, that the Gods do not exist, ever continued in the same till he was old. The two other notions certainly do continue in some cases, but not in many ; the notion I mean, that the Gods exist, but take no heed of human beings, and the notion that they do take heed of them, but are easily propitiated[1] with offerings and prayers. Now, if you will take my advice, you will continue to examine whether the opinion which might seem to you to have been established to the best of your power, is really true or not, asking help both of others and above all of the legislator. And meanwhile beware of committing any impiety against the Gods'. After this prelude the speaker proceeds to give a proof of theism from the essential and necessary priority of mind to matter, and from the movements of the heavenly bodies.

A 'divine word' needed to dispel the darkness of the future.

Simmias and Cebes are not quite satisfied with the grounds alleged by Socrates for his belief in the immortality of the soul, but they shrink from saying anything which could disturb the serenity of his last hours. Socrates encourages them to speak fearlessly, since his patron, Apollo, has granted to him that same foretaste of future blessedness, which makes the dying swan burst forth into its hymn of praise. Simmias, thus encouraged, excuses his own hardness of belief in the following

---

[1] By 'propitiation' here, as in the 2nd book of the *Republic*, Plato means the supposed power, on the part of an unrepentant sinner, to avert the Divine wrath by votive offerings.

words: 'I do not doubt, Socrates, that you are as fully convinced as we are of the impossibility, or at least the extreme difficulty, of arriving at actual certainty in regard to these matters, whilst we are on earth. Still you would justly blame our faint-heartedness, if we desisted from the search for truth, before we had tried every possible means of attaining it. You would tell us that, if a man has failed to learn the truth from another, or to discover it for himself, it is his duty at any rate to find the best and most irrefragable of human words, and trusting himself to this, as to a raft, to set forth on the hazardous voyage of life, unless it were possible to find a surer and less dangerous way on board a stronger vessel, some word of God[1].'

I conclude with one example of Plato's allegorical style, the famous simile of the Cave from the Seventh book of the *Republic.*

'Imagine human beings living in a sort of underground den which has a mouth wide open towards the light: they have been there from childhood and, having their necks and legs chained, can only see before them. At a distance there is a fire, and between the fire and the prisoners a raised way, and a low wall built along the way, like that over which marionette players show their puppets. Above the wall are seen moving figures, who hold in their hands various works of art, and among them figures of men and animals, wood and stone, and some of the passers-by are talking and

---

[1] τὸν γοῦν βέλτιστον τῶν ἀνθρωπίνων λόγων λαβόντα καὶ δυσεξ-ελεγκτότατον, ἐπὶ τούτου ὀχούμενον, ὥσπερ ἐπὶ σχεδίας, κινδυνεύοντα διαπλεῦσαι τὸν βίον, εἰ μή τις δύναιτο ἀσφαλέστερον καὶ ἀκινδυνότερον ἐπὶ βεβαιοτέρου ὀχήματος, λόγου θείου τινὸς, διαπορευθῆναι.

others silent. The captives see nothing but the shadows which the fire throws on the wall of the cave ; to these they give names; and, if we add an echo which returns from the wall, the voices of the passengers will seem to proceed from the shadows. Suppose now that you suddenly turn them round and make them look with pain and grief to themselves at the real images; will they believe them to be real? Will not their eyes be dazzled, and will they not try to get away from the light to something which they are able to behold without blinking? And suppose further, that they are dragged up a steep and rugged ascent into the presence of the sun himself, will not their sight be darkened with excess of light? Some time will pass before they get the habit of perceiving at all; and at first they will be able to perceive only shadows and reflexions in the water; then they will recognize the moon and the stars, and will at length behold the sun in his own proper place as he is. Last of all they will conclude : This is he who gives us the year and the seasons, and is the author of all that we see. How will they rejoice in passing from darkness to light ! How worthless to them will seem the honours and glories of the den or cave out of which they came ! And now imagine further that they descend into their old habitations. In that underground dwelling they will not see as well as their fellows, and will not be able to compete with them in the measurement of the shadows on the wall; there will be many jokes about the man who went on a visit to the sun and lost his eyes; and if those imprisoned there find any one trying to set free and enlighten one of their number, they will put him to death if they can catch him.

Now in this allegory, the cave or den is the world of sight, the fire is the sun, the way upwards is the way to knowledge; and in the world of knowledge the Idea of Good is last seen and with difficulty, but, when seen, is inferred to be the author of good and right, parent of the lord of light in this world and of truth and understanding in the other. He who attains to the beatific vision is always going upwards; he is unwilling to descend into political assemblies and courts of law; for his eyes are apt to blink at the images or shadows of images which they behold in them; he cannot enter into the ideas of those who have never in their lives understood the relation of the shadow to the substance. Now blindness is of two kinds, and may be caused either by passing out of darkness into light, or out of light into darkness, and a man of sense will distinguish between them, and the blindness which arises from fulness of light he will deem blessed, and pity the other. There is a further lesson taught by this parable of ours. Some persons fancy that instruction is like giving eyes to the blind, but we say that the faculty of sight was always there, and that the soul only requires to be turned round towards the light. And this is conversion : other virtues are not innate but acquired by exercise like bodily habits; but intelligence has a diviner life and is indestructible, turning either to good or evil according to the direction given. Did you never observe how the mind of a clever rogue peers out of his eyes, and the more clearly he sees, the more evil he does? Now, if you take such an one and cut away from him the leaden weights which drag him down and keep the eye of the soul fixed on the ground, the same faculty in him will be turned round, and he will behold the truth as clearly as he now discerns his meaner ends. And have we not decided that our rulers must neither be so uneducated as to have no fixed rule of life, nor so over-educated as to be unwilling to leave their paradise for the business of the world? While we must choose out the natures who are most likely to ascend to the light and knowledge of the good, we must not allow them to remain in that region of light, but must force them to descend again among the captives in the den to partake of their labours and honours. Nor is this unjust to them, for our purpose in framing the State was not that our citizens should do what they like, but that they should serve the State for the common good of all. May we not fairly say to the philosopher:—In other states philosophy grows wild, and a wild plant owes nothing to the gardener, but you we have trained to be the rulers of our hive, and therefore we must insist on your descending into the darkness of the den? You must each of you take your turn and become able to use your eyes in the dark, and with a little practice you will see far better than those who quarrel about the shadows, whose knowledge is a dream only, whilst yours is a waking reality. It may be, the saint or philosopher who is best fitted, may also be the least inclined to rule, but necessity is laid upon him, and he must no longer live in the heaven of ideas. And this will be the salvation of the State.'

Aristotle 'the master of the wise,' according to the great poet of the Middle Ages, the tyrant of the schools, and champion of the Obscurantists, according to Bacon and the Renaissance, was born at Stagira, a Greek colony in Thrace, in the year 385 B.C. He came to Athens in his 17th year and studied under Plato for twenty years. On Plato's death in 347 B.C. he went with Xenocrates to reside at the court of his former pupil Hermias, the ruler of the Mysian cities of Assos and Atarneus. On the overthrow and death of Hermias in 344, he retired to Mitylene, from whence he was invited in 342 by Philip, King of Macedon, to superintend the education of his son Alexander, then a boy of 13. When Alexander set out on his Persian expedition in 335 B.C. Aristotle returned to Athens and taught in the Lyceum. As he lectured while walking his disciples were called Peripatetics[1]. On the death of Alexander, Aristotle left Athens to escape from a charge of impiety, 'desiring', as he said, 'to save the Athenians from sinning a second time against philosophy', and settled at Chalcis in Euboea, where he died 322 B.C.

It is worth while to pause and reflect for a moment on the succession here brought before us; Alexander the disciple of Aristotle, the disciple of Plato, the disciple of Socrates. That four such names, each supreme in his own line, should have been thus linked together, is a fact unparalleled in the history of the world; and its momentous nature is seen in its consequences, the Hellenizing of East and West by the sword of Alexander and by the writings of Plato and Aristotle. The work of Alexander might perhaps have been done by a meaner instrument, but without the 'great twin brethren' the whole course of human development must have been different. Science, Law, Philosophy, Theology, owe their present form and almost their existence to them. When Plato, griev-

---

[1] The form shows that the word is derived from περιπατέω not from περίπατος.

ing over the helplessness and the isolation of the solitary
thinker, sighed for a philosophic governor to carry out
his ideas in action, he little dreamt that he was laying
the foundation of a spiritual kingdom which was to embrace the whole of the civilized world. Then again,
reflect on what is meant by twenty years of philosophic
intercourse between a Plato and an Aristotle. Zeller has
conclusively shown the falsehood of various scandalous
anecdotes in which the latter is represented as guilty,
among other faults, of disrespect and ingratitude towards
his master. On the contrary there seems every reason to
believe that tradition has preserved the spirit, if not the
precise facts, of the relationship between them, when it
attributes to Plato the saying that 'Aristotle was the
intellect of his school' ($\nu o \hat{v} s \ \tau \hat{\eta} s \ \delta \iota a \tau \rho \iota \beta \hat{\eta} s$), and to Aristotle the epitaph in which Plato is described as 'one
whom it would be profanity in a bad man even to praise'
($\dot{a} \nu \delta \rho \dot{o} s, \ \ddot{o} \nu \ o \dot{v} \delta' \ a \dot{\iota} \nu \epsilon \hat{\iota} \nu \ \tau o \hat{\iota} \sigma \iota \ \kappa a \kappa o \hat{\iota} \sigma \iota \ \theta \dot{\epsilon} \mu \iota s$). No wonder
that the mind of the disciple became to such a degree
saturated with the thoughts of his master that, in the words
of Sir A. Grant, 'almost every page of Aristotle's Logical,
Rhetorical, Ethical, Political and Metaphysical writings
bears traces of a relation to some part or other of Plato's
dialogues[1].'

But though it would hardly be going too far to say
that Aristotle's philosophy, setting aside his Logic and
Natural History, was, in the main, little more than an
expansion and elaboration of the guesses and hints of
Plato ; though the groundwork of the two systems is the
same, yet nothing can be more dissimilar than the impressions produced by the writings of the two men. The

[1] *Ethics of Aristotle*, Vol. I. p. 180.

vague mysticism, the high poetic imagination, the reform-
ing and revolutionary tendencies of the master, were
altogether alien to the scholar. While Plato's aim was
to modify or reform existing fact or opinion by the standard of the idea in his own mind, Aristotle's aim is to
correct and develop the idea, which he usually accepts
from Plato, by a reference to existing fact or opinion[1].
While Plato is overpowered by the sense of a surrounding infinity, which the intellect of man is powerless
to grasp, but to which it is nevertheless drawn by an
irresistible attraction; while he appears oppressed by
the consciousness of the necessary incompleteness of all
human knowledge, and seeks rather to throw new lights
on the various objects of thought, than to bring them
under fixed and definite formularies; Aristotle on the
contrary cared only for what is clear, precise, defined,
and made it his chief aim to map out the whole of
existing knowledge in definite compartments and to
sum up results in technical formulas of universal application. Probably one reason for his popularity in
the Middle Ages was the almost magical virtue which
he thus appears to attribute to formulas. Corresponding
with this difference in tone and feeling is the difference
of style: there is an inimitable charm and grace in almost
every sentence of Plato, but Aristotle, of set purpose,
adopts a style which is, for the most part, as dry and
unadorned as Euclid, though perhaps we may be dis-

---

[1] See *Ethics*, x. 8, συμφωνεῖν τοῖς λόγοις ἐοίκασιν αἱ τῶν σοφῶν
δόξαι. πίστιν μὲν οὖν καὶ τὰ τοιαῦτα ἔχει τινά, τὸ δ' ἀληθὲς ἐν τοῖς
πρακτοῖς ἐκ τῶν ἔργων καὶ τοῦ βίου κρίνεται· ἐν τούτοις γὰρ τὸ κύριον.
σκοπεῖν δὴ τὰ προειρημένα χρὴ ἐπὶ τὰ ἔργα καὶ τὸν βίον ἐπιφέροντας,
καὶ συνᾳδόντων μὲν τοῖς ἔργοις ἀποδεκτέον, διαφωνούντων δὲ λόγους
ὑποληπτέον.

posed to think, as we study his writings more carefully, that no other style could have given so strong an impression of the earnest truthfulness and the philosophic calm of the author[1]. For a further account of the relation between them, I borrow again from Sir Alexander Grant.

'While Aristotle is far more scientific, he is wanting in the moral earnestness, the tenderness, and the enthusiasm of Plato...On the other hand he is more safe than Plato. He is quite opposed to anything unnatural (such as communism) in life or institutions...And on all questions he endeavours to put himself in harmony with the opinions of the multitude, to which he thinks a certain validity must be ascribed' (p. 215). 'Plato's rich and manifold contributions to logic, psychology, metaphysics, ethics, and natural religion, were too much scattered up and down in his works, too much overlaid by conversational prolixity, too much coloured by poetry or wit, sometimes too subtly or slightly indicated, to be readily available for the world in general, and they thus required a process of codification. Aristotle with the greatest gifts for the analytic systematizing of philosophy that have ever been seen, unconsciously applied himself to the required task' (p. 181.)

Thus Plato's Dialectic method was developed by Aristotle into the strict technical science of Logic: Plato's Ideas, though shorn of their separate supra-mundane existence, still survived in the Aristotelian Form, as opposed to Matter. Aristotle distinguished three movements or aspects of the former, and, by adding to these the antagonistic principle of Matter, he arrived at his

---

[1] For a more unfavourable view of Aristotle's style, see Cope, *Introduction to Aristotle's Rhetoric*, p. 132.

famous classification of the four Causes, the strictly formal (εἶδος, τὸ τί ἦν εἶναι[1], ἡ πρώτη οὐσία), the material (ὕλη, τὸ ὑποκείμενον, τὸ ἐξ οὗ), the efficient (τὸ κινοῦν, τὸ ὑφ' οὗ), the final (τέλος, τὸ οὗ ἕνεκα), which are really four kinds of antecedent conditions required for the existence of each thing. For instance, in order to the production of a marble statue by Phidias there is needed (1) the pre-existence in his own mind of the ideal form which is subsequently impressed upon the stone; (2) the existence of the stone; (3) the act of carving; (4) the motive which induced the sculptor to make the statue, as for instance the desire to do honour to the God whose statue it is. Or again, we may illustrate Aristotle's doctrine on this point, and shew how the three aspects of

---

[1] This curious phrase, applying most properly to the creative idea in the mind of the artist, is thoroughly characteristic of the plastic genius of Greece. We may ask, in regard to any work, τί ἐστι; what is its actual nature? or we may ask τί ἦν; what is the idea it was intended to embody? And by putting this in a substantival form, 'the being what it was intended to be,' we get an expression for its essential nature or true definition; see Trendelenburg's note on the *De Anima* I. 1, 2, Waitz on *Anal. Post.* I. 11. Every concrete object is a combination of pre-existing matter and form: matter being regarded as indefinite, without character or quality, (cf. *Met.* VII. 10, p. 1036 *a*. ἡ δ' ὕλη ἄγνωστος καθ' αὑτήν), all that is characteristic in the object must come from the other element, viz. form, which may therefore be described as that which the thing was, previous to its state of concrete existence. Thus a house consists of bricks or other materials adapted to a certain end, but the thought of this adaptation preceded the actual existence of the house: so, in nature, the tree is a combination of materials grouped according to a certain law or form, but this law was pre-existent in the seed before it was made manifest in the tree, and again it pre-existed in the parent tree before it received a latent embodiment in the seed.

Form tend to run into one another, by considering what was the cause of the virtue of Socrates. The material cause here is the existing Socrates with a yet unrealized potentiality of virtue; the formal cause is the virtuous ideal presented to his mind; and this formal cause will also be the efficient cause, in so far as it tends to actualize itself in the concrete Socrates, and the final cause, in so far as the virtuous character is its own end. But the opposition of Form and Matter is not confined to such simple cases; it covers the whole range of existence from the First Matter, which is mere potentiality of being (δύναμις) at the one extreme, to the First Form which is pure immaterial actuality (ἐνέργεια), the Divine Being, at the other extreme. The intermediate links in the chain are matter or form according as they are viewed from above or below, as marble for instance is form in reference to stone generally, matter in reference to statue; vitality is form in reference to the living body, matter in reference to rationality. In this way Matter becomes identified with the logical Genus, Form with the Differentia : as Matter can only attain to actual existence in some concrete shape by the addition of Form, so the Genus is by itself only potential, but attains actual existence in its Species through the addition of the Differentia[1].

The First Form of Aristotle, like the ἰδέα τοῦ ἀγαθοῦ of Plato, is also the First Mover, the cause of the upward striving of the universe, of the development of each thing from the potential into the actual; and this not by any act of creation, for He remains ever unmoved in His own eternity, but by the natural

[1] See Zeller III. p. 210, Bonitz on Arist. *Met.* IV. p. 1024 *b*, Grote *Arist.* II. 341.

tendency which all things have towards Him as the
absolutely Good, the object and end of all effort, of all
desire[1]. The universe itself is eternal, a perfect sphere
the circumference of which is composed of the purest
element, ether, and is carried round in circular motion
by the immediate influence of the Deity. In it are the
fixed stars, themselves divine. All above this Primum
Mobile is the abode of divinity, in which there is
no body, no movement, no void, and therefore no
space and no time. The lower planetary spheres
have a less perfect movement and are under the
guidance of subordinate divinities. Still, throughout the
whole space, from the outermost sidereal sphere down to
the lunar sphere, all is ordered with perfect regularity
according to Nature. It is only in the sublunary region
extending from the moon to the earth, which is fixed in
the centre, furthest removed from the First Mover and
composed of the four inferior elements with their rectilinear movements, centripetal or downwards in the
case of earth and water, centrifugal or upwards in
the case of air and fire, that the irregular forces of
Spontaneity and Chance make their appearance, and
impede or modify the working of Nature. Yet even
here we find a constant progressive movement from
inorganic into organic, from plant into animal, from life
which is nutritive and sensitive only into life which is
locomotive and finally rational in man. The human soul
is a microcosm, uniting in itself all the faculties of the
lower orders of animated existence, and possessing,

[1] Aristotle's words κινεῖ ὡς ἐρώμενον (*Met.* XII, 7), remind us
of the yearning after the First Fair, treated of in the *Symposium* and
other dialogues of Plato.

besides, the divine and immortal faculty of reason. As each thing attains its end by fulfilling the work for which it is designed by nature, so man achieves happiness by the unobstructed exercise of his special endowment, a rational and virtuous activity. Pleasure is the natural accompaniment of such an activity. Virtue, which may be described as perfected nature, belongs potentially to man's nature, but it becomes actual by the repetition of acts in accordance with reason. It is subdivided into intellectual and moral, according as it is a habit of the purely rational part of the soul, or as it is a habit of the emotional part, which is capable of being influenced by reason, but not itself rational. Every natural impulse is the potential basis of a particular virtue which may be developed by repeated actions freely performed in accordance with the law of reason so as to avoid either excess or defect. Since man is by nature gregarious, his perfection is only attainable in society, and ethical science is thus subordinate to political science.

I have here given the briefest possible summary of Aristotle's general system, as it is contained in the *Physica*, the *Metaphysica* (so called as following the *Physica*) and the *Nicomachean Ethics*. Of the latter and of the *Politics* I have added a fuller analysis below, in order to enable the reader to compare them with Plato's *Republic*. In the remaining works we have a sort of encyclopaedia of science. The *Organon*[1] contains the theory of deductive reasoning. It includes (1) the *Categories* in which

---

[1] There is an excellent edition by Waitz with Latin notes : Mr Poste has brought out an English translation of the *Posterior Analytics and Fallacies*, with introduction and notes. See also Trendelenburg's *Elementa Logices Aristoleae*.

all predications are classified under ten heads, Substance (οὐσία), Quantity (πόσον), Quality (ποῖον), Relation (πρός τι), Place (ποῦ), Time (πότε), Situation (κεῖσθαι), Possession (ἔχειν), Action (ποιεῖν), Passion (πάσχειν). Their use may be thus illustrated, 'Socrates is a man, seventy years old, wise, the teacher of Plato, now sitting on his couch, in prison, having fetters on his legs, instructing his disciples, and questioned by them'. It has been often pointed out that the classification here given errs both in excess and in defect, but it has the merit of being the first attempt of the kind. Trendelenburg suggests that it was borrowed from the grammatical division of the Parts of Speech. The 2nd of the Logical treatises is the *De Interpretatione*, dealing with the Proposition, in which the distinction between Contrary and Contradictory, and between Possible and Necessary ('Modal') Propositions, is for the first time clearly explained. In the 3rd, the *Analytica*, we have the doctrine of the Syllogism set forth with as much completeness as in Whately or Aldrich, together with an account of applied reasoning under the two heads of Demonstration (ἀπόδειξις) and Dialectic (διαλεκτική). It further distinguishes between Induction (ἐπαγωγή), arguing upwards to Universals from Particulars, which are γνωριμώτερα ἡμῖν, more familiar and intelligible to the learner or investigator, and Deduction (συλλογισμός), arguing downwards to Particulars from Universals, which are φύσει γνωριμώτερα, naturally and in themselves clearer and more intelligible. But though Aristotle thus derives the major premiss of the Syllogism from previous Induction, he has nowhere attempted to state the laws of the Inductive process, as he has done those of the Syllogism. He only tells us that the general idea, which

Plato thought to be a separate existence known to the soul in a previous state of being, was simply a truth attained by gradual process of Induction, and certified by the unerring principle of reason (νοῦς). The steps were perception (αἴσθησις), memory (μνήμη), experience (ἐμπειρία); and the half-conscious judgment contained in the last, when taken up, examined and approved by the supreme faculty νοῦς, was stamped as absolutely and universally true. Dialectical reasoning is the subject of the 4th of Aristotle's logical treatises, called the *Topica*, because it treats of the 'places' or 'storehouses' (τόποι) in which arguments are to be found. In it Aristotle gives the principles and rules of the Socratic dialogue, the original 'Dialectic' before the term had been twisted by Plato to mean not only the art of philosophical discussion, but the highest part of philosophy itself. Aristotle on the contrary carefully separates it from science (ἐπιστήμη) and connects it more with rhetoric, since both deal with matters of opinion and make use of probable arguments. Its end is not so much to prove truth as to expose inconsistency : it is useful both as a stimulating mental exercise, and as clearing the ground for a scientific treatment of a subject by bringing to light the difficulties on all sides. The τόποι are arranged under the four Predicables, *genus, differentia, proprium, accidens,* which express the various relations which the predicate may bear to the subject. The last of the logical treatises is the *Sophistici Elenchi,* in which we have a careful enumeration of the various kinds of Fallacies. The fundamental axioms of Logic, viz. the Maxim of Contradiction and the Maxim of the Excluded Middle are treated of in the *Metaphysica.*

From the art of reasoning we proceed to the art of

persuasion, which forms the subject of the *Rhetoric.*[1]
Aristotle begins by clearing this art, which he calls an
off-shoot of Dialectic, from the reproach which had been
brought upon it by its sophistical misuse, and which had
caused it to be repudiated with such contempt by Plato.
He defines it as 'the power of discovering in each case the
possible means of persuading,' (δύναμις περὶ ἕκαστον τοῦ
θεωρῆσαι τὸ ἐνδεχόμενον πιθανόν, *Rhet.* I 2), and shows that
it is really an art founded on scientific principles, and
that, if it is liable to abuse, that is common to it with all
other methods of increasing human power. The fault
lies in the motive (προαίρεσις) of the speaker, not in the
command of the resources of speech supplied by the art.
It is unfair to expose justice unarmed to the attack of injustice armed with rhetoric. The means of persuasion
are divided into the scientific, supplied by the speech
itself, and the unscientific, which exist independently of
the speech, such as the evidence of witnesses, &c. The
scientific means are of three kinds, (1) probable proofs
(πίστεις) contained in the speech, (2) the moral weight
(ἦθος) of the speaker, (3) the emotions of the audience
(πάθος). The proofs are either of the nature of Deduction, or of Induction. The former is the 'consideration,' or enthymeme (ἐνθύμημα), a probable syllogism con-
structed out of signs and likelihoods (σημεῖα καὶ εἰκότα)
with the major premiss omitted[2]; the latter is the example

---

[1] See Cope's edition with the *Introduction.*

[2] See Cope, *Introduction*, p. 103. In *Rhet.* II. 21 it is said that
a maxim (γνώμη) is turned into an enthymeme by adding a reason.
Among the examples given is one from the *Medea* 294 foll. in which
over-education is blamed for the envy it excites. As a syllogism
this would require the additional statement of the major, 'the envy

(παράδειγμα). Besides giving proof of fact, the speech should impress the audience with a certain idea of the ἦθος of the speaker, i.e. of his wisdom (φρόνησις), virtue (ἀρετή) and goodwill towards themselves (εὔνοια); and it should appeal to the appropriate feelings, of which a classification is given. There are three branches of rhetoric, distinguished by the aim of the speaker, (1) Deliberative (συμβουλευτικόν) which advocates or deprecates some course to be taken in the future, on the ground of expediency, (2) Judicial (δικαστικόν) which defends or accuses some person as having acted justly or unjustly in time past ; (3) the least important of the three, Declamatory (ἐπιδεικτικόν) the subject of which is commonly eulogy of honorable conduct in reference to present time. The last book of the *Rhetoric* deals with style (λέξις) and the arrangement of the topics of the speech (τάξις).

In the *Poetic* [1] Aristotle takes Plato's view of Poetry as a branch of Imitation, and divides it into three kinds, Epic, Tragic, and Comic. All imitation is a source of pleasure, but the imitation of the poet or artist is not simple representation of ordinary fact, but of the universal and ideal which underlies ordinary fact; whence poetry is more philosophical than history. This is most conspicuous in Tragedy, where the characters are all on a grander scale than those of common life; but even Comedy selects and heightens in its imitation of the

of the citizens is to be avoided.' Another example is the anonymous line ἀθάνατον ὀργὴν μὴ φύλασσε θνητὸς ὤν, where the full syllogism would be ' the feelings of mortals should be mortal like themselves ; you are mortal; therefore your wrath should have an end.'

[1] Translated into English with full commentary by Twining, 1789. See also the German edition by Susemihl, and Döring's *Die Kunstlehre des Aristoteles.*

grotesque. Tragedy is not, as Plato thought, a mere
enfeebling luxury; rather it makes use of the feelings of
pity and terror to purify similar affections in ourselves (δι'
ἐλέου καὶ φόβου περαίνουσα τὴν τῶν τοιούτων παθημάτων
κάθαρσιν), i.e. it gives a safe vent to our feelings by
taking us out of ourselves, and opening our hearts to
sympathize with heavier woes of humanity at large, typi-
fied in the persons of the drama, while it chastens and
controls the vehemence of passion by never allowing its
expression to transgress the limits of beauty, and by
recognizing the righteous meaning and use of suffering.

Aristotle's treatises on the science and philosophy
of Nature may be classed under the Physical, including the *Physica Auscultatio*, the *De Caelo*, *De
Generatione et Corruptione* and *Meteorologica;* and the
Biological, including the *Historia Animalium*, with its
appendages the *De Partibus Animalium, De Generatione
Animalium*, *De Incessu Animalium*, and the *De Anima*
with its appendages the *De Motu Animalium* and the
collection of tracts known as *Parva Naturalia.*

The Physical treatises, which deal not so much with
what we should now call Natural Philosophy as with the
underlying metaphysical ideas, are those which especially
provoked the animadversions of Bacon. Thus in the
Novum Organum 1 *Aph.* 63 he says 'Of Sophistical
philosophy the most conspicuous example was Aristotle
who corrupted natural philosophy by his logic, fashioning
the world out of categories,...disposing of the distinction
of Dense and Rare by the frigid distinction of Act and
Power, asserting that single bodies have each a single
and proper motion......and imposing countless other
arbitrary restrictions on the nature of things, being
always more anxious to find a ready answer in words

than to ascertain the inner truth of things.' Bacon no
doubt, is disposed to make Aristotle responsible for all
the short-comings of the Scholastic philosophy; but
more impartial and better-instructed writers are hardly
more favourable in their judgments. Thus Dr Whewell
writes (*Hist. of Ind. Sc.* 1 52[3].) 'The Aristotelian physics
cannot be considered as otherwise than a complete failure.
It collected no general laws from facts; and consequently,
when it tried to explain facts, it had no principles which
were of any avail.' And he explains this failure not so
much by the absence of observation, as by the absence of
clear and appropriate Ideas to arrange the facts observed
(p. 54 foll.). In illustration he quotes Aristotle's proof of
the *Quinta Essentia*, the eternal celestial substance[1], from
the fact of circular motion: 'The simple elements must
have simple motions; thus fire and air have their natural
motions upwards, and water and earth have their natural
motions downwards; besides these rectilinear motions
there is the motion in a circle, which is a more perfect
motion than the other, because a circle is a perfect line,
and a straight line is not; there must therefore be some
simple and primary body more divine than the four
elements, whose nature it is to be carried round in a
circle, as it is the nature of earth to move downwards,
and of fire to move upwards. It is impossible that the
revolving bodies can revolve contrary to nature, for their
motion is continuous and eternal, whereas all that is
contrary to nature speedily dies away[2].' It must not be
supposed however that the physical reasoning of Aristotle

[1] *De Caelo*, 1 2.

[2] See too Herschel's Natural Philosophy, p. 109, and Lewes'
Aristotle *passim*.

is all of this description.   In the *Physica Auscultatio* II 8
there is a very interesting discussion on the evidences
of Design in Nature, in which he gives his reasons against
Empedocles' theory of Development.   Still on the whole
we too often find ourselves balked with phrases and
formulas, where we looked for facts and ideas.

In Biology Aristotle was more successful.   Cuvier
speaks in ecstatic terms of his *History of Animals*, and
though Dr Whewell and G. H. Lewes[1] have shown that
he has greatly exaggerated its merits, and that Aristotle
has not attempted anything like a scientific classification
of animals, yet all admit 'that it is a marvellous work
considering the period at which it was produced and the
multiform productions of its author[2].'   The spirit in
which Aristotle entered on his investigations is shown in
a striking passage of the *Part. An.* I. 5, the substance of
which is as follows, 'It remains for us to speak of the
nature of animals, omitting nothing as too mean.   For
even in those things which are least agreeable to the
sense, creative nature affords a wonderful delight to those
who are able to understand their causes.   Therefore we
must not shrink in disgust, like children, from the examination even of the meanest animals, for there is something
admirable in all nature's handiwork.   As Heraclitus said,
when his friends were reluctant to enter a mean apartment
(ἱπνός), "Enter, for here too there are Gods," so every
work of nature is beautiful as exhibiting evidences of
design.   There is much that is offensive in the sight of
flesh, bones, veins, &c, but we disregard this in our desire
to master the principle of construction which they embody.'

[1] See his *Aristotle*, ch. XV.   [2] Lewes, p. 290.

We need not dwell upon any of the treatises classed under this head except the *De Anima*, of which Lewes says 'the extreme interest of its problems and the profundity of its views render it the most valuable of ancient attempts to bring the facts of life and mind into scientific order[1].' Aristotle here examines the theories of previous philosophers, Democritus, Empedocles, Plato &c., and then proceeds to give his own view as follows. The Soul (ψυχή) is the vital principle of all organized bodies, manifesting itself in an ascending scale of functions, nutritive, sentient, locomotive, appetitive, imaginative, rational, throughout the range of animated existence, from plant up to man. Each higher function involves the lower, so that all the functions are found conjoined with rationality in man, while the nutritive function exists separately in vegetables. The soul is the Form of which body is the Matter, it brings into actuality[2] the capacities which are latent in body and is itself limited by those capacities. It is also the Final and the Efficient Cause of the body, since this exists for the sake of the soul, and is set in motion by it. The highest function of soul is not inherent in the body and has no special organ with which it is connected,

---

[1] P. 221. The book is also analysed by Grote, *Aristotle* vol. II. ch. 12, and in A. Butler's *Lectures*.

[2] This actualizing power is expressed by the technical term ἐντελέχεια, whence the definition ψυχή ἐστιν ἐντελέχεια ἡ πρώτη σώματος φυσικοῦ δυνάμει ζωὴν ἔχοντος; which Grote explains as 'the lowest stage of actuality, the minimum of influence required to transform potentiality into actuality'; 'it is not indispensable that all the functions of the living subject should be at all times in complete exercise : it is enough if the functional aptitude exist as a dormant property, ready to rise into activity when the proper occasions present themselves.' *Aristotle* II. 186.

like the other functions; it is an emanation from the celestial sphere, and is the only part of the soul which survives the death of the body; but though it survives, it apparently loses its individuality and becomes merged in the universal reason.   There is much that is interesting in the account of the Senses and of the 'Common Sensibles' (*i.e.* primary qualities); in the distinction drawn between the Active and Passive Reason, between Memory and Reminiscence and, as connected with this, in the theory of the Association of Ideas[1]; but the pleasure of reading the book is lessened, as is so often the case in Aristotle, by his over-fondness for logical distinctions, by confused arrangement and extreme conciseness, made up for at times by unnecessary repetitions.

I proceed now to give an analysis of the book in which the true greatness of Aristotle is most conspicuous, the *Nicomachean Ethics*, commencing with a translation of the first three chapters[2].

'Every art and every science, and so too every act and purpose, seems to aim at some good. Hence people have well defined the supreme good to be that at which all things aim.   Sometimes the end consists in the exercise of a faculty for its own sake, at other times in certain external results beyond this.   Where the end consists in such external result, the result is more important than the activity to which it is due.   Now as there are many kinds of action and of art and science, there must also be many ends, the end of medicine for instance being health, of ship-building a ship, of strategy victory, of domestic

[1] See his short treatise on Memory.

[2] See Grant's 3rd edition and the English translation by Chase or Williams.

economy wealth. But where the arts themselves fall under some higher art, as bridle-making under the general art of riding, and this again and the whole business of war under the master art of strategy,—in all such cases the end of the master art, whether it be a simple activity or some further tangible result, is more important than the ends of the subordinate arts, the latter being pursued for the sake of the former. If then, there is some end for all that has to do with action, and if everything else which we desire is relative and subordinate to this final end, and we do not go on interminably making every choice for the sake of something beyond (in which case our desires would be frustrate and void of effect), then this must be the Summum Bonum or chief good. And, if so, must not the knowledge of this be of great importance for the conduct of life; and shall we not be more likely to know what we ought to do, when we have this before us, as a mark to aim at? Can we form any conception of the science to which this highest end belongs? Plainly it must be the highest and most comprehensive science. And such is πολιτική, the science of society, as it ordains what other sciences shall find a home in States, what sciences shall be learnt by different classes, and to what degree of proficiency. Even the most esteemed of the arts and faculties are subordinate to this; for example, strategy, domestic economy, and rhetoric. Seeing then that the science of society makes use of the various sciences concerned with action and production, and lays down the law as to what men should do and should abstain from doing, the end of this will embrace the ends of all other sciences and will consequently be the highest good of man. For even supposing it to be the case that the end of the individual is identical with that of the State, yet the end of the State is at any rate more comprehensive and complete. Granted that even in the case of the individual the Summum Bonum is an aim to be cherished, yet for a nation and for States it is certainly more noble and divine. Our science therefore is of the nature of πολιτική.

'In regard to method, the subject will be adequately treated if it be elucidated with as much clearness as the subject matter admits. Rigorous exactness must not be looked for, to the same extent, in all subjects of discussion, any more than an equal perfection of finish in all the different products of handicraft. And there is so much controversy and uncertainty in regard to what is honorable and what is just,—questions with which our science is concerned—that they have been thought to depend on custom only and to have no natural foundation. Similarly with regard to good things; for sometimes these are found to be injurious in their results, as men have been ruined owing to their wealth or their courage. Arguing then, as we are, upon such varying phenomena and from such uncertain premisses, we must be satisfied if we can set forth the truth roughly and in outline. Where the premisses, no less than the subject matter, are only probable and contingent, we must be content to draw inferences of a corresponding nature. It is the characteristic of an educated man not to require scientific precision upon any subject under inquiry beyond what the nature of the case admits; *e.g.* to demand scientific demonstration from an orator would be as improper as to accept probable reasoning from a mathematician. A man judges aright only of what he

himself knows; and only to that extent is he a good
critic. Special points will be judged best by him who
has received a special education, and general questions
by him who has been generally educated. It follows
that a young man is no fit student of our science, having
no experience in the affairs of real life, from which our
reasonings must be drawn and with which they are
concerned. Moreover, as he is prone to follow his
passions, it will be idle and profitless for him to listen
to moral truths, of which the end is not intellectual but
practical. Whether such a student be young in age or
only childish in character, is immaterial, as his incompe-
tence is not measured by length of time, but is due to his
living, and pursuing his several objects, under the rule of
the passions. To such persons knowledge is useless, as
it is to those who have no self control; on the other
hand to those who shape their desires and regulate their
conduct in accordance with reason, it will be highly
profitable to be informed on these points.

'These remarks may serve as an introduction to
indicate who are the proper students of morals, what is
the spirit and method with which the subject must be
treated, and what is the precise scope of the present
treatise.'

Aristotle then proceeds, in his usual manner, to examine the opinions current on the subject of the chief good,
first premising that, as our reasoning must be drawn from
experience, he who is to appreciate its force must have
been so brought up as to have this experience at command, *i.e.* to have the feeling of honour and right, in
his own mind. He points out that, while all agree in
calling the Chief Good by such names as Happiness,

Living-well, Doing-well, there is great dispute as to what these consist in. Judging from people's lives, we may distinguish three main views : the mass hold that happiness consists in bodily pleasure ; those of a higher class, who are engaged in active life, make it consist in honour; the philosopher makes it consist in thought. The 1st is an animal view, the 2nd assumes an end which is precarious, and is sought rather as a means to assure ourselves of our own excellence than as being in itself an end: the consideration of the 3rd is postponed. Then, though reluctantly, he criticizes Plato's ideal good, for ' friends and truth being equally dear, we are bound to prefer the truth[1].' The arguments are not very clear[2], but their general purport is to prove that the 'Ideal Good' is something unintelligible, and in any case of no use for practice. Having thus cleared the ground, Aristotle developes his own conception of happiness. It is final, it is self-sufficing (αὐταρκες), it must be found in the proper work or function (ἔργον) of man.

The reasoning by which man's happiness is inferred from his ἔργον appears to be as follows. Everything which exists is specially adapted to some special good end (τέλος). This adaptation is called the nature (φύσις) of the thing. The process by which it arrives at its end is its ἔργον. Its special excellence (ἀρετή) consists in the per- fection of its φύσις. Therefore, φύσις being given, we may find the other terms. Life is the function of all living things. Amongst these man is distinguished by the possession of reason ; his ἔργον therefore will be not life simply but rational life, and this must be

---

[1] ἀμφοῖν φίλοιν ὄντοιν ὅσιον προτιμᾶν τὴν ἀλήθειαν.

[2] See Essay II. of the *Introduction* to Grant's *Ethics.*

actively rational, and such as is found in the best specimen of man. Thus we obtain the definition: 'the good
of man is a putting forth of the faculties of the soul in
accordance with his highest excellence, (τὸ ἀνθρώπινον
ἀγαθὸν ψυχῆς ἐνέργεια γίνεται κατὰ τὴν ἀρίστην ἀρετήν). And
further we must add ἐν βίῳ τελείῳ 'in a complete life,' so that
nothing may hinder the full development of the ἐνέργεια.
It is shown that this definition embraces all the various
characteristics of happiness distinguished by previous
philosophers, not excluding pleasure, because virtue is
essentially productive of pleasure, and that the highest
pleasure. Hence we learn that man is himself the chief
source of his own happiness, and that Solon was wrong
in saying that no man is to be called happy during his
life.

Aristotle then proceeds to give a further account
of human excellence. Man is a compound of a rational
and an irrational nature. Of the irrational nature part
is merely nutritive and entirely unparticipant of reason,
part is appetitive and impulsive (ἐπιθυμητικὸν καὶ ὀρεκτικὸν)
and is capable of being brought into subjection to reason.
Human excellence therefore will be twofold, according
as it is seen in the purely rational or the semi-rational
part. The excellence of the former is intellectual, δια-
νοητική, the excellence of the latter moral, ἠθική. (In
speaking of the latter the word ἀρετή will be translated by
'virtue.') Moral virtue is acquired by practice, just as
manual skill is acquired. According to the practice will
be the resulting character; by a repetition of brave
acts we become brave, &c.[1] We start with a capacity
(δύναμις) which may be developed in either direction by

---

[1] ἐκ τῶν ὁμοίων ἐνεργειῶν αἱ ἕξεις γίνονται. II. 1. 7.

a series of acts of a definite quality, and thus become fixed in a corresponding habit or tone of mind (ἕξις).

In order to become virtuous then, we must first know how to do virtuous actions, to act, that is, in accordance with right reason or the right standard; and this we shall do by avoiding excess or defect. When a man does such actions wittingly, intentionally, choosing them for their own sakes and taking pleasure in them, and when he is also firmly set in this course, he exhibits all the marks of a formed habit of virtue; of which let this be our definition, 'a fixed habit of mind, resulting from effort and principle, which, with reference to our own particular nature, is equidistant from excess or defect;' to which we must add, that the mean must be determined by reason and as a sensible man would determine it[1]. It must be confessed however that there are exceptions to the definition. We sometimes find a virtue which has nothing to do with a mean, and it frequently happens that a virtue is more opposed to one extreme than to another. A good practical rule is to shun the worse extreme or that to which we are most prone.

The Third Book commences with an inquiry into moral responsibility. It is only voluntary acts, that are praised or blamed. An act is involuntary when done ignorantly or under constraint. Of constraint there are two kinds, physical or moral; it is only the former which is, strictly speaking, involuntary. So of ignorance there are two kinds, ignorance of principles, which is a mark of utter depravity, and ignorance of particular facts, which is excusable if the agent, when better informed, repents

---

[1] ἕξις προαιρετική, ἐν μεσότητι οὖσα τῇ πρὸς ἡμᾶς, ὡρισμένῃ λόγῳ καὶ ὡς ἂν ὁ φρόνιμος ὁρίσειεν. II. 6.

of his act done in ignorance. Thus we may define voluntary action as 'that which originates with the agent's self, knowing the circumstances of the action, (τὸ ἑκούσιον δόξειεν ἂν εἶναι οὗ ἡ ἀρχὴ ἐν αὐτῷ εἰδότι τὰ καθ' ἕκαστα ἐν οἷς ἡ πρᾶξις). It is a mistake to suppose that actions done from anger or desire are involuntary. One particular form of the Voluntary is Purpose or Volition, (προαίρεσις). It is distinguished from Wish (βούλησις) because that refers to the end, this to the means; as well as from Desire, Anger, and Opinion. It implies previous deliberation (βούλευσις) and may be defined 'a grasping after something within our own power after previous deliberation' (βουλευτικὴ ὄρεξις τῶν ἐφ' ἡμῖν).

A question has been raised as to the nature of the End which is the object of our wish. The true account seems to be that abstractedly, and to the virtuous man, good itself is the end wished for, but to others the apparent good. And then arises the question whether vice is really voluntary, if we of necessity wish for the apparent good, which may not after all be the real good. To this it may be answered that it is in our power to be virtuous (and so, to wish rightly), because it is in our power to do the acts which lead to the formation of virtuous habits, and avoid the opposite acts: and that we are thus free, is witnessed to by the whole constitution of society. If it is further argued that we are born different, one with an eye for what is good and right, and another without it, we may at least reply that in any case virtue and vice must stand on the same footing as regards freedom, and that our own actions do at any rate contribute to intensify this difference.

Aristotle then proceeds to the discussion of the

several virtues which may be presented in a scheme
as follows with their corresponding extremes.

Sphere.	Defect.	Virtue.	Excess.
anticipated evils.	δειλία, timidity.	ἀνδρεία, courage.	θρασύτης, foolhardiness.
bodily pleasures.	ἀναισθησία, insensibility.	σωφροσύνη, temperance.	ἀκολασία, intemperance.
property.	ἀνελευθερία, avarice.	ἐλευθερία, liberality.	ἀσωτία, prodigality.
wealth.	μικροπρέπεια, meanness.	μεγαλοπρέπεια, magnificence.	ἀπειροκαλία, ostentation. βαναυσία, snobbishness.
greatness.	μικροψυχία, littleness of mind.	μεγαλοψυχία, magnanimity.	χαυνότης, pompousness.
honour.	ἀφιλοτιμία, want of spirit.	φιλοτιμία, right ambition.	φιλοτιμία, wrong ambition.
provocation.	ἀοργησία, dullness.	πραότης, gentleness.	ὀργιλότης, irascibility.
companionship.	ἀπέχθεια, rudeness.	φιλία, sociableness.	κολακεία, flattery.
conversation.	εἰρωνεία, self-disparagement.	ἀλήθεια, sincerity.	ἀλαζόνεια, boastfulness.
recreation.	ἀγροικία, sullenness.	εὐτραπελία, urbanity.	βωμολοχία, buffoonery.
facing of men.	ἀναισχυντία, impudence.	αἰδώς, modesty.	κατάπληξις, bashfulness.
the fortunes of others.	ἐπιχαιρεκακία, malignant pleasure.	νέμεσις[1], indignation.	φθόνος, envy.

[1] Νέμεσις is a 'mean,' because the indignant man is pained only
at undeserved prosperity, while the envious, exceeding him, is pained
at all prosperity, and the malicious is so far defective in feeling pain
that he even rejoices at—not prosperity, but adversity, *Eth.* II. 7. By
the time he wrote the *Rhetoric*, Aristotle had come to see the absurdity
of this opposition, and identifies ἐπιχαιρεκακία with envy, *Rhet.* II. 9.

As a specimen of Aristotle's analysis of character, I give an abstract of his remarks on the Brave Man and the Magnanimous or high-minded man.

He begins by limiting the sphere of Bravery. Bravery is not concerned with all objects of fear; *e.g.* a man is not called brave for being fearless as to disgrace, or to injury which may threaten his family; but we call him brave who does not shrink from death. He is truly brave who in presence of danger behaves as reason directs and under a sentiment of honour. Suicide is a mark of cowardice rather than of courage. There are five imperfect forms of courage, (1) that which is produced by a regard to the opinion of others, (2) that which comes from experience, as the sailor's in a storm, (3) that which comes from passion or spirit; when joined to reason this becomes true courage, (4) that which comes from a hopeful temperament, (5) that which comes from ignorance of danger.

High-mindedness or loftiness of spirit is an accompaniment and ornament of the other virtues combined. The high-minded man is one who is worthy of the highest honour and rates himself at his true worth. If a man has small worth and rates himself accordingly, we should call him modest. The vicious excess is where a man rates himself above his worth, the vicious defect where he is too humble and rates himself below his worth. The high-minded man will always bear himself with calmness and moderation. He will despise dishonour, knowing it to be undeserved, and honour too, for this can never be an adequate reward of virtue, though he will accept it as his due from the good. He is ready to bestow favours on others, but scorns to receive them;

is proud to the great, but affable to the lowly; will not compete for common objects of ambition; is open in friendship and hatred; cares for reality more than for appearance, dislikes personal talk, wonders at nothing, bears no malice, disregards utility in comparison with beauty, is dignified in all his actions and movements.

The Fifth, Sixth and Seventh books are taken bodily from the *Eudemian Ethics*, a sort of paraphrase of the *Nicomachean Ethics*, written by a pupil of Aristotle. Some suppose that the *Nicomachean Ethics* were never completed; perhaps it is a more probable view that these three books were accidentally lost, and that their place was supplied from the paraphrase. Sir A. Grant and others have pointed out slight divergences between the genuine Aristotelian doctrine and that put forward in these books; but, though inferior in force and perspicuity, they may be accepted as supplying a generally faithful representation of the ideas of Aristotle. Justice is the subject of the Fifth Book. The writer begins by distinguishing two meanings of the term: it either means 'the fixed habit of fulfilling the law,' which is equivalent to virtue in general as displayed towards our neighbour; or it is used in a narrower sense and means 'fair dealing with regard to property.' It is the latter or Civil Justice which is our subject. It is divided into two kinds, Distributive (διανεμητική) and Corrective (διορθωτική). The former assigns to each citizen his due in regard to the honours and burdens of civil life: and that which is due or equal will be discovered here by a 'geometrical proportion;' as man is related to man, so must the honour done to the one be related to the honour done to the other. Corrective Justice takes no account of persons, but, when inequality has been occasioned by injustice, it endeavours to restore equality by an 'arithmetical proportion,' simply subtracting so much from one side and adding it to the other. This latter Justice is the principle of commerce. The simple 'retaliation' of Pythagoras is too rude for either Distributive or Corrective Justice. Just dealing is a mean between injuring and being injured, so that Injustice is both an excess and a defect. Justice in the strict sense exists only between equals who are subject to the same law. It is partly natural, partly conventional. One form of justice is Equity, ἐπιείκεια. This is a rectification of law in the spirit of the Law-giver, where the law fails to prescribe what is just in the particular case, owing to its generality.

The Sixth Book returns to the definition of virtue, and explains the phrase 'right reason' there employed. The soul has been already analyzed into Irrational and Rational; and we have shown that the Moral Excellences, though having their foundation in the former, must be regulated by the latter. It remains to explain how this is done. We begin by sub-dividing the rational soul into the Scientific part (ἐπιστημονικόν) which is concerned with necessary truth, and the Calculative or Deliberative (λογιστικόν, βουλευτικόν), answering to the δόξα of Plato, which is concerned with contingent matter. It is this latter kind of Reason which, when combined with Impulse (ὄρεξις), becomes προαίρεσις and leads to action. Action itself is of two kinds, Making (ποίησις) and Doing (πρᾶξις). The rational excellence which is concerned in making is τέχνη, Art, that which is concerned with doing is φρόνησις, Practical Wisdom or Prudence. Returning to the ἐπιστημονικόν, we find two forms of excellence which belong to this head, Intuitive Reason, νοῦς, the faculty which supplies first principles (ἀρχαί), and Discursive Reason, ἐπιστήμη, which arrives at truth by reasoning from the principles supplied by νοῦς; the combination of the two is called σοφία, Philosophy; which is the perfection of Reason dealing with that which is divine and eternal, as Prudence is the perfection of Reason dealing with that which concerns human well-being. As regards first principles, Prudence is the opposite to the Intuitive reason, being concerned chiefly with particulars which are below demonstration; it is indeed a sort of moral sense which only acts rightly in the temperate man; (whence Temperance is called σωφροσύνη, the guard of Prudence), and is strengthened by experience. Without moral virtue, Prudence would be mere cleverness, and without Prudence moral virtue would be only a generous instinct liable to perversion. For complete virtue we need both the impulsive and the rational element. This explains the mistake of Socrates in confounding Virtue with Knowledge.

In the Seventh Book we have a fuller account of Temperance and the allied and contrasted qualities, which bears no relation to the previous discussion on the subject. It contains a graduated scale of good and evil states in reference to our power of resisting pleasures and pains. Thus, between divine or heroic goodness on the one side and bestial depravity on the other, we have σωφροσύνη, where passion is entirely subject to reason; ἐγκράτεια Continence or Self-control, where reason prevails over resisting passion; ἀκρασία Incontinence, where passion prevails in spite of the resistance of reason; ἀκολασία Intemperance, where reason is entirely subject to passion.

Corresponding to ἐγκράτεια and ἀκρασία in reference to pleasure, we have two states distinguished in reference to pain, καρτερία endurance, and μαλακία effeminacy.

The account above given of ἀκρασία seems at variance with Socrates' principle that men never do wrong except through ignorance. In what sense is it true that the incontinent man sins against knowledge? Before he is under the influence of passion, he certainly knows that the act is unlawful. But a man may have knowledge without using it, as in slumber; and a man may unconsciously practise sophistry towards himself, allowing the general principle 'excess is wrong,' but shutting his eyes to the particular premiss 'to drink this would be excess,' and attending to another principle suggested by passion, 'drinking is pleasant.' Incontinence in Anger is not so bad as incontinence in respect to Lust, because Anger, which kindles on suspicion of wrong, does in a way listen to Reason, though it listens amiss; also Anger is less deliberate than Lust, and it is accompanied with pain and is less wanton. There are two kinds of incontinence, the one proceeding from hastiness of temper, where a man acts without deliberation; the other from weakness of will, where he deliberates but cannot hold to his resolve; the latter is less easily cured. Holding to one's resolve is not always a mark of continence; it may even be a kind of incontinence, as when a man sticks to a wrong opinion merely from self-will.

In Book VIII. we return to the genuine Aristotle. I have thought it worth while to give a somewhat full analysis of the beautiful treatise on φιλία contained in this and the following book, as supplying a Pagan counterpart to the description of Christian ἀγαπή contained in the thirteenth chapter of the First Epistle to the Corinthians.

Friendship, by which we understand 'mutual affection mutually known,'[1] deserves a place in a treatise on Morals, because it is a great help to leading a virtuous and happy life, and because the best friendship is impossible without virtue. It is also deeply rooted in human nature, and is the chief bond in civil society. There are three chief kinds of friendship, based respectively on the good, the pleasant, the useful. As the useful merely means that which conduces to good or to pleasure, the three are ultimately reducible to two. Of the three, the first alone is perfect. It is possible only for the good, who wish each other's real good. It is unselfish, unaffected by external considerations, permanent, trustful, built on similarity of tastes, and surpasses the other forms even in their special characteristics of utility and pleasantness. Such friendship is rare and slowly formed. The friendships founded on pleasure and on utility are not disinterested, and therefore they are liable to come to an end when they cease to produce these effects. Still such friendships may pass into the true friendship, if virtue is joined to them. Friendship may exist potentially in separation, but for its active exercise frequent intercourse is needed; otherwise it passes into simple good-will (εὔνοια). For the formation of friendships sensibility and amiability are needed; for these make intercourse delightful; and therefore the young are more prompt to make friends than the old. Mere fondness, however, will not suffice: the judgment and the will must combine with the affection to promote the welfare of the beloved. This ideal friendship can

---

[1] ἀντιφίλησις οὐ λανθάνουσα, VIII. 3.

only be exercised towards a few, but the friendship of interest or of pleasure may be spread over a large circle. Men in power will have friends of these imperfect kinds, but not a perfect friend, unless they excel in virtue as well as in power. All the forms of friendship imply a kind of equality or reciprocity of good for good, or pleasure for pleasure, or pleasure for use. Where the parties to friendship stand in a position of relative inferiority and superiority, as parents and children, the balance should be made up by a larger proportion of honour and affection on the part of the inferior. Extreme inequanty, as between a man and a God, renders friendship impossible. The essence of friendship is to love rather than to be loved, but the majority prefer to be loved, taking it as a sign of honour. Every association implies something of friendship, as well as of justice. The end of Civil Society is the same as that of friendship, viz. the common good, and all subordinate associations are but parts of the great society of the state. The family union presents counterparts to the various forms of Civil Government. In the family, friendship varies according to the different relationships. Parents love their children as being a part of themselves; children gradually come to love their parents as benefactors. Brothers love each other as being of common blood, and also from companionship and long intimacy and similar tastes. The friendship of husband and wife has its root in instinct, and is increased by the sense of mutual help and common interests and pleasures and, if they are good, by the delight in each other's virtue. Quarrels and complaints occur most frequently in the case of interested friendships, where each party seeks a surplus of advantage to accrue to himself. Such friendship may be either on a business footing, corresponding to legal justice, or it may have more of a moral element, resembling unwritten law. In the latter, no precise stipulation is made, yet still the benefactor expects an equivalent and grumbles if he does not receive it. He may please himself with the idea of acting disinterestedly, but when it comes to the point, he prefers payment. It is well therefore to have a clear understanding before receiving the favour, and to do one's best afterwards to repay it in full. The amount returned should be determined by the receiver in proportion to what he would have been prepared to give to obtain the favour at first.

Questions of casuistry arise in reference to conflicting claims of friendship. In general it may be said that the payment of a debt must take precedence of conferring a favour, and that claims will vary with the nearness of the relationship. Another question relates to the termination of friendships. Where friendship is only for pleasure or use, the connexion ceases with the motive. Where a more ideal friendship is professed, it may be broken off if one of the parties finds that the other has been acting from an inferior motive, or if he finds him out to be a vicious man; but in the latter case, he is bound to make every effort to reclaim him before breaking off the connexion. Where one party improves and the other remains stationary, it may be impossible for friendship to continue, but there should be kindly feeling for the sake of old association. It is often said that 'a friend is a second self,' and it would seem that a good man's feeling towards a friend is an extension of his feeling towards himself. For he is at unity with himself, and desires and does with all his

powers all that is good for himself, *i.e.* for the intellectual
principle within him, which is his true self; and he
desires his own continued existence, and takes pleasure
in his own society, for his memories of the past are
sweet, and he has good hopes for the future, and his
mind is fully stored with subjects for contemplation, and
his days are 'joined each to each by natural piety.' And
just such are his feelings towards his friend. But with a
bad man all this is changed: he is at variance with himself, and lusts after one thing but wishes for another, and
chooses what is pleasant, though he knows it to be
hurtful, and shrinks in cowardice from what he knows to
be best; and at length, having committed many crimes,
he comes to hate his life and puts an end to himself.
Moreover the bad man cannot endure his own society,
for his memories of the past and his expectations of the
future are alike unpleasant; and it is only when in company with others that he can escape from these thoughts.
He cannot sympathise with himself, because his soul is
torn in sunder by faction, one part grieving at what
pleases another part. And thus he is incapable of
friendship, either for himself or for another. Good-
will and Unanimity are akin to friendship, but not
the same. The first may be felt towards strangers;
it is usually called out by the sight of some noble or
excellent quality, and forms the natural prelude to friendship. By unanimity we understand a unity of sentiment
on practical matters, especially among citizens of the
same state. The bad are incapable of such unanimity,
as they are always seeking to get an advantage over each
other.

What is the explanation of the superior strength of

affection in the benefactor as compared with the bene-
fited? It is not enough to say that this is a case of a
creditor desiring the prosperity of the debtor. The
benefactor is like an artist who loves his work as
increasing his sense of his own powers; he has also the
lasting consciousness of doing an honourable act, while
the recipient of kindness has only the consciousness of
the present profit. Finally the active part taken by the
benefactor has more affinity with the active principle of
loving. Another question which is asked is whether self-
love is good or bad. On the one hand, the worse a man
is, the more selfish (φίλαυτος) he is thought to be: on the
other hand, we have pointed out that love for self is the
original type of love for others. The explanation is that
the word self-love (τὸ φίλαυτον) is used in two senses,
having reference to two different selves. When we use
the name 'self-love' of those who are eager to give to
themselves the larger share of honours, riches and bodily
pleasures, we mean the love of the lower self, that is, of
the appetites and passions and generally of the irrational
part of the soul. If on the contrary a man sets himself
to do always what is just and temperate and thus wins
honour to himself, we should not generally speak of such
a man as loving himself; and yet it is plain that he
seeks the best and noblest things for himself, and
gratifies that principle of his nature which is most
rightfully authoritative (χαρίζεται ἑαυτοῦ τῷ κυριωτάτῳ);
and such a principle we must consider to constitute the
man's true self, just as it does in the case of the State or
any other system. In this sense then the good man
ought to love himself, for his reason chooses what is in
itself best, and in obeying reason he performs noble

actions, which not only benefit himself but also do good to others. On the other hand the bad man ought not to love himself, for he will only do harm both to himself and to others by following his evil propensities. It is true that the good man will seem at times to be sacrificing himself for his friends or for his country; for, for their sakes, he will throw away money and honours and even life itself, if so be he may win true glory (τὸ καλόν). Nay he will even surrender to his friend the doing of noble deeds; and yet, in all, he does what is best for himself and chooses what is best; for to help his friend to honour is more honorable than to win honour for himself, and the rapture of one glorious moment is worth years of common-place life.

Another question raised is whether the happy man needs friends? Those who deny this take the view that the only use of friends is to supply a want, and the happy man has no wants. But this is plainly a mistake. For (1) the possession of friends being one of the greatest of external goods is necessarily included in perfect happiness: (2) the happy man will need friends, not as givers, but as recipients of kindness: (3) companionship is a natural want to him as to others: (4) the good man's happiness consists in doing and seeing good, and he can see goodness in a friend more clearly than he can in himself: he delights in a good action for its own sake, and he delights in it still more because it is his friend's: (5) the performance of good acts is made easier and pleasanter and consequently more continuous by their being done in company with others: and (6) to be in the society of the good is a sort of schooling in virtue. The argument may be put in a more metaphysical form as follows, 'Life is good, especially to the good man; but man's life consists in consciousness[1]; the more of consciousness the more of life; if then he doubles his consciousness in a good friend, he has so much more of life and therefore of good.' But to enjoy this sympathetic consciousness it is necessary to live in the company of the friend and share his words and thoughts.

The number of friends for use or pleasure is limited by convenience. The number of true friends is limited by our incapacity to feel the highest kind of affection for many, and also by the difficulty of harmonious association among many; οἱ δὲ πολύφιλοι οὐδενὶ δοκοῦσιν εἶναι φίλοι, 'the man of many friends is thought to be no one's friend.'

Friendship is more beautiful in prosperity, more necessary in adversity. In the latter the presence of friends has a mixed effect. While it is sweet to see a friend and be conscious of his sympathy, and while a friend, if he has tact (ἐὰν ᾖ ἐπιδέξιος), is the best of all comforters; yet, on the other hand, it is inconsistent with a manly character to cause unnecessary pain to friends. We should invite our friends to share our good fortune, and we should go unasked to comfort them in their misfortunes, but not solicit their help ourselves unless the service they are able to do would far outweigh the pain it costs. On the other hand we must beware of the appearance of sullenness in declining offers of help or sympathy. In the ordinary course of life friendship proves itself in companionship. Whatever a man makes the chief interest of his life, from drinking to philosophy, he wishes his friend to share in it. And thus it is that

---

[1] ἔοικε τὸ ζῆν εἶναι κυρίως τὸ αἰσθάνεσθαι ἢ νοεῖν. IX. 9.

the bad are made worse, and the good better by their friendships.

The subject of the Tenth Book is Pleasure. This forms a part of ethics, because it is an essential element of human life and also of virtuous training; for to take pleasure in what we ought is the foundation of a good moral character. Two opposite views have been put forward by philosophers, (1) that it is the Summum Bonum, (2) that it is altogether bad. Some of the supporters of the latter view have probably overstated the case in order to correct man's common proneness to pleasure; but this is a mistaken policy. The exaggeration is soon exposed, and its exposure brings the truth itself into disrepute.

The first argument alleged in favour of pleasure is that pleasure is the one thing which all creatures, rational and irrational, desire; which proves that it must be the Summum Bonum, because all creatures are led by nature to their good, as they are to their proper food. Aristotle defends this argument in so far as it is founded on a universal instinct; ὃ γὰρ πᾶσι δοκεῖ τοῦτ᾿ εἶναι φάμεν. 'Those who dispute this will hardly find any better ground of certainty. Even in the inferior animals nature has infused something of a higher strain which aims at that which is good for them.' I will not dwell on the somewhat technical argumentation which follows, but pass on at once to Aristotle's own view of Pleasure, which comes in, like a virtuous mean, between the two extreme views. Pleasure is something complete in itself at each successive moment of time. It is an accompaniment of the natural activity of the healthy organ or faculty, and is better in proportion to the excellence of the faculty.

It is thus a sort of crowning perfection or consummation of the activity [1]. Uninterrupted pleasure is an impossibility, because our faculties are not capable of uninterrupted exercise. Since pleasure is thus bound up with the activity, and is sweetest when that is best, it is evident that, in seeking to exercise their living powers, all things seek the pleasure which is the accompaniment and token of their most perfect exercise. Thus we may say indifferently that we desire pleasure for the sake of life, or life for the sake of pleasure.

Pleasures are of different kinds in accordance with the differences of the faculties and activities to which they are attached. Each activity is promoted and intensified by its own pleasure; for instance, he who takes pleasure in a particular study is likely to succeed best in it. On the other hand the activity is impeded by an alien pleasure, as the sound of a flute makes it difficult for a musician to attend to a speech.

Since activities differ in a moral point of view, and we call some good, some bad; there must be the same difference among pleasures. Again, the pleasures of intellect differ in purity from those of sense; and the pleasures of sight, hearing, and smell, from those of taste and touch. Each species of animal has its own specific pleasures, as it has its own powers and activities. Even among men we find great varieties of liking, for instance the healthy man and the sick man have a different judgment as to what is sweet. Amid these varieties we shall make the perfect man our standard: that is true pleasure which is pleasure to

---

[1] τελειοῖ τὴν ἐνέργειαν ἡ ἡδονὴ, οὐχ ὡς ἡ ἕξις ἐνυπάρχουσα, ἀλλ᾽ ὡς ἐπιγινόμενόν τι τέλος, οἷον τοῖς ἀκμαίοις ἡ ὥρα, X. 4.

him[1]. But it is no wonder that these pleasures are not agreeable to corrupt and degraded natures, nor on the other hand that what they think pleasures are abhorrent to the virtuous man.

Aristotle here reverts to his definition of happiness, 'an activity in accordance with excellence,' and preeminently with the highest excellence, which is that of the highest part of the soul, the reason (νοῦς). The highest happiness therefore consists in activity of the reason, i.e. in philosophy (ἐνέργεια θεωρητική). This activity is capable of being sustained longer than any other. It is also the pleasantest, the least dependent on circumstances, and the freest from care; and it is sought for its own sake without reference to any further result to be gained by it. Such a life of calm contemplation (θεωρία) continued through an adequate period is the highest human happiness[2]. Nay, it is more than human, for it is only by virtue of the divine element within him that man is capable of living such a life. And in whatever proportion that

---

[1] ἔστιν ἑκάστου μέτρον ἡ ἀρετὴ καὶ ὁ ἀγαθός, ᾗ τοιοῦτος, καὶ ἡδοναὶ εἶεν ἂν αἱ τούτῳ φαινόμεναι καὶ ἡδέα οἷς οὗτος χαίρει, X. 5.

[2] This high estimate of the philosophic life is common to all the great thinkers of antiquity; see Grant I. p. 197. It is echoed in Virgil's *Me vero primum dulces ante omnia Musae accipiant, caelique vias et sidera monstrent*, G. II. 475; and in the description of Elysium, *Aen.* VI. 721. The distinction between the Active and the Contemplative life was familiar in the Middle Ages, and supposed to be symbolized in the persons of Leah and Rachel, Martha and Mary; see Aquinas *Summa Sec. Sec. Qu.* 180. But our word 'contemplation' is scarcely an equivalent for Aristotle's θεωρία, suggesting rather the *Imitatio Christi* than the speculations of a Newton or a Kant, or the poetic musings of a Milton or a Wordsworth; which would certainly approach nearer to Aristotle's conception of what constituted the joy of the philosophic life.

divine element transcends man's mixed and composite
nature, in the same proportion will his purely rational
activities transcend those which are inspired by the other
virtues[1]. We often hear it said, that man should be content
with his lot and not seek to rise above the limits of
mortality; but, if we would attain the highest happiness, we
must do the very contrary to this, train ourselves, as far as
may be, to think and feel as immortals, and to live with a
constant reference to that which is best and highest in our
nature[2]. For that, after all, is the man's truest self; and
it would be absurd to prefer another's life to that which
is in the truest sense our own proper life. All other
virtues, and the happiness which flows from them, are,
in comparison with contemplation, human as opposed
to divine. They are necessary for society and for the
business of life; they are bound up with man's composite
nature, with the passions as well as with the reason,
with the corporeal as well as with the spiritual; they are
more or less dependent on circumstances, (thus the liberal
man and the just man need some amount of property
if they are to give proof of their justice and liberality),
while the contemplative life needs only the minimum of
external prosperity. On the other hand the contemplative life is the only one which we can ascribe to the
Gods. For what sort of actions would be congruous
with our idea of the divine nature? Not just acts; for

---

[1] See, on the divine principle in man, Grant's *Aristotle* I. p. 296,
and the passage quoted there from *Gen. Anim.* II. 3. 10, λείπεται
τὸν νοῦν μόνον θύραθεν ἐπεισιέναι καὶ θεῖον εἶναι μόνον.

[2] οὐ χρὴ κατὰ τοὺς παραινοῦντας ἀνθρώπινα φρονεῖν ἄνθρωπον ὄντα
οὐδὲ θνητὰ τὸν θνητόν, ἀλλ' ἐφ' ὅσον ἐνδέχεται ἀθανατίζειν καὶ πάντα
ποιεῖν πρὸς τὸ ζῆν κατὰ τὸ κράτιστον τῶν ἐν αὐτῷ, Χ. 7.

what have they to do with contracts and deposits? nor brave acts; for what danger can threaten them? nor temperate acts; for what passions have they to need restraint? And yet the Gods are in the full enjoyment of conscious life. If then this life is not one of action, still less one of production, nothing remains but that it should be a life of contemplation. And thus it is in the contemplative life that man approaches most nearly the eternal blessedness of the Gods. The other animals have no share in happiness because they are incapable of contemplation.

Something of external prosperity is needed for the putting forth of that activity which constitutes happiness, but the wisest of men are agreed that what is needful is very small. And if there is any providential care of mankind, surely it is reasonable to suppose that he who cherishes reason above all things, and passes his life in harmony with reason, will be dear to those to whom reason is dear, and consequently under the special charge of the Gods and receive from them all he needs.

Our theory is now complete, but theory has little influence except with the small minority who are pre-disposed to virtue. The mass of mankind are insensible to appeals to reason or honour. Living by the rule of their passions they know of no higher pleasures than can be obtained through these. What is to be done, if such as these are to be reformed? Some hold that goodness is a gift of nature, some that it comes from teaching, others that it comes from habituation. If the first is a true account, we can ascribe it only to a special divine blessing; the second, as we have said, is only efficacious where the soul of the learner has been duly prepared,

as soil to receive good seed, by being accustomed to like
and dislike as he ought; when a man is once enslaved
to his passions, there is no reasoning with him. We must
therefore begin a course of habituation early in life. It
is a part of the duty of the State to provide a system of
public education and to enforce discipline by punishments, and this authoritative control should be continued through the whole of life, as at Sparta. Where
such a system does not exist, private individuals should
do their best to train and influence for good those who
come within their reach. For this purpose it is necessary
that they should endeavour to acquaint themselves with
the principles of legislation and gain something of the
spirit of a legislator. But where and how is this to be
learnt? Up to the present time we have nothing but
the empirical politics of the statesman, or the doctrinaire
politics of the sophist. Aristotle proposes to construct
a science of Politics from which to determine the nature
of the best State and the laws by which it will train its
citizens to virtue.

The sequel to the *Ethics*, as we might infer from the
last sentence, is to be found in the *Politics*. Before
proceeding to the analysis of the latter, I will make one
or two brief remarks upon the former. First, as to
Aristotle's general conception of Ethics, is he to be called
a Eudaemonist? So it has often been said, because he
makes εὐδαιμονία the end to which man's life and actions
should be referred. But the well-being and well-doing,
the εὐζωία and εὐπραξία, which constitute the εὐδαιμονία
of Aristotle, are carefully distinguished from any form of
pleasurable sensation. Εὐδαιμονία with him is a particular

kind of putting forth of the powers of the soul, which is intrinsically good by itself, quite apart from the pleasure which, as a matter of fact, attends it like its shadow. Virtuous activity does not become good because it is a means to pleasure; it is good as being itself the end we should aim at. We admire it in and for itself, as we admire a beautiful statue. This view is of course very far removed from the Epicurean and also from the modern Utilitarian. It agrees with these in so far as it determines the quality of our actions by referring them immediately to an end, instead of to an absolute law, or intuitive conception ot right; but the end is neither pleasure to self nor pleasure to others, but the perfect fulfilment of the ἔργον of man. And to know what this perfect fulfilment is, we must fall back on reason embodied in the judgment of the wise man. It is no doubt a grave defect in Aristotle's system, as compared with Utilitarianism or with Christianity, that in determining the quality of actions, he only incidentally, as in the discussion on friendship, notices their influence on the well-being of others; in fact, he nowhere gives any clear statement of the grounds of reason on which the wise man founds his judgment as to the virtuous mean. Secondly, as to the doctrine of the 'Mean' itself, I think every one must feel that, while it is highly important to insist on balance, proportion, moderation, as an element of a perfect character, yet to make this the *differentia* of virtue, is both superficial and misleading. Aristotle himself confesses that the definition is not always strictly applicable; and, if we try to apply it to the higher Christian conception of virtue, as love towards God and Man, it of course fails utterly: there can be no excess of such love. But confining ourselves to cases which Aristotle gives, and where the doctrine of the mean might seem least unsatisfactory, as in the definition of courage, this would seem to imply that there is a certain quality or instinct, which is found existing in three different degrees; a small degree constituting cowardice, a somewhat larger amount courage, a larger still rashness. Whereas the truth is that, while courage and rashness do differ in degree, and spring from the same instinctive root, cowardice differs from them both in kind, and springs from an entirely different instinct. There cannot be less of the natural impulse which, moralized and rationalized, becomes courage, than none at all; yet such a negative state would never give rise to the impulse to run away, which springs from another positive principle, the desire of self-preservation. Aristotle's 'Mean' is in fact an attempt to express two distinct circumstances in regard to the moral constitution of man, one that the several instincts are indeed the raw material of as many virtues, but that, if untrained and unchecked, they run to excess and become vices; and, secondly, that the perfect character is one in which all the various instincts are harmoniously developed, so that the adventurous instinct, for instance, is balanced by the cautious instinct; one giving rise to the virtue of courage, the other to the virtue of prudence. The last point on which I shall touch is the divergence between the Aristotelian and Christian ethics. I have mentioned the absence of benevolence from Aristotle's list of virtues. In this he fails to give a right idea of our relation towards our fellow-men; but the main defects of his system arise from his defective idea of our relation to God. In regard to theology, as in regard to every thing else, Aristotle seeks to find some confirmation for his own view in the ordinary belief of men. He thinks that the human race is for ever passing through alternate cycles of barbarism and civilization, and that in the traditional beliefs of men we may see, as it were, a ray of earlier light which has not been entirely extinguished in its passage through succeeding darkness[1]. [Such is Aristotle's matter-of-fact rendering of the 'Reminiscence' (ἀνάμνησις) of Plato[2].] It is this primaeval tradition which teaches us that all nature is encompassed by Deity, and that the heaven itself and the heavenly bodies are divine. But this original belief has got incrusted with mythological additions, partly owing to man's natural tendency to generalize his own experience[3], and attribute to the Gods whatever belongs to himself; and partly to design on the part of legislators with a view to moral or political expediency. While Aristotle considers these fables unworthy of serious attention[4] he is not roused like Plato, to protest against their immoral tendency. Nor, again, will he accept Plato's idea of God as the Creator and Governor of the world. Such an idea appears to him unworthy of the Deity and inconsistent with the blessedness which we ascribe to Him. The supreme God of Aristotle is the perfection of wisdom, the never-ceasing cause of all the beauty and order of the universe; but we cannot speak of Him as acting, or, as

[1] Cf. Zeller, II. 2. p. 792 with the references, especially *Met.* XII. 8.

[2] See above p. 43.

[3] Cf. *Pol.* I. 2, ὥσπερ τὰ εἴδη ἑαυτοῖς ἀφομοιοῦσιν οἱ ἄνθρωποι, οὕτω καὶ τοὺς βίους τῶν θεῶν.

[4] *Met.* II. 4, περὶ τῶν μυθικῶς σοφιζομένων (such as Hesiod) οὐκ ἄξιον μετὰ σπουδῆς σκοπεῖν.

M. P. 9

displaying moral virtue; He is not in any sense a moral Governor; no idea of Duty or of Sin arises in us at the thought of the relation in which we stand to Him. The same reason may probably explain why humility is treated as a failing; why nothing is said of purity, as distinct from self-mastery; and why the description of the crowning virtue of magnanimity, presents so much that is offensive to our present feeling. There is a further difference between the Aristotelian and the Christian views as to the immortality of the soul. Aristotle, it is true, allows immortality to νοῦς, the rational element in man, but his statements in regard to the continuance of a separate individual existence after death are extremely vague[1]. The thought of immortality is far from having the same practical influence with him, as it had with Plato.

I proceed now to the analysis of the *Politics*[2], which commences, as is usual in Aristotle's writings, with a broad generalization[3].

Every association aims at some good, and the State, as the highest and most comprehensive association, at the highest and most comprehensive good. The elements of

[1] See Grant, *Ethics of Aristotle* I. p. 294 foll.

[2] English editions by Eaton, 1855, and Congreve, ed. 2, 1874; a better one of books 1, 3, 4 with translation by Bolland and Lang, 1878. See Oncken *Staatslehre des Aristoteles*, 1877, and an essay on 'Aristotle's conception of the State' by A. C. Bradley in *Hellenica*.

[3] It is a great drawback to this interesting and admirable book that it has come down to us in such a confused and fragmentary state. In my analysis I have arranged the topics in the order which seemed to me most natural, disregarding altogether the order of the books after the first two.

the State, in the ultimate analysis, are male and female, ruler and ruled. Society originates in the instinctive and necessary combination of these elements, for the sake of the preservation and perpetuation of the race. The simplest form of society is the family, consisting of husband, wife, children, slave. Out of a combination of families is produced the village (κώμη), governed by the eldest progenitor; out of a combination of villages is produced the complete and self-sufficing organization of the State (πόλις) still under the government of One. Though later in time, this is essentially prior (πρότερον φύσει) to the family or the individual, as every whole is prior to its parts, because man is by nature a political animal, and only attains his perfection in the State. Whoever is unfitted for the State must be either above or below humanity (ἢ θεὸς ἢ θηρίον). Without political society man is without justice and law, and becomes the worst of animals, as he is the best armed with courage and craft.

The theory of the Family has to do with persons and with possessions. In regard to the former it embraces the relations of master to slave, of husband to wife, of father to child. To these relations correspond three forms of government, despotism, civil magistracy, monarchy. As to the question whether slavery is natural and lawful or not, it would seem that, if there are any men whose ἔργον consists in bodily activity alone, and who can only be said to have a share in reason in so far as, without possessing it themselves, they are capable of receiving it from others, from whom they differ as much as the body differs from the soul,—then slavery is the best condition for them, and they are by nature slaves :

9—2

but where this difference is not found, as in the case of
Greeks enslaved by Greeks, there slavery is unnatural and
unlawful. The slave, not possessing the deliberative
faculty, is only capable of the inferior virtues, such as
temperance, in the degree in which they are needed for
his work. There is a corresponding difference between
the virtue of a man, a woman and a child[1].

In treating of wealth we have to distinguish between
what is real and what is factitious. In increasing
the former we actually increase the general stock of
useful things by agriculture, hunting, or otherwise; in
increasing the latter we merely add to our own store of
money, which is simply a convenient token. The worst
and most unnatural form of accumulation is usury.

The Second Book commences with a criticism of
Plato's *Republic*. It is founded on the wrong principle,
that unity is the perfection of the State. So far from this
being the case, the State, as it approaches unity, loses its
character of a community, becoming first a family, then
an individual. Even if unity were the perfection of the
State, Socrates (Aristotle prefers to make him the nominal
opponent) uses the wrong means to attain it. For (1) as
regards community of women, it is impossible for 'all to
have all in common,' if we use the word 'all' distributive-
ly; and, if it is used collectively, (affirming a general

---

[1] ὁ μὲν δοῦλος ὅλως οὐκ ἔχει τὸ βουλευτικόν, τὸ δὲ θῆλυ ἔχει μέν,
ἀλλ' ἄκυρον, ὁ δὲ παῖς ἔχει μέν, ἀλλ' ἀτελές...ὥστε οὐχ ἡ αὐτὴ
σωφροσύνη γυναικὸς καὶ ἀνδρός, οὐδ' ἀνδρία καὶ δικαιοσύνη, καθάπερ
ᾤετο Σωκράτης, ἀλλ' ἡ μὲν ἀρχική, ἡ δ' ὑπηρετική. Compare, on the
difference of the male and female character, *Œcon.* I. 3, and the
very elaborate comparison in the *Hist. An.* IX. 1, quoted by Zeller
II. 2. p. 688.

right, without granting to each the enjoyment of that right), this would have no tendency to produce harmony. (2) Such policy would lead to an absence of interest: every man's duty being no man's duty. The sonship proposed would be a weaker tie than the most distant relationship now recognized. (3) It is impracticable: resemblance would betray the closer relationship. (4) Concealment of relationship would open the door to offences against nature. (5) As regards property, Communism destroys the charm of property and the virtue of liberality[1]. (6) The State is split up into two nations differing altogether in manners and institutions. (7) The argument from the customs of animals (οἷς οἰκονομίας οὐδὲν μέτεστιν) to the customs of men, ignores the moral difference between the two. After urging these and similar objections, Aristotle proceeds to point out defects in the more practical Ideal contained in the *Laws*, as also in the ideal commonwealths of Phaleas and others. He discusses, by the way, how far it is desirable to make changes in laws. On the one hand, laws need constant improvement; men should not care for antiquity but for utility. On the other hand, since laws derive their force from custom, every change must weaken the reverence which the citizens should have for the constitution. The book ends with an account of the constitutions of Sparta, Crete &c.

Existing forms of government may be classified as follows. A State may be ruled by One, by the few who are rich, or by the many who are poor; and the rule is just or unjust, as it is for the public good, or for the good of the

[1] See p. 1263 βέλτιον εἶναι μὲν ἰδίας τὰς κτήσεις, τῇ δὲ χρήσει ποιεῖν κοινάς.

rulers only. We shall thus have three normal or legitimate forms of government and three perversions (παρεκβάσεις), monarchy (βασιλεία) with its perversion tyranny (τυραννίς), aristocracy (ἀριστοκρατία) with its perversion oligarchy (ὀλιγαρχία), and republic (πολιτεία) with its perversion democracy (δημοκρατία). Each of these is better or worse in proportion as it is adapted to the nature and position of the people, and as it approaches to the ideal State, the true ἀριστοκρατία, of which the end is to dispose all the citizens to a noble and virtuous activity; not simply to train for war, as Lycurgus sought to do, but far more to foster the peaceful virtues of self-control, justice, wisdom, since all war is undertaken for the sake of peace, as all business for the sake of leisure. This ideal State requires certain external advantages (as the good man his βίος τέλειος). It must not be too small for strength, or too large for unity[1]; must possess a country fruitful, not luxurious, well situated for commerce and for defence. The people must neither have the fierceness of the North, nor the softness of the East, but combine spirit with intelligence like the Greeks, who are the mean between these two extremes. None can be admitted to citizenship who are incapable of exercising the virtues of the citizen, which in the ideal State will be identical with all human virtue. That is to say, all the citizens will be gentlemen enjoying an honorable and virtuous leisure (σχολάζοντες ἐλευθερίως ἅμα καὶ σωφρόνως *Pol.* VII. 5 p. 1326), supported in part by the State and in part by their hereditary allotments, which will be worked for them

---

[1] It is remarkable that Aristotle, writing after the conquests of Alexander, seems to have no suspicion that the State of the future would exceed the limits of a Greek πόλις.

by slaves or other dependents. They will have common meals, as at Sparta, and form the standing army during the military age, after which they will be employed in civil duties and such magistracies as they may be appointed to by the common vote. Their highest work, however, will be thought and study, the advancement of science and the superintendence of education. When age unfits them for more active duties they will become eligible for the priesthood. The number of citizens and allotments being strictly limited by law, it will be the duty of the magistrates to regulate marriage with a view to restrict the number of children and to prevent any but the healthiest and strongest being reared. Children born under the conditions sanctioned by the law will be taught at home till their 7th year, and will then be sent to the public schools, where the education will be directed to train the body, the feelings, and the reason for a noble life.

Unfortunately we have only an incomplete account of the subjects of education. Besides Reading and Writing, Drawing is recommended as training the eye to beauty of form; Music is praised, not only for the pleasure it gives, but for its power of calming the passions and generally for its moral influence: it is the natural expression of emotion and tends to produce the emotion which it expresses; it is therefore of great importance to exclude all music which is of a vulgar or debasing character. Education should be general and liberal, not utilitarian or professional[1]. One of its chief uses is to teach the proper use of leisure (σχολάζειν καλῶς).

---

[1] τὸ ζητεῖν πανταχοῦ τὸ χρήσιμον ἥκιστα ἁρμόζει τοῖς μεγαλοψύχοις καὶ τοῖς ἐλευθέροις. *Pol.* v. p. 1338 *a.*

To return to existing constitutions, Monarchy is allowable where one citizen far surpasses all the others in wisdom and virtue, or where the mass of the people are only fit for subjection, as in the East. Aristocracy is allowable where the qualitative superiority of the wealthy more than counterbalances the quantitative superiority of the poor. A republic is best where the citizens are nearly on a level in respect to the contribution of service which they bring to the State. It has an advantage because it interests the majority in the government; and though, taken separately, the poor may be inferior to the rich, yet in combination they may surpass them; as for instance the popular judgment is decisive in works of art. They should share in any part of government which can be safely intrusted to a number, and have a voice in electing the higher officers. Each of these three normal constitutions is better in itself and more likely to be permanent, the more it borrows from the other two, and the more influence it allows to the middle class which forms the link between rich and poor. Revolutions are brought about by the excess of the characteristic quality of each constitution, as an oligarchy is overthrown by the temper shown in the oligarchical oath ' I will be an enemy of the Commons and do them all the harm I can [1].' The true policy is the exact contrary; the government should show special tenderness to the interest which it does not itself represent. It is a sign of a good, i.e. an appropriate constitution, when no portion of the body politic is desirous of organic change. The functions of government are Deliberative, Administrative

---

[1] τῷ δήμῳ κακόνους ἔσομαι καὶ βουλεύσω ὅ τι ἂν ἔχω κακόν. *Pol.* v. 9.

and Judicial. General principles should be as far as possible laid down by the Law, leaving only questions of fact and details of application to be determined by votes of assemblies or the judgment of the magistrate. When the Law rules, it is the rule of Reason and of God; when man rules, without law, he brings with him the wild beast of passion[1].

Aristotle treats at considerable length of the varieties of each kind of constitution, e.g. of the difference caused in the nature of a democracy, according as the citizens are mainly agricultural or manufacturing, and as the franchise is higher or lower. He points out, with very full historical illustrations, the characteristics of each variety, the dangers to which it is exposed and the means of guarding against them. Many of the maxims of Machiavelli's *Prince* are taken from Aristotle's chapters on the Tyrant. The broad distinction between the normal constitution and its perversion seems here to pass into a gradation of varieties, a view which is perhaps more in accordance with actual facts.

It is strange that, in constructing his Ideal State, Aristotle should have fallen into some of the errors which he condemns in Plato. As far as we can judge from the imperfect sketch which he has left, there would have been less of common feeling between his gentleman-citizens and the urban and rural population by whose labour they are supported, than between Plato's Guardians and Artizans. The latter had at any rate the name of citizens, and Plato

---

[1] ὁ μὲν οὖν τὸν νόμον κελεύων ἄρχειν δοκεῖ κελεύειν ἄρχειν τὸν θεὸν καὶ τὸν νοῦν μόνους, ὁ δ' ἄνθρωπον κελεύων προστίθησι καὶ θηρίον. *Pol.* III. 16.

makes provision for raising promising boys from the lower class into the higher. Probably Aristotle thought that the disaffection of citizens was likely to be more dangerous than that of slaves or Metoeci, who were sure to recognize their own unfitness to rule. The philosophic disbelief in the possibility of virtue, i.e. of thoughtfulness and a sense of honour, in artizans and labourers (θῆτες and βάναυσοι), becomes more remarkable when we remember that many of the philosophers themselves belonged to this class, from the time of Protagoras the porter, and the Socratics Aeschines and Simon, down to the time of the slave Epictetus. Again Aristotle, no less than Plato, is open to the charge of making regulations παρὰ φύσιν, when he sanctions abortion and exposure of infants.

The contrast between Aristotle's philosophy of Man and his philosophy of Nature, between the richness of ideas, the exhaustive analysis, the firm grasp of fact, the sound judgment, which characterize the former, and the barren notionalism which is too prevalent in the latter, is a striking justification of Socrates' resolve to keep clear of physics. Aristotle indeed is unfortunate even as compared with other ancient writers on the same subject. While Parmenides and Plato, as we have seen, profess to give nothing more than guesses as to the nature of the Universe, Aristotle puts forward his views with an air of scientific precision which makes his mistakes seem all the more absurd; and he often deliberately rejects anticipations of later science which may be found in the writings of his predecessors. Thus Pythagoras having guessed that the earth was a planet moving round the central fire of the Universe, Aristotle rebukes him for not squaring his causes and theories with the apparent facts, but endeavouring to force facts to suit his fancies (*De Caelo*, II. 13)[1]. So Democritus had already exploded the doctrine of the four elements, substituting for it the more scientific conception of atoms; similarly he had explained circular movement as a resultant of various rectilinear movements; and Epicurus afterwards distinctly controverted the attribution of a natural upward movement to air and fire[2], as well as the Aristotelian limitation of Space[3].

And yet, if we hold Plato right in describing the philosopher as one who is enamoured of all truth and all knowledge[4], we can hardly blame Aristotle either for his boundless curiosity in seeking to ascertain facts and causes, or for his endeavour to harmonize all facts, whether of inner or outer experience, and so to build up one all-embracing body of science. No doubt he, like his predecessors, thought the human microcosm to be a truer mirror of the macrocosm than it really is, and was disposed to assume as a law of the objective universe whatever appeared to satisfy our subjective needs and tastes; and yet he made a decided advance by insisting on the importance of observation, and on the necessity of testing theory by comparison with the actual phenomena[5]. Again it is no doubt true that when he

[1] It is probable, however, that, in this criticism, Aristotle is thinking chiefly of the Anti-Chthon, invented for the purpose of making up the sacred number Ten.

[2] See Lucr. II 185.

[3] Lucr. I 958.

[4] *Rep.* V. 475.

[5] See *Gen. An.* III. 10. § 25. 'From our reasoning and from the apparent facts, such would seem to be the truth about the bees; but the facts have not yet been fully ascertained : when they have been,

ventured into the province of Physical Science, Aristotle was endeavouring to map out a *terra incognita* which he had no means for exploring. He had neither the methods nor the instruments which were needed: but were men to wait for the microscope and telescope, or for the full development of the various branches of mathematical and physical science, before formulating any ideas on the general character of the universe in which they were placed? Now, that we know that Aristotle was following a blind path in his endless refinements on the meaning of 'motion' and similar terms, we may find his physical treatises 'inexpressibly fatiguing and unfruitful[1];' but the question is, whether it was not worth while to make some attempt at a working hypothesis which might supply men with a framework in which to arrange their thoughts and feelings with regard to the nature of the world around them. There is a value in the prophet's vision as well as in the historian's narrative; and men may be thankful to the philosopher who gives wings to their imagination and extends the limit of their mental horizon, however much he may have failed to anticipate the revelations of modern science.

To turn now to the history of Aristotle's writings. All readers of Aristotle have had to complain of the defective arrangement and the general abstruseness of

---

then we must trust observation more than theory, and only trust our theory if it gives results corresponding to the phenomena,' τοῖς λόγοις πιστευτέον ἐὰν ὁμολογούμενα δεικνύωσι τοῖς φαινομένοις. Compare a multitude of similar passages in Bonitz's *Index* under φαινόμενα.

[1] Lewes *Aristotle*, p. 127.

his works. This has been accounted for, partly, by the supposition that the treatises which have come down to us under his name, consist of notes for lectures hastily revised by himself, or edited after his death by his disciples, and partly by the story, reported by Strabo and others, of their concealment for nearly 150 years in the cellar of Neleus. According to this story, the Library and MSS. of Aristotle passed, at the death of his successor Theophrastus, into the hands of Neleus, a pupil of the latter, and were taken by him to Scepsis, a city which was then under the rule of the kings of Pergamus. These kings appear to have paid little regard to the rights of property in their desire to augment the royal library, which was almost as renowned as that of the Ptolemies; and the descendants of Neleus could only preserve their treasures by hiding them in a cellar where they suffered much from worms and damp. When the last Attalus left his kingdom to the Romans in 133 B.C., the then owner of the MSS. brought them out from their concealment and sold them to Apellicon, a Peripatetic residing at Athens, who at once had copies made, and endeavoured, not very succesfully, to restore the text where it was defective. The library of Apellicon was seized by Sulla on his conquest of Athens in 86 B.C., and transported to Rome, where the Aristotelian MSS. once more fell into the hands of a competent reader in the person of the Rhodian Andronicus, who brought out a new edition in which the treatises were rearranged and the text much improved. This edition is considered to be the foundation of our existing text of Aristotle. There seems no doubt that somehow or other the abstruser works of Aristotle had been lost to common use not many years after his death. Strabo tells us that only a few of the more popular treatises were in the possession of the Peripatetic school at Athens, and this is what we might infer from the manner in which Cicero speaks of the style of Aristotle,[1]—using expressions which are certainly anything but appropriate to the books which have come down to us,—as well as from the comparative frequency of his references to the lost Dialogues. Again we find in Diogenes Laertius a list taken probably from the catalogue of the Alexandrine Library, containing the names of 146 separate Aristotelian treatises, of which more than twenty are dialogues. This would represent Aristotle as he was known at the beginning of the 2nd century B.C. Our existing Aristotle consists of 46 treatises, very few of which appear in the list of Diogenes.

As a specimen of the more popular style by which Aristotle was best known during the interval from Theophrastus to Andronicus I insert here a translation of a passage from his dialogue *De Philosophia* preserved by Cicero (*N. D.* II. 95).

'Imagine a race of men who had always lived under ground in beautiful houses adorned with pictures and statues and every luxury of wealth. Suppose that some dim rumour of a divine being had reached them in their subterranean world. Then suppose that the earth were to open and they ascended up from their dark abodes and saw before them all the wonders of this world. Could they doubt, when they beheld the earth and the sea and the sky with its gathering clouds and its mighty winds, and the glory and majesty of the sun as he floods the heaven with the light of day, and then the starry

---

[1] See *Acad.* II. 119, *veniet flumen orationis aureum fundens Aristoteles*, and the other passages cited in Grote's *Aristotle*, I. 43.

heaven of night, and the varying brightness of the waxing and the waning moon, and the regular movements of all the heavenly bodies and their risings and settings governed by an everlasting and unchanging law,—could they doubt that the Gods really existed, and that these mighty works were theirs ?'

With the death of Aristotle a new age begins. The fearless spirit of Greek thought which had soared upwards as on eagle wings to the empyrean, gazing with Plato on the Ideas clustered around the one supreme Idea of Good, contemplating with Aristotle the Thought of Thought, the Form and End and Cause of all existence, sank back to earth in weariness when once the spell of the mighty masters was removed. A feebler generation followed whose lot was cast in a more ungenial time. As the great prae-Socratic movement had terminated in the scepticism of the Sophists, so this greater movement produced its natural reaction in the scepticism of Pyrrho and the later Academy. Even the dogmatic systems which sprang up along with them, while asserting man's claim to know, yet changed the object and limited the range of knowledge, as it was understood by the preceding age. Lofty idealist systems require strenuous effort of thought and imagination on the part of their adherents, if they are not to wither into mere empty phrases and barren formalism. While the founders live, enthusiastic faith gives a motive for effort, and supplies any deficiency in the evidence demanded by reason: when that first enthusiasm has died away, slumbering doubts awake in the minds of the more independent disciples, and the ruder and coarser among them are likely to seize on some one portion or aspect of the master's teaching, losing sight of its more subtle and refined elements, and to make that stand for the whole ; or perhaps they break away altogether and fall back on some earlier and simpler philosophy.

So here, men were not only repelled by the difficulty of understanding what Plato and Aristotle really meant; they had further positive grounds for departing from them when they found them opposed to each other on essential points, such as the nature and import of ideas, when they saw the weaknesses of the former laid bare in the criticisms of the latter, and became aware of the vagueness and uncertainty which characterized the the critic's own utterances in regard to questions of deep practical interest such as the nature of God and the providential government of the world. Under these circumstances those who still believed that it was possible for men to attain to knowledge, practically limited the range of knowledge to what had reference to man's own immediate use ; all that they asked for was knowledge so far as it is needed to direct the life of man ; and by man they meant the individual standing alone, not man as the citizen of a Greek πόλις. We shall see, when we come to speak of the Stoics, in what way the political circumstances of the time contributed to this change of view. Again, the abstruseness and indefiniteness, which offended them in preceding philosophers, were especially connected with Ideas and Forms, with the depreciation of the senses and the glorification of incorporeal spirit. All this might be avoided by the assumption that the sole ground of knowledge is sensation, and that body is the only thing which can either act or be acted upon. The post

Aristotelian schools therefore were predominantly ethical, sensationalist, and materialist, as opposed to the idealistic metaphysics of the preceding age.

Of these schools the least original and the least important is the Peripatetic. The immediate successor of Aristotle was Theophrastus, whose *Characters* and treatises on Botany we still possess, together with fragments of other works. He appears to have carried further his master's investigations upon particular points, without diverging from his general principles. Cicero charges him with assigning too much weight to fortune as an element of happiness. Strato, who succeeded him as head of the Lyceum in 287 B.C., dethroned the *Nous* of Aristotle, and explained the ordered movement of the universe by ascribing ' to the several parts of matter an inward plastic life, whereby they could artificially frame themselves to the best advantage according to their several capabilities without any conscious or reflexive knowledge [1].' Cicero says that he is *omnino semovendus* from the true Peripatetics, as he abandoned ethics and departed very widely from his predecessors in physics, to which he confined himself. Aristoxenus and Dicaearchus were contemporaries of Theophrastus; the former is chiefly known as the writer of the first scientific treatise on Music, the latter was a voluminous popular writer much esteemed by Cicero. He denied the immortality of the soul. After the time of Andronicus, mentioned above, the Peripatetics were chiefly known as laborious commentators. Cratippus presided over the school during the lifetime of Cicero, who sent young Marcus to Athens to attend his lectures.

[1] Cudworth I. p. 149.

The first name among the Sceptics is Pyrrho of Elis (fl. about 320 B.C.), who is said to have had some connexion with the Megarian and the Atomic schools, and to have accompanied Alexander on his expedition into India, and thus learnt something of the doctrines of the Magi and the Indian Gymnosophists. Perhaps the influence of the latter may be traced in the three positions attributed to him, (1) that the wise man should practise ἐποχή, suspension of judgment, (2) that all external things are ἀδιάφορα, matters of indifference to him, (3) that he will thus be free from passion and anxiety, and arrive at the condition of complete ἀταραξία, imperturbability. Pyrrho left no writings, but his pupil, Timon of Phlius (fl. 280 B.C.), was a voluminous writer. We have a few fragments of his *Silli*, a satirical poem in which he ridiculed the tenets of other philosophers. When the Academy became sceptical there was no room for an independent Pyrrhonist school, but it revived in the person of Aenesidemus when the Academy became identified with an eclectic dogmatism under Antiochus. The sceptical argument was summed up in ten τρόποι, and is given in full in the works of Sextus Empiricus (fl. 200 A.D.). The most important points in it are as follows: (1) the discrepancy of opinions among wise and honest men, (2) the relativity of all knowledge, *i.e.* the manner in which it varies with the physical and mental conditions of the observer or thinker, (3) the impossibility of proving the first principles on which proof is based, (4) the *petitio principii* involved in the syllogism, the major premiss assuming the truth of the conclusion.

We turn back now to trace the fortunes of the Academy,

which may be conveniently divided into three schools, the Old, the Middle or Sceptical, and the Reformed or Eclectic Academy[1]. To the first belong the names of Speusippus Xenocrates and Polemo, who successively presided over the school between 347 and 270 B.C., as well as those of Heraclides of Pontus, Crantor and Crates. They appear to have modified the Platonic doctrines mainly by the admixture of Pythagorean elements. Crantor's writings were used by Cicero for his *Consolatio* and *Tusculan Disputations.* The chief expounders of the Middle Academy were its founder **Arcesilaus** 315—241 B.C., (characterized in a line borrowed from the Homeric description of the Chimaera as πρόσθε Πλάτων, ὄπιθεν Πύρρων, μέσσος Διόδωρος, implying that by his dialectic quibbling he had changed the Platonism, which he professed, into a mere Pyrrhonism), **Carneades** of Cyrene 214—129 B.C., one of the Athenian ambassadors to Rome in 155 B.C.[2], and **Clitomachus** of Carthage, the literary exponent of the views of his master Carneades, who is said to have never written anything himself. They neglected the positive doctrine of Plato, and employed themselves mainly in a negative polemic against the dogmatism

---

[1] Cicero only recognized the Old and the New Academy, the latter corresponding to what is above called the Middle Academy, but including Philo. Antiochus himself claimed to be a true representative of the Old Academy. Later writers made five Academic schools, the second founded by Arcesilaus, the third by Carneades, the fourth by Philo, the fifth by Antiochus.

[2] Carneades had an extraordinary reputation for acuteness and skill in argument, as is shown by a line of Lucilius (preserved by Lactantius v. 15), in which Neptune speaks of some question as insoluble even to a Carneades, *nec si Carneaden ipsum ad nos Orcu' remittat.*

of the Stoics, professing to follow the example of Socrates, though they thought that even he had approached too near to dogmatism in saying that he *knew* that he knew nothing. Probable opinion was the furthest point in the direction of knowledge to which man could attain.

Cicero, in his *Natura Deorum* and *Academica,* and Sextus Empiricus have preserved to us several specimens of the arguments used by Carneades in order to prove the impossibility of the attainment of knowledge in the abstract, as well as to expose the errors and inconsistency of the knowledge professed by the Dogmatic schools of his time. Thus, if there is such a thing as knowledge, it must rest ultimately on the senses; but the senses are constantly deceptive, and we have no means of distinguishing between a true and a false sensation, the difference between objects being often so imperceptible that we are liable to mistake one for another. The impotence of reasoning as an instrument for the attainment of certain truth is shown by the Sorites and other logical puzzles. Dialectic only tests formal accuracy of procedure, it cannot assure us of the truth of that which we assume as the foundation of our reasoning. Like the polypus which feeds on its own limbs, it can destroy, but never establish proof. The Stoics allege universal consent as a proof of the existence of God. But this consent is not proved, and, if it were, the opinion of the ignorant has no weight. The Stoics further maintain that the world exhibits the perfection of reason in its constitution and that Divine Providence directs all things for the good of men. But many things exist for which we can see no reason, many which are distinctly injurious to mankind. Even the possession of reason is a very doubtful advan-

tage; and we do not find that the wise and virtuous man
is always prosperous. Granting that the world is perfect,
why may not this perfection be the result of the unconscious working of nature? Why are we bound to
attribute it to the action of an intelligent Being? Again
it is impossible to form any consistent conception of God.
The ideas of personality and infinity are mutually contradictory. Even to think of Him as the living God or the
good God, is opposed to reason. For animal life is
necessarily joined with feeling, and feeling implies
consciousness of pleasure and pain, but whatever is
capable of pain is liable to destruction by excess of pain.
And how can we ascribe virtue to a Being who is
supposed to have no weaknesses to conquer, no temptations to resist; who being all-powerful can have no need
of prudence to devise means for attaining his ends, no
need of courage to sustain him against danger? It is
equally impossible to think of God either as corporeal or
incorporeal. If he is the former, he must be either
simple or compound: if he is compounded of different
elements, he is naturally liable to dissolution; if he is a
pure elementary substance, he must be without life and
thought. On the other hand that which is incorporeal can
neither feel nor act. In like manner it may be shown that
it is impossible to make any assertion whatever about God.

But though knowledge and certainty are unattainable,
we are not left simply to act at hazard. Probability was
the guide of life to Carneades, as to Bp. Butler; and he
carefully distinguished degrees of probability. Thus a
sensation might be of such a nature as to produce in us
belief involuntarily; this he called φαντασία πιθανή, a
persuasive presentation. Again, no sensation comes

singly, and any one sensation is liable to be confirmed or weakened by the connected sensations. We may believe, for instance, that we see the figure of Socrates; and this belief will be confirmed if we think we recognize his voice. If then all the associated sensations agree in confirming our belief, such a belief is called φαντασία ἀπερίσπαστος, an undisturbed presentation. The highest degree of probability is when we have further investigated the conditions under which the sensation occurred (such as the soundness of the organ, the distance from the object etc.), and find nothing to raise suspicion as to its reality; belief is then called φαντασία περιωδευμένη, a thoroughly explored presentation. We have very little information as to the particular doctrines to which Carneades assigned probability. One tradition says that in his old age, he relaxed in his irony, and became more free-spoken[1], but his successor Clitomachus professed that he had never been able to ascertain what his real belief was[2].

The Reformed Academy may be regarded as commencing with **Philo** of Larissa, a pupil of Clitomachus and one of Cicero's teachers. In it we see a return to dogmatism combined with an eclectic tendency which showed itself most strongly in Philo's pupil **Antiochus**, who endeavoured to strengthen the Academy by uniting Stoic and Peripatetic doctrines with the original Platonism. Further details will be given when we come to speak of the influence of the Roman spirit on the development of philosophy.

We turn now to the two most important developments of post-Aristotelian philosophy, Stoicism and Epicureanism. To understand them it is necessary to look for a

---

[1] See Zeller III. I. p. 531[3].   [2] Cic. *Acad.* II. 139.

moment at the changes which had been brought about by
the conquests of Alexander. While Greece proper lost
its national life, the Greek language and Greek civilization
spread throughout the world, and the Greeks in their turn
became familiarized with Oriental thought and religion.
Thus the two main supports of the authoritative tradition
by which practical life had hitherto been regulated, the
law of the State and the old religion of Greece, were
shaken from their foundations. The need which was
most strongly felt by the best minds was to find some
substitute for these, some principle of conduct which
should enable a man to retain his self-respect under the
rule of brute force to which all were subject. It must be
something which would enable him to stand alone, to defy
the oppressor, to rise superior to circumstances. Such a
principle the Stoics boasted to have found[1]. **Zeno,**
the founder of the school, was a native of Citium in
Cyprus. He came to Athens about 320 B.C. and attended
the lectures of Crates the Cynic and afterwards of Stilpo
the Megarian and of some of the Academics, and began
to teach in the στοά ποικίλη about 308 B.C. He was
succeeded by **Cleanthes** of Assos in Asia Minor about
260 B.C. Among his other pupils were Aristo of Chius,
Herillus of Carthage, Persaeus, who like his master
was a native of Citium, and Aratus of Soli in Cilicia, the
author of two astronomical poems translated by Cicero
(*N. D.* II. 104—115). Cleanthes was succeeded by
Chrysippus of Soli (b. 280, d. 206), who did so
much to develop and systematize the Stoic philosophy
that he was called the Second Founder of the

[1] See the interesting treatise on Stoicism by W. W. Capes in the
S. P. C. K. series, and *Essay* VI of the Introduction to Grant's *Ethics*.

school[1]. Next came Zeno of Tarsus and Diogenes of Babylon, one of the three ambassadors to Rome in 155 B.C. From this time forward Stoicism begins to show a softened and eclectic tendency, as we may see in **Panaetius** of Rhodes (180—111 B.C.), and also in his pupil **Posidonius** of Apamea in Syria, of whom we shall have more to say hereafter.

The end of philosophy with the Stoics was purely practical. Philosophy is identical with virtue. But since virtue consists in bringing the actions into harmony with the general order of the world, it is essential to know what this order is, and thus we arrive at the famous triple division of philosophy into *physics*, including cosmology and theology, which explains the nature and laws of the universe; *logic*, which ensures us against deception and supplies the method for attaining to true knowledge; *ethics*, which draws the conclusion for practical life. The Stoics were famed for their logical subtilties, and are often referred to under the name *Dialectici*. They included in Logic both Rhetoric and Grammar, and made great improvements in the theory of the latter subject. The chief point of interest however in their Logic is their theory as to the *criterion*. They considered the soul to resemble a sheet of blank paper[2] on which impressions (φαντασίαι) were made through the senses[3].

---

[1] Cf. the line εἰ μὴ γὰρ ἦν Χρύσιππος οὐκ ἂν ἦν στοά.

[2] Plut. *Plac. Phil.* IV. 11.

[3] Cleanthes held that each impression was literally a material impression on the soul, like that of a signet-ring on wax: Chrysippus thought this inconsistent with the infinite variety of impressions which we are continually receiving, and preferred to speak of them as modifications (ἑτεροιώσεις) of the soul. See Sext. *Math.* VII. 228.

The concept (ἔννοια) was produced from the impressions by generalization, which might be either spontaneous and unconscious, giving rise to common ideas or natural anticipations (κοιναὶ ἔννοιαι, ἔμφυτοι προλήψεις), or it might be conscious and methodical, giving rise to artificial concepts. In entire opposition to Plato they held that the individual object alone had real existence; the universal, the general term, existed only in the mind as subjective thought. The truth or falsehood of these impressions and conceptions depended on their possession of τὸ καταληπτικόν, the power of carrying conviction. An impression which was not merely assented to, but forced itself irresistibly on the mind, was a καταληπτικὴ φαντασία a perception that has a firm grasp of reality[1]. The same irresistible evidence attaches to a πρόληψις[2], but artificial concepts required to have their truth proved by being connected with one or other of these criteria. The ten Categories of Aristotle were reduced by the Stoics to four, (1) the substratum, τὸ ὑποκείμενον, (2) the essential quality, τὸ ποιόν, (3) the condition, τὸ πῶς ἔχον, (4) the relation, τὸ πρός τι πῶς ἔχον.

The *physical* theory of the Stoics is a *pantheistic materialism.* The only real existences are such as can act and be acted upon, and these are bodies, for like can

---

[1] Zeno compared the simple impression or sensation (φαντασία) to the touching of an object with the outstretched fingers; the mental assent which follows (συγκατάθεσις) to a half closure of the hand upon the object; the distinct apprehension (κατάληψις) to a tight grasp ; knowledge itself to the grasping of the fist by the other hand, so as to keep it more firmly closed.

[2] Cicero's renderings of the above technical terms are as follows: φαντασία *visum,* κοιναὶ ἔννοιαι *communes notiones,* ἔμφυτοι προλήψεις *insitae anticipationes,* κατάληψις *comprehensio,* συγκατάθεσις *assensio.*

only act on like[1]. But these bodies are not moved simply by mechanical laws, as Democritus supposed. The whole universe is an embodied spiritual force, of which we may call one part passive, one part active, but all is alike material. The active portion is soul, a fiery ether pervading the whole, but having its principal seat in the heaven which encompasses it on every side; the passive portion consists mainly of the inferior elements, water and earth. These latter proceed from the former and are periodically reabsorbed into it in the world-conflagration. The universe itself, as a perfect living creature, is rightly called God, but the name is more particularly given to the soul of the universe, who is also known by many descriptive appellations, Rational or Artistic Fire ($\pi\hat{\upsilon}\rho$ $\nu o\epsilon\rho\acute{o}\nu$, $\pi\hat{\upsilon}\rho$ $\tau\epsilon\chi\nu\iota\kappa\acute{o}\nu$), All-penetrating Air, Spirit, Reason, Nature, Providence, Destiny, Law, Necessity, the Ruling Principle ($\tau\grave{o}$ $\dot{\eta}\gamma\epsilon\mu o\nu\iota\kappa\acute{o}\nu$), and, with reference to his creative and 'informing' power, the Generative Reason ($\lambda\acute{o}\gamma os$ $\sigma\pi\epsilon\rho\mu a\tau\iota\kappa\acute{o}s$). The gods of the popular religion represented different activities of the one true Deity. Thus Zeus, one God under many names as Cleanthes calls him, is denominated Hera, when we think of him as pervading the air, Poseidon as pervading water, Demeter as pervading earth: again Demeter is the name we give to Zeus when we think of him as the giver of corn, Dionysus, when we think of him as the giver of wine.

---

[1] Not only substances, but feelings and attributes were regarded as corporeal. Thus the virtues, and even the seasons of the year, were called animals or bodies. These paradoxical modes of speech were explained by saying, that virtue denoted a certain tension or elasticity ($\tau\acute{o}\nu os$) of the psychical element, ether; that when we speak of summer, we mean air of a certain temperature, &c.

The foolish or immoral stories told by the poets were explained as allegories intended to convey some moral or physical truth. For instance, when Hera is represented as suspended by a gold chain from heaven with weights round her feet ἐν αἰθέρι καὶ νεφέλῃσιν, this is interpreted to mean the order of nature binding the four elements together[1]. The human soul is an emanation from Deity, and is often spoken of as the God within us[2]. Although it outlives the body, it will only retain its individual existence till the next conflagration, and that only in the case of the wise. The stars being made of pure fire are divine.

In all this we see the influence of Heraclitus, who was much quoted by the Stoics; but in their distinction between the active and passive elements of the universe they probably had in mind the Aristotelian distinction between Form and Matter, only substituting for the mysterious attraction exercised on Matter by the transcendent First Form of Aristotle, the quickening influence of an ever-active all-pervading Spirit. They agreed with Aristotle also in holding the unity, finiteness and sphericity of the world, but, unlike him, considered that there was an unlimited void beyond it. That which was peculiarly Stoical was the strong moral colouring which they gave to their materialistic system. The all-pervading fire was at the same time the all-seeing Providence, who creates and governs all things for the best ends, and makes each several existence, each several fact, conspire together for the good of the whole. It is the privilege of

[1] Heracl. *Alleg. Hom.* p. 463 Gale.

[2] See Seneca *Epp.* 31 and 41, and other passages quoted in Zeller III. 1. p. 319[3].

man to be able knowingly and willingly to act as a rational part of the rational whole, instead of yielding himself up to irrational and selfish impulse: but however he acts, he must perforce carry out the divine purpose, as Cleanthes says in the noble lines:

> ἄγου δέ μ' ὦ Ζεῦ, καὶ σύ γ' ἡ Πεπρωμένη,
> ὅποι ποθ' ὑμῖν εἰμὶ διατεταγμένος·
> ὡς ἕψομαι γ' ἄοκνος· ἢν δὲ μὴ θέλω,
> κακὸς γενόμενος, οὐδὲν ἧττον ἕψομαι.

From this it follows that the *summum bonum* is to live according to nature, both universal nature, *i.e.* the reason embodied in the universe, and the particular nature[1], not only of man in general, but of the individual concerned; or, to express the same principle in other words, each man is to act in accordance with his own particular nature in so far as that is in harmony with universal nature: and it is through virtue or wisdom that we are enabled to do this; wisdom being not only *speculative*, judging what is in accordance with nature or the divine law, but *practical*, strongly willing what is thus determined to be right.

The stages of rational development in the individual were thus described. The first impulse in every animal is to its own self-preservation[2]. This appetite manifests itself in little children before any pleasure or pain is felt. We begin by loving our own vitality; and we come, by association, to love what promotes our vitality; we hate destruction or disablement,

---

[1] Cf. Diog. L. VII. 88 τέλος γίγνεται τὸ ἀκολούθως τῇ φύσει ζῆν, ὅπερ ἐστὶ κατά τε τὴν αὑτοῦ καὶ κατὰ τὴν τῶν ὅλων, and Cic. *De Off.* I. 107.

[2] This was called the *prima conciliatio naturae*, ἡ πρώτη οἰκείωσις, see Cic. *Fin.* III 16 with Madvig's note.

and we come to hate whatever produces that effect. But these *prima naturae*[1] are not good in themselves, and there is nothing virtuous in the effort to attain them. It is only as the dawning reason of the youth becomes conscious of a wider nature of which his own nature is a part, and of a higher Reason revealing itself in the order and harmony of nature and of human society, that the true Good becomes possible for him, not in the attainment of those primary ends, but in the right choice of the means by which to attain them. And the right choice is one which is always in accordance with reason and with nature. If he takes the right course, whether he attains those lower ends or not, he has attained the highest end of man, the true *Bonum* or *Honestum*. Just as the archer's excellence is shown in aiming rightly, and there is no independent value in the mere act of hitting the target; so there is no independent value in those *prima naturae;* the acting in accordance with nature is all in all[2]. One who has thus learnt to live in accordance with nature is αὐταρκής, in need of nothing. He alone is free, for he has all he wishes: his will is one with the universal Will. External good, external evil are matters of indifference (ἀδιάφορα): intrinsically and in themselves they are neither bad nor good, though they may become such according to the manner in which they are used. Nothing can be called really good which is not always and under all circumstances good. What are commonly regarded as goods, such as wealth, station, &c., only provide the field in which virtue is to exercise itself;

[1] See on the *prima naturae,* πρῶτα κατὰ φύσιν, Madvig's *De Finibus, Exc.* 4.

[2] Grote's *Aristotle* II. p. 444, R. and P. § 420.

they are not essential to its exercise, as the Peripatetics thought. If ivory and gold are wanting, the art of Phidias will show itself in baser materials : so the wise man will show his mastery in the art of life, alike in poverty as in wealth, in adversity as in prosperity. Nay, the less favourable his circumstances are, the greater is the call on the resources of his art, and the more glorious his success if he succeeds in acting the virtuous part. A good man struggling with adversity is a spectacle worthy of God[1]. Until we have learnt the lesson that our happiness can neither be increased nor diminished by the presence or absence of anything outside of ourselves, anything which is not in our own power, we can never attain to that inner calm, which is the essence of true happiness.

This distinction between things in our power[2], and things not in our power, is one on which the Stoics laid great stress. By the former they meant things which we could do or acquire if we willed, such as our opinions, our affections, desires and aversions ; by the latter they meant things which we could not do or acquire if we willed, such as natural constitution of body, wealth, honour, rank, &c., but in regard to these last our judgment of them *is* in our own power, we *can* train ourselves to think of them as unimportant. Thus it is in our power to discipline the mind in the way of controlling or suppressing some emotions, generating and encouraging others. The grand aim of the Stoical system was to strengthen the governing reason and to enthrone it as a

---

[1] Seneca *Epist.* LXXXV, *De providentia*, c. 2.

[2] τὰ ἐφ᾽ ἡμῖν, the sphere of προαίρεσις according to Aristotle *Eth.* III 4.

fixed habit and character, which would control by counter-suggestions the impulse arising at each special moment, particularly all disturbing terrors or allurements, by the reflection that the objects which appear to be desirable, or the contrary, are not really such, but are only made to appear so by false and curable associations. Nothing can really harm us unless we choose to make it do so by allowing it to conquer our reason and will[1].

Pleasure is a natural concomitant (ἐπιγέννημα) of activity, but is not a natural end : not even if we count as pleasure that high delight (χαρά as opposed to ἡδονή), which belongs to virtuous activity, for pleasure regarded in itself has a tendency to lead man away from the true end, viz. acting not for self, but for the whole. On this ground Chrysippus condemned Plato and Aristotle for preferring the contemplative to the practical life, alleging that the former was merely a higher kind of self-indulgence. Man is born for society, he is a member of the great body[2] which includes all rational creatures within it : if he forgets his relation to other men, and only cares to gratify his intellectual tastes, he abnegates his proper place in the world. The feeling of common membership in one body binds each not to justice only but to beneficence and to mutual help[3]: above all it constitutes the firmest bond of friendship between those who act up to that membership, so that every wise man is dear to all who are wise, even though he may be personally unknown to them[4].

---

[1] See Grote's *Aristotle*, II. p. 446.

[2] Seneca *Ep.* XCV. 52 *membra sumus corporis magni. Natura nos cognatos edidit*; Cic. *Off.* III. 32.

[3] Cic. *Off.* I. 20.   [4] Cic. *N. D.* I. 121.

But while on the one hand the consciousness of our being thus bound up with others, as parts of a common whole, supplies a motive for action and forbids all exclusive self-regard, as far as feeling is concerned; on the other hand the consciousness that the individual reason (τὸ λογιστικόν, τὸ ἡγεμονικόν) in each man is a portion of the Universal Reason, a revelation to him personally of the Divine Will[1],—this preserves intact the individuality of each, and enables and requires him to act and think for himself, and to stand alone, regardless of the opinions and wishes of the world outside. It is this sense of independence towards man and of responsibility towards God which especially distinguishes the Stoic morality from that which preceded it. The Stoics may be said to have introduced into philosophical ethics the conception of Duty, involving obligation[2], as distinguished from that of Good, regarded as the desirable or the useful or the beautiful, and of Virtue as the way to this. Not that Duty is with them mere obedience to an external law;

---

[1] See Chrysippus in Diogenes VII. 88, 'We call by the name of Zeus the Right Reason which pervades the universe;' Zeno in Cic. *N. D.* I. 36 'God is the divine law of nature, commanding what is right, forbidding what is wrong,' Cic. *Leg.* II. 10, and I. 18, 'Law is first the mind and reason of Jupiter, and then reason in the mind of man;' *Leg.* I. 33, 'To whom nature has given reason, to them she has given law;' Chrysippus in Plut. *Comm. Not.* p. 1076 'not even the smallest particle can exist otherwise than as God wills' (ἄλλως ἔχειν ἀλλ᾽ ἢ κατὰ τὴν τοῦ Διὸς βούλησιν); also passages from Seneca referred to in a previous note.

[2] Compare the Stoic definition of right and wrong as that which is commanded or forbidden by law, τὸ κατόρθωμα νόμου πρόσταγμα εἶναι, τὸ δ᾽ ἁμάρτημα νόμου ἀπαγόρευμα Plut. *Sto. Rep.* II. 1, and other passages quoted by Zeller p. 245.

it is also the following of the highest natural impulse (ὁρμή)[1]. But impulse by itself is no trustworthy guide. On the contrary it is one chief work of reason in man to subdue and eradicate his irrational impulses. These passions (πάθη), as they are called, originate in a perversion of the reason itself. The four principal are pleasure and pain, which may be defined as false beliefs of present good or evil; hope and fear, which are similar beliefs in reference to the future. No man can be called virtuous who has not got rid of all such beliefs and arrived at the state of pure ἀπάθεια. We may distinguish different virtues in thought, as the Stoics themselves summed up their teaching on this subject under the four Cardinal Virtues, which represent four principal aspects of the one *Honestum* or *Decorum;* but in fact no virtue can exist apart from the rest[2]. He who has a right judgment and right intention is perfectly virtuous, he who is without right judgment and intention is perfectly vicious. There is no mean. The wise man is perfectly happy, the fool perfectly miserable : all the actions of the former are wise and good ; all the actions of the latter foolish and bad. There may be a progress towards wisdom, but, until the actual moment of conversion, even those who are advancing (οἱ προκόπτοντες) must still be classed among the fools[3].

Thus in the original Stoicism we have the strange

[1] See Zeller III. 1, p. 223[3].

[2] So Aristotle had said that all other virtue is involved in φρόνησις. *Eth.* VI. 13, VII. 2.

[3] See Plut. *Mor.* p. 1058. 'Among the Stoics you go to bed stupid and ignorant and unjust and intemperate, a pauper and a slave ; you wake up in a few hours a king, or rather a God, rich and wise and temperate and just.'

union of a highly ideal ethics with a materialistic philosophy. But it was impossible to maintain this uncompromising idealism in practice. The later Stoics
found themselves compelled to admit that, apart from
virtue and vice, the absolute Good and Evil, there were
preferences to be made among things indifferent. Some
of these, such as bodily health, mental endowments, even
wealth and position, were allowed to have comparative
value, and, as such, were called προηγμένα, *producta*
or *praeposita*, 'preferable,' while their opposites were
termed ἀποπροηγμένα, *rejecta*, 'undesirable'; and the name
ἀδιάφορα was now limited to such things as were entirely
neutral and could not influence choice. In like manner
it was allowed that, besides the perfectly virtuous actions
of the wise man (κατορθώματα, *perfecta officia*), there was
a subordinate class of appropriate actions (καθήκοντα,
media officia), which might be performed by one who had
not attained to perfection, or which might have reference
to some preferable end other than the absolute good.
Again, since they were compelled to allow that their
perfectly wise man, whom they vaunted to be equal to
Zeus, had never existed, they found it necessary to
allow a positive value to προκοπή, progress towards
wisdom, and to self-control as contrasted with absolute
apathy.

The Stoics paid great attention to the subject of Natural
Theology and pleased themselves with discovering evidence, in the external universe, of a creative intelligence
and a providential care for man. Cicero gives the
Stoical argument on this head in the Second Book of his
Natura Deorum. Holding, as they did, the optimist
theory of the perfection of the universe, they were bound

to reconcile this with the apparent existence of moral and physical evil. They endeavoured to do so by the following reasoning. What we call evil is only imperfection; and in a system compounded of parts, the imperfection of the parts taken separately is essential to the perfection of the whole. What we call physical evil is a necessary result of natural causes, and is in itself a matter of indifference: it only becomes evil to the man who uses it wrongly. Many things which are commonly regarded as evil are really beneficial; as an instance, Chrysippus cited the prevention of over-population by means of war[1]. Moral evil, which arises like disease from human weakness, is the necessary foil and condition of virtue. How could prudence and courage display themselves, if there were no choice to be made between good and evil; if there were no injustice and fraud to guard against and endure? In the end however all evil will be converted into good. If we sometimes see virtue unrewarded, this is because the government of the world proceeds by general laws, which, though best for the whole, necessarily involve the possibility of what seems to be individual hardship[2]. But this is, after all, only appearance, for good and evil lie not in feeling, but in action. He who acts fittingly is happy, and it is always in our own power to act fittingly to the circumstances in which we are placed. If in no other way, it is at least in our power to quit a world in which we are hindered from action. God has placed in our hands, as the last safeguard of our freedom,

---

[1] Compare Plut. *Stoic. Rep.* 32, and other passages quoted by Zeller III. 1. p. 174[3].

[2] The same argument is used by Bp. Butler in the *Analogy* Pt. 1. ch. 7.

this highest privilege of self-removal ($\epsilon\ddot{v}\lambda o\gamma o\varsigma$ $\dot{\epsilon}\xi a\gamma\omega\gamma\dot{\eta}$), not to be used at random, but to save another's life, or to escape from being forced into anything degrading, or at the lowest to cut short unprofitable years.

One other characteristic doctrine of the Stoics may be mentioned here. It will have been noticed that none of the above-named representatives of the school were of pure Greek birth, and that most were only connected with Greece by the Macedonian conquests. It was easy to rise from this fact to the higher doctrine which flowed naturally from their first principle, the doctrine namely that all men were members of one State, that the world is the common City of Gods and men, that all men are brethren as having the same Divine Father. Sir A. Grant has further called attention to the fact that Zeno himself and some of his most distinguished followers belonged to Semitic towns or colonies; and he suggests that the characteristic features of Stoicism, its stern morality, its deep religious earnestness, may perhaps be traced to this connexion.

There is indeed a very striking resemblance, mixed with no less striking contrasts, not only between particular sayings of individual Stoics, especially Seneca[1], and the language of the New Testament, but between Stoicism and Christianity in regard to their general view of the facts of the physical and moral universe. The Stoic pantheism, i.e. the doctrine of the interpenetration and transfusion of all nature by a Divine Spirit, has its Christian counterpart in St Paul's words, 'in Him we live

---

[1] Cf. the appendix on *St Paul and Seneca* in Bp. Lightfoot's edition of the Epistle to the Philippians.

and move and have our being,' 'of Him, through Him
and to Him are all things[1],' and still more markedly in the
language of the great Christian poet of this century:

> "And I have felt
> A presence which disturbs me with the joy
> Of elevated thoughts; a sense sublime
> Of something far more deeply interfused,
> Whose dwelling is the light of setting suns,
> And the round ocean and the living air,
> And the blue sky, and in the mind of man :
> A motion and a spirit, that impels
> All thinking things, all objects of all thought,
> And rolls through all things[2]."

This indwelling Spirit was known to the Stoics, as to the
Christians, under the name of the Logos[3]. He fashions
the universe according to His own will and upholds it
and governs it by His wisdom; but His principal seat is
in the highest heaven and in the heart of man. He is
the Father of lights and the Father of spirits, the source
of all spiritual and rational life, an ever-present inward
witness, monitor, and guide to those who submit themselves to His guidance. He orders all things for our
good and for the good of all this universe. To follow
and to imitate Him is the perfection and happiness of
man. Where, we might ask, is the inconsistency between
this and Christian theology? Bp. Lightfoot[4] answers
the question as follows : 'The basis of Stoic theology is
gross materialism,...the supreme God of the Stoics had
no existence distinct from external nature...the different

---

[1] Acts XVII. 28, Rom. XI. 36.
[2] Wordsworth *Tintern Abbey*.
[3] See Heinze, *Die Lehre vom Logos* ch. 3.
[4] *Philippians* p. 294 foll.

elements of the universe, such as the planetary bodies, were inferior Gods, members of the Universal Being.'

It is however only fair to remember that the views of many of the early Christians were far from clear on these points, and that individual Stoics differed much in the explanations they gave of the formulas of their system. Tertullian was as thorough-going a materialist as any Stoic or Epicurean[1]; and Origen thought it necessary to argue against those who interpreted the words 'Our God is a consuming fire,' 'God is a spirit,' ($\pi\nu\epsilon\hat{\upsilon}\mu\alpha$ = breath), as implying some kind of corporeity[2]. I confess it seems to me that, while metaphysically it is a solecism to talk of 'thinking matter,' yet practically, if the supposition is once admitted that thought itself can be somehow material, it makes little difference whether we conceive the one eternal Being, who constitutes the universe by his thought, to be absolutely incorporeal and immaterial, or to be, as the Stoics held, a pure etherial substance, generating all existence out of itself and taking it back into itself. Probably the incongruous compound 'thinking matter' resolved itself, more or less consciously, into one or other element according to the idiosyncrasy of the individual philosopher, God being regarded in the one case as self-determining Reason residing in its fiery vehicle and impelling baser matter through that instrumentality; in the other as the material universe developing itself according to necessary law. In either case, the

---

[1] Compare *De Carn. Christi* c. 11. *Omne quod est, corpus est sui generis : nihil est incorporale, nisi quod non est* (quoted with apparent agreement by the Lutheran Bp. Martensen *Christian Ethics*, p. 71 *tr.*).

[2] *De principiis* I. 1.

Stoic might say, no less than the Christian, looking forward to the cyclical conflagration, and contrasting nature with the God of nature, the *mundus* with the *anima mundi*, the passive with the active elements of the universe, 'they (i.e. all that we see in the world around) shall perish, but thou remainest; yea, all of them shall wax old as doth a garment; as a vesture shalt thou change them and they shall be changed; but thou art the same and thy years shall have no end[1].'

The contrast between the second view mentioned above, which gives the name of God to the material universe developing itself according to necessary law, and the Christian view, has been well expressed by St Augustine in a splendid passage of his Confessions. 'Seeking to find an answer to the question "What is God," I asked', he says, 'the earth, the sea, the air, the heaven, the sun, the moon and the stars: all gave the same answer "we are not God, but we are made by Him." *Interrogavi mundi molem de Deo meo, et respondit mihi: non ego sum, sed ipse me fecit[2].'* I doubt however whether such a frank identification of the Deity with external nature as that supposed, is to be found in any genuine Stoic writer, and whether it is not in fact rather the limit (to speak mathematically) of Stoic materialism, than a positive doctrine taught in their schools. The world, like every other system, must have its ἡγεμονικόν, its guiding principle; and, as the soul which guides and governs the body, though material, is still distinct from the body; so God, the guide and ruler of the world, is distinct from the world, though that too may be called divine or even God, in virtue of the divine principle pervading it. When we are told that

[1] Psalm 102. 26.　　　　[2] x. 7.

Necessity is one of the Stoic names for God, this does not mean that God is Himself subject to a Necessity supposed higher than Himself, but that His own Reason constitutes the universal law which He Himself and all things obey[1]. Some Stoics, such as Boethus, even denied the animality of the universe, and said that it was guided by the Deity, as the car by the charioteer or the ship by the pilot; and it would be hard to say that the hymn of Cleanthes is addressed to an impersonal God. On the other hand, it must be granted that, though we never find a Stoic going so far as to say, with Strauss, that the universal Reason only becomes self-conscious in man, we do find Chrysippus asserting the equality of reason in man and reason in God, and speaking of the wise man as the equal of Zeus, no less useful to Zeus than Zeus to him, both being alike divine[2].

Still more marked is the opposition between the Christian and the Stoic idea of the *character* of God. To the Stoic He is perfect reason and justice, to the Christian He is preeminently the God of love. So, while the Logos represents both to Stoic and to Christian the rational element in the universe, the light that lighteth every man, the latter regards Him, first, as existing with the Father before all worlds, and secondly, as made

[1] The Stoics were the first to discuss with any fulness the difficulties connected with the doctrine of Necessity, see Heinze *l. c.* pp. 153—172.

[2] Compare Cic. *N. D.* II. 154, 'The life of the wise man is in no respect inferior to that of the Gods except in duration,' and other passages cited by Zeller, p. 252[3]. Yet, objectionable as is the tone of these passages, they need not be regarded as asserting more than the doctrine of a Divine presence in the heart of man, and of the sameness of the Divine nature under all circumstances.

man in the person of Jesus Christ, and so revealing the truly Divine under the perfectly human.

If we turn now to man and compare the teaching of the two systems in reference to the ideal of man, his duty and his happiness, we find again great apparent agreement. There is the same uncompromising tone in both; the one thing needful is a righteous will; Stoicism is no less emphatic than Christianity in asserting that the gain of the whole world can never counterbalance the loss of the soul. Both demand from their followers the practice of stern self-denial, they call upon them to make the will of God their rule of life[1], and to shine as lights in the midst of prevailing darkness. Both use the same language in reference to the corruption of the unregenerate man. If we read in the Bible ' the whole world lieth in wickedness,' 'there is none that doeth good, no, not one;' we find Cleanthes in like manner saying that, though man is the highest being on earth, it is plain there must be somewhere a higher and more perfect being, for 'man walks in wickedness all his life through, or at least for the greater part of it, only attaining to virtue in late old-age[2];' and Seneca still more strongly 'we are all thoughtless and foolish, all ambitious and complaining, in a word, we are all wicked;' 'we have all sinned, some more, some less grievously, some in malice, some in haste, some led away by others. Even if there be one who has so cleansed his heart that nothing can henceforth agitate or deceive it, still it was through sin that he finally arrived at innocence;' also Cicero, ' Even an

---

[1] Hence the Stoics held that every wrong action was an act of impiety, πᾶν ἁμάρτημα ἀσέβημα, Stob. *Ecl.* II. p. 216.

[2] Sext. *Math.* IX. 90.

Aristides was not perfect in justice, nor a Scipio in courage, nor a Laelius in wisdom; all have fallen short of the standard of the sage[1].' On the other hand the excellency of the ideal life is described by both in equally glowing terms. The Wise Man of the Stoics is the only freeman, he alone is self-sufficient, he possesses all things, he is the true king and the true priest: whatever he does, though it be no more than the putting forth of a finger, is done in accordance with perfect virtue and the highest reason: there is no mean between virtue and vice; he who is guilty of one vice is guilty of all, and he who can act rightly in one point must act rightly in all; it is impossible for him to sin, as it is impossible for him to lose his firm conviction that the only evil is vice, the only good virtue[2]; virtue is the ground of all his preferences; what is virtuous he loves however far removed from him, what is vicious he hates however closely connected[3]: he knows no ties but those of virtue. In like manner the Christian holds that he whom the truth has made free is the only freeman, that we are made kings and priests unto God, that all things are ours; and St Paul speaks of himself and the other Apostles 'as sorrowful, yet alway rejoicing; as beggars, yet making many rich; as having nothing, but yet possessing all

---

[1] Seneca *De Ira*, III. 26, *De Clementia*, I. 6, *Benef.* IV. 27, Cic. *Off.* III. 16, cited among other passages by Zeller, p. 253, foll.

[2] The question of Final Perseverance, so much debated among Christians afterwards, was not unknown to the Stoics; Cleanthes with the Cynics maintaining it, Chrysippus on the other hand arguing that it was possible for the Wise Man to fall away and become a reprobate; see Zeller, p. 271.

[3] Diog. L. VII. 33.

things[1]. He tells his converts that, whether they eat or drink or whatever they do, they may do all to the glory of God; and St John asserts boldly that 'whatsoever is born of God cannot commit sin,' of which we have the converse again in St Paul's 'whatever is not of faith is sin,' and in St James's 'whosoever shall keep the whole law and yet offend in one point is guilty of all.' Again the weakness of earthly ties, as contrasted with that which unites men to Christ and to each other, as members of Christ's body, appears in the constant allusion to brotherly love in the Epistles, as well as in the words of Christ himself 'Whosoever shall do the will of God, the same is my brother and my sister and mother,' and still more strongly in the warning 'if any man come to me and hate not father and mother...yea, and his own life also, he cannot be my disciple.'

Yet on closer examination we find a great gulf concealed under this apparent agreement. The Christian, while he claims all these high prerogatives, owns that none of them are his by his own right; in himself he is poor and blind and naked; all the good that is in him flows to him from Christ, through whom he is made a partaker in the divine nature, and with whom he is connected as the branch with the vine, as the hand

---

[1] Compare Plutarch's paradoxical account of the Stoic Wise Man (*Mor.* p. 1057) with St Paul's description of himself in 2 *Cor.* vi. 4—10. ὁ Στωικῶν σοφὸς ἐγκλειόμενος οὐ κωλύεται, καὶ κατακρημνιζόμενος οὐκ ἀναγκάζεται, καὶ στρεβλούμενος οὐ βασανίζεται, καὶ πηρούμενος οὐ βλάπτεται, καὶ πίπτων ἐν τῷ παλαίειν ἀήττητός ἐστιν, καὶ περιτειχιζόμενος ἀπολιόρκητος, καὶ πωλούμενος ὑπο τῶν πολεμίων ἀνάλωτος, and just above, ἄφοβος δὲ μένει καὶ ἄλυπος καὶ ἀήττητος καὶ ἀβίαστος, τιτρωσκόμενος, ἀλγῶν, στρεβλούμενος, ἐν κατασκαφαῖς πατρίδος, ἐν πάθεσι τοιούτοις.

with the body. Once alone has the ideal life been fully revealed on earth, in the man Christ Jesus; but each Christian is encouraged to strive after it as that to which he is called, and to which he may continually approximate in proportion as he yields himself to the sanctifying influence of Christ's Spirit within him.

On the other hand, while some of the Stoics, as we have seen, claimed for their wise man a moral equality with God; most of them confessed that they were unable to point to any actual example of the ideal life; or, if some thought that they saw it exemplified in a Hercules, a Socrates or a Diogenes, they never imagined that virtue was attainable for themselves only through the virtue of one of these. The victory of Socrates might be an encouragement to another to struggle against weakness after his example, but it contained no ground or assurance of victory, as that of Christ does to the Christian. There is no personal feeling of loyalty or devotion to Socrates as to an ever-present, all-powerful Saviour and friend. Again, while Christian and Stoic both agree in regarding pleasure in itself as utterly worthless in comparison with virtue and the calm of mind which accompanies self-mastery; Stoic apathy is, in the first place, a very poor and colourless substitute for the Christian 'peace that passeth all understanding,' 'the joy unspeakable and full of glory;' in the next place, it is itself un-Christian, since the Gospel stimulates to the utmost the unselfish affections which Stoicism represses, and makes virtue consist at least as much in warmth and energy of feeling as in rational self-control; thirdly, though the mere life of pleasure, the living for pleasure, is everywhere condemned in the New Testament, yet asceticism, as such, is reprobated in the Epistle to Timothy, as a doctrine of devils, and pleasure is recognized as a good gift of God in the words 'every creature of God is good, and nothing to be refused if it be received with thanksgiving.' So too with regard to its opposite, though there may be occasions on which the Christian will rejoice in tribulation, yet he is not bound to pretend, like the Stoic, that pain is not in itself an evil: on the contrary, the great Pattern of Christians, as He had always the tenderest sympathy for the sorrow of others, so in his own case He combined the utmost sensitiveness to pain with the unshaken resolution to do and to bear His Father's will. Lastly, the Christian belief in the immortality of each individual man, the belief that virtue, inchoate here, will be finally perfected hereafter, and have full scope for its exercise, that the ideals which nature even now suggests will there be more than realized,—this sheds over life a warm and genial ray, in contrast to the grim austerity of the Porch, and supplies a solid basis for that which with them was scarcely more than a romantic and irrational optimism[1]. Christianity

---

[1] The contrast between the Christian conception of an uninterrupted progress continued throughout eternity, and the Cyclical Regeneration by which the Stoics imagined that, after the general conflagration, all things would be reproduced in the same order, so that each Great Year should be an exact copy of its predecessors, is well pointed out in Dean Mansel's posthumous lectures on *Gnosticism*, p. 4, and illustrated by the beautiful chorus from Shelley's *Hellas* :

> The world's great age begins anew,
>   The golden years return ;
> The earth doth like a snake renew
>   Her winter weeds outworn ;
> Heaven smiles, and faiths and empires gleam
> Like wrecks of a dissolving dream.

may in fact be regarded as the fulfilment of the dreams of Stoicism, as St Paul seems to suggest when he took a line of Cleanthes for his text in preaching at the Areopagus. The noblest things in Stoicism are the analogues to the three Christian Graces, the faith which led them to believe that all things were ordered by a good and wise Governor, the hope that made them look forward to the more perfect revelation of the City of God after death, the love which taught them that they were made for the world and not for themselves, that all mankind were one body. 'The poet sings of beloved Athens, and shall not we sing of thee, O beloved City of Zeus[1],'—do we not seem to hear in these words of Marcus Aurelius the tuning of the harp of Zion by the waters of Babylon?

> A brighter Hellas rears its mountains
>   From waves serener far;
> A new Peneus rolls its fountains
>   Against the morning star.
> Where (Here?) fairer Tempes bloom, there sleep
> Young Cyclads on a sunnier deep.
>
> A loftier Argo cleaves the main,
>   Fraught with a later prize;
> Another Orpheus sings again,
>   And loves, and weeps, and dies.
> A new Ulysses leaves once more
> Calypso for his native shore.
>
> *   *   *   *   *
>
> O cease! must hate and death return?
>   Cease! must men kill and die?
> Cease! drain not to its dregs the urn
>   Of bitter prophecy.
> The world is weary of the past,
> O might it die, or rest at last!

See further Zeller, p. 154, foll.

[1]Anton. **IV.** 23.

But if Stoicism is admirable, as promise of better things to come, what are we to say of it when it shows itself as the residuum of a dying faith? We may at least find it easier to understand the attraction which it had for the Thraseas and Arrias of the Empire, when we find pure Stoicism preached as the Gospel for our own day in such words as those of Carlyle. 'This fair universe, were it in the meanest province thereof, is in very deed the star-domed City of God: through every star, through every grass-blade, and most through every Living Soul the glory of a present God still beams[1].' 'The situation which has not its Duty, its Ideal, was never yet occupied by man. Yes, here, in this poor, miserable, hampered, despicable Actual, wherein thou even now standest, here or nowhere is thy Ideal: work it out therefrom, and working, believe, live, be free. Fool! the Ideal is in thyself, the impediment too is in thyself: thy condition is but the stuff thou art to shape that same Ideal out of: what matters whether such stuff is of this sort or that, so the Form thou give it be heroic, be poetic[2]?' 'Does not the whole wretchedness of man's ways in these generations shadow itself for us in that unspeakable Life-philosophy of his: the pretension to be what he calls happy?...We construct our theory of Human Duties not on any Greatest-Nobleness Principle, but on a Greatest-Happiness Principle...But a life of ease is not for any man nor for any god[3].' Again, what else is the 'New Faith'

---

[1] *Sartor Resartus*, Bk. III. ch. 8.

[2] *Sartor Resartus*, Bk. II. ch. 9.

[3] *Past and Present*, Bk. III. ch. 4. Compare with the last clause the continual reference in Epictetus to the Labours of Hercules, as giving a pattern of the life which all men should lead; e.g. *Diss.* III.

put forward by Strauss than a revival of the least Christian side of Stoicism together with even an exaggeration of its old unrealities? The nature of this Neo-Stoicism[1] will be sufficiently apparent from the following passage. 'In regard to the Cosmos we know ourselves as part of a part; our might as naught in comparison to the almightiness of Nature; our thought only capable of slowly and laboriously comprehending the least part of that which the universe offers to our contemplation as the object of knowledge... As we feel ourselves absolutely dependent on this world, as we can only deduce our existence and the adjustment of our nature from it, we are compelled to conceive of it as the primary source of all that is reasonable and good in ourselves as well as in it...That on which we feel ourselves thus dependent is no mere rude power to which we bow in mute resignation, but is at the same time both order and law, reason and goodness, to which we surrender ourselves in loving trust. More than this: as we perceive in ourselves the same disposition to the reasonable and the good, which we seem to recognize in the Cosmos, and find ourselves to be the beings by whom it is felt and recognized, in whom it is to become personified, we also feel ourselves related in our inmost nature to that on which we are dependent, we discover ourselves at the same time to be free in this dependence: and pride and humility, joy and submission, intermingle in our feeling for the Cosmos...We consider it arrogant and profane on the part of a single individual

---

26, 31 τρυφᾶν με οὐ θέλει ὁ θεός, οὐδὲ γὰρ τῷ Ἡρακλεῖ παρεῖχε τῷ υἱῷ τῷ ἑαυτοῦ.

[1] *The Old Faith and the New*, Eng. tr. p. 161.

to oppose himself with such audacious levity [as the Pessimists do] to the Cosmos, whence he springs, from which also he derives that spark of reason [compare the ἀπόῤῥοια and ἀπόσπασμα of the Stoics] which he misuses. ...We demand the same piety for our Cosmos that the devout of old demanded for his God[1].'

The hymn of Cleanthes may fitly conclude our account of the Stoics. 'O Thou of many names, most glorious of immortals, Almighty Zeus, sovereign ruler of Nature, directing all things in accordance with law; Thee it is right that all mortals should address, for Thine offspring we are, and, alone of all creatures that live and move on earth, have received from Thee the gift of imitative sound[2]. Wherefore I will hymn thy praise and sing thy might for ever. The universe, as it rolls around this earth, obeys Thy guidance and willingly submits to Thy control. Such a minister Thou holdest in thine invincible hands, the two-edged thunderbolt of ever-living fire, at whose strokes all nature trembles...No work is done without Thee, O Lord, neither on earth, nor in the heaven, nor in the sea, except what the wicked do in their foolishness. Thou knowest how to make the rough smooth[3], and bringest order out of disorder, and things not friendly are friendly in Thy sight: for so hast Thou fitted all things together, good and evil alike, that there might be one eternal law and reason for all things. The wicked heed it not,

[1] It is worthy of note that Strauss also accepts the Stoic conflagration, see p. 180.

[2] The Stoics thought that names were given φύσει οὐ νόμῳ, and that in some way they represented the real nature of the thing, μιμουμένων φωνῶν τὰ πράγματα, see Orig. *c. Cels.* I. 24.

[3] Literally 'to make what is odd even.'

unhappy ones, who, though ever craving for good, have
neither eyes nor ears for the universal law of God, by
wise obedience to which they might attain a noble life.
But now they think not of right; but hasten each after
their own way, some painfully striving for honour, others
bent on shameful gains, others on luxury and the pleasures of the body. But do Thou, all-bounteous Zeus, who
sittest in the clouds and rulest the thunder, save men,
from their grievous ignorance : scatter it from their souls,
and grant them to obtain wisdom, whereon relying Thou
dost govern all things in righteousness; that so, being
honoured, we may requite Thee with honour, as it is
fitting for man to do, since there is no nobler office for
mortals or for gods, than duly to praise for evermore the
universal law.'

The broad distinction which we noticed at the beginning of our history between the Italic or Doric and
the Ionic Schools, reappears in the marked contrast
between the two materialistic schools of later times. As
the Stoics are preeminently Doric and Roman in character, so the Epicureans are Ionic and Greek. The one
might be said to represent the Law, the other the Gospel
of Paganism. The former not unfrequently made themselves odious and ridiculous among the more educated
class by their obstinacy, pride and intolerance, their
exaggeration, pedantry and narrow-mindedness; while the
latter won general favour in society by their freedom from
prejudice, their good sense and amiability. But, in spite
of this, it was the Porch which was the nurse and school
of all that was noblest in the Graeco-Roman world; from
it came the patriot, the martyr, the missionary, the hero :

it set the example of that renunciation which was followed by the ascetic orders of Christendom; it supplied to the technicalities of Roman law that ideal element which fitted it to become so important a factor in our modern civilization. On the other hand, if we ask what results proceeded from the Garden of Epicurus, we may point to such a life as that of Atticus, who passed unscathed through the Civil Wars of Rome, retaining the esteem of all parties, and using his influence to alleviate the sufferings of all; we may see in Epicureanism a needful protest in behalf of the rights of human nature and the freedom of individual thought and feeling, against the oppression of a superstitious religion and an over-strained morality. But it is only as protest and correction that it is of value; its own view of human nature is poorer and narrower than that put forward by any of the systems which it sought to supersede; it cares not for science in itself, it has no serious regard for truth as such, it offers no spirit-stirring ideal for action; there is nothing great, generous or self-sacrificing in the temper of mind which it tends to foster and encourage. And popular opinion, which only recognizes broad contrasts, fastened upon the essential differences in the two schools; it regarded with admiration the lofty character of a Zeno or a Cato, and looked with suspicion upon their Epicurean rivals, as undermining the foundations of religion and morality, and advocating a life of selfish enjoyment.

We have comparatively few remains of Epicurean writers, none in fact but the poem of Lucretius, together with some letters of Epicurus and the scarcely legible fragments of Philodemus and others discovered at Herculaneum; while we have several complete treatises on

the other side, such as those of Seneca, Epictetus, M.
Aurelius, and Cicero's philosophical dialogues. The
Christian Fathers also sided strongly with the Stoics
against the Epicureans, even going so far as to count
Seneca one of themselves, so that the traditional literary
view had till lately followed the old popular view. But
of late years the pendulum has swung in the other
direction, partly owing to more accurate research, which
has brought to light the exaggerations of the old view,
partly to the present rage for rehabilitating whatever has
been condemned by former ages, but more particularly
because Epicureanism was identified with the cause of
freedom, intellectual, social, moral and religious; because
it was regarded as the forerunner of positive science and
of utilitarian morality; and in a lesser degree because,
the great poem of Lucretius having been better edited
and more widely studied, admiration for the poet has led
to an increased sympathy with the philosophy which he
advocates[1]. To what extent these advantages may fairly
be claimed on behalf of Epicureanism will perhaps be
made clear as we proceed. For my own part I am inclined to think Cicero was not very wide of the mark when
he spoke of it as a '*bourgeois* philosophy[2].' Whether we
have regard to his expressed opinions on science and
literature and ethics; or to the *naïveté* of his assumptions,
the narrow scope of his imagination, the arbitrariness and
one-sidedness shown in his appeals to experience, and
the want of subtlety and thoroughness in his reasonings,

[1] An example of this change of view, in quarters where it would
hardly have been expected, is to be found in Dean Alford's Note on
Acts XVII. 18.

[2] *Plebeii philosophi, Tusc.* I. 55.

Epicurus seems to me to stand out among philosophers as the representative of good-natured, self-satisfied, un-impassioned, strong-willed and clear-headed Philistinism. No doubt it was doing a service to mankind to give any-thing like philosophical expression to such a very im-portant body of sentiment as that with which we are familiar under this name; but I think Epicurus himself would be not a little surprised, if he could return to life and see the kind of supporters, aesthetic and other, who have lately flocked to his standard.

Historically speaking, Epicureanism may be roughly described as a combination of the physics of Democritus with the ethics of Aristippus[1]. Epicurus (341—270 B.C.) was an Athenian, born in Samos, where he is said to have received instruction in the doctrines of Plato and Demo-critus, though, like Hobbes and Bentham and Comte in later times, he himself always denied his indebtedness to previous thinkers, and stoutly maintained his entire independence and originality of thought. He founded his school at Athens about 306 B.C., teaching in his own 'Garden,' which became not less famous than the Stoic 'Porch.' Here he gathered around him a sort of Pytha-gorean brotherhood, consisting both of men and women, united in a common veneration for their master[2], and in a mutual friendship which became proverbial in after

[1] See the excellent, though somewhat apologetic, account of Epicureanism by W. Wallace, in the S. P. C. K. series.

[2] For the extravagant terms in which the Epicureans were accustomed to speak of their founder, see Lucretius v. 8, *deus ille fuit, deus, inclute Memmi, qui princeps vitae rationem invenit eam quae nunc appellatur sapientia*, and other passages quoted in my note on Cic. *N. D.* I. 43. His disciples kept sacred to his memory not only his birthday, but the 20th day of every month, in ac-

years. All Epicureans were expected to learn by heart
short abstracts of their master's teaching, especially
the Articles of Belief, κύριαι δόξαι[1], still preserved to
us by Diogenes Laertius; and it is said that the last
words addressed by Epicurus to his disciples, were to bid
them 'remember the doctrines,' μεμνῆσθαι τῶν δογμάτων.
The scandalous tongue of antiquity was never more
virulent than it was in the case of Epicurus, but, as
far as we can judge, the life of the Garden joined to
urbanity and refinement, a simplicity which would have
done no discredit to a Stoic; indeed the Stoic Seneca
continually refers to Epicurus not less as a model for
conduct, than as a master of sententious wisdom. It is
recorded that, though partly supported by the contributions of his disciples, Epicurus condemned the literal
application of the Pythagorean maxim κοινὰ τὰ φίλων, much
as Aristotle had done before, because it implied a want
of trust in the generosity of friendship. Among the most
distinguished members of the school were Metrodorus,
(*paene alter Epicurus*, as Cicero calls him) Hermarchus the
successor of Epicurus, Colotes, Leonteus and his wife
Themista, to whom Cicero jestingly alludes in his speech
against Piso, as a sort of female Solon, and Leontium the
hetaera, who ventured to attack Theophrastus in an essay
characterised, as we are told, by much elegance of style[2].
Cicero mentions among his own contemporaries Phaedrus,
Zeno of Sidon, called the *Coryphaeus Epicureorum*

cordance with the instructions in his will. Hence they were called
in derision εἰκαδισταί, see Diog. L. x. 15, Cic. *Fin.* II. 101.

[1] Cf. Diog. x. 12, 16, and Cic. *Fin.* II. 20, *quis enim vestrum
non edidicit Epicuri κυρίας δόξας?*

[2] Cic. *N. D.* I. § 93.

(*N. D.* 1 59,) and Philodemus of Gadara [1]: and his account of the Epicurean doctrines is probably borrowed from these. Epicureanism had great success among the Romans [2]; but, with the exception of the poet Lucretius, none of the Latin expounders of the system seem to have been of any importance [3].

The end of the Epicurean philosophy was even more exclusively practical than that of the Stoics. Logic (called by Epicurus 'Canonic,' as giving the 'canon' or test of truth) and physics were merely subordinate to ethics, the art of attaining happiness. Knowledge, as generally understood, is in itself of no value or interest, but tends rather to corrupt and distort our natural judgment and feeling. Hence we are told that Epicurus preferred that his disciples should have advanced no further in the elements of ordinary education than just so far as to be able to read and write [4]. In particular we are informed that he condemned not only the study of Poetry, Rhetoric and Music, but also those sciences which Plato had declared to be the necessary Propaedeutic of the philosopher, Arithmetic, Geometry, Astronomy and Dialectic or Logic, as being at best a frivolous waste of time, dealing with words and not with things, if not

---

[1] Several treatises of Philodemus have been found among the Herculanean papyri. On the relation between his Περὶ Εὐσεβείας and Cicero's *De Natura Deorum* see my edition of the latter, pp. XLII—LV.

[2] Cic. *Tusc.* IV 7, *Fin.* I 25.

[3] Cf. Cic. *Tusc.* II 7, and Zeller III 1. p. 372.

[4] Compare his words reported by Diogenes X 6, παιδείαν δὲ πᾶσαν, μακάριε, φεῦγε; Quintil. *Inst.* XII § 24, *Epicurus fugere omnem disciplinam navigatione quam velocissima jubet;* and Sext. Emp. *Math.* I I and 49.

actually erroneous and misleading[1]. It is possible that these strictures may have had reference not so much to Art and Literature and Science in themselves, as to the manner in which they were then prosecuted, to the 'learned' poetry of Alexandria with its recondite mythological allusions[2], to the hair-splitting logic of the Megaric and Stoic schools, and the unreal interpretations of Nature propounded by the great idealistic philosophies; but there is not the least appearance of any real speculative interest among the early Epicureans[3]. If there had been, we can hardly suppose, that they would have spoken of geometry as 'utterly false,' just at the time when the Elements of Euclid, the elder contemporary of Epicurus, had made their appearance amid the general applause of the scientific world[4]. Even their supposed strong point[5], Physical Science, was not studied by them for its own sake. Epicurus himself distinctly says that

[1] See Cic. *Fin.* I § 72, II § 12, *Acad.* II § 106, and § 97.

[2] Metrodorus, however, told his disciples they need feel no shame in confessing that they could not quote a line of the Iliad, and did not know which side Hector took in the Trojan war.

[3] Hirzel has shown in his *Untersuchungen zu Ciceros philosophischen Schriften*, p. 177 foll. that there was an important section among the later Epicureans (probably alluded to in Diog. X 25, as those οὓς οἱ γνήσιοι Ἐπικούρειοι σοφιστὰς ἀποκαλοῦσιν) who set a higher value on logic and literary culture generally than their master had done. One of these was Philodemus, of whom Cicero speaks as *litteris perpolitus* (*In Pis.* 70), the author of numerous treatises on rhetoric, music, poetry, dialectic, &c.

[4] See *Art.* in *Dict. of Biog.* by De Morgan, 'the Elements must have been a tremendous advance, probably even greater than that contained in the *Principia* of Newton;' 'their fame was almost coaeval with their publication.'

[5] Cic. *Fin.* I § 63: *in physicis plurimum posuit.*

'we must not think there is any other end in the knowledge of τὰ μετέωρα, celestial phenomena, beyond tranquillity of mind and freedom from superstitious fears,'...'if it had not been for the anxieties caused by our ideas about death and about the influence of these heavenly powers, there would have been no need for Natural Philosophy (φυσιολογίας)[1].'...'The minute inquiries of the astronomers do not tend to happiness: nay the constant observation of the phenomena of the heavens, without a previous knowledge of the true causes of things, is likely to generate a timid and slavish turn of mind[2].' The indifference of Epicurus to scientific truth comes out still more strongly in the explanations which he offers of particular phenomena. His one object being to guard against the hypothesis either of divine agency or of necessary law[3], he tells his disciples that it is madness to suppose that similar effects must always proceed from the same causes, and provides them with a choice of various hypotheses on which to explain the rising and setting of the sun, the changes of the moon, the movements of planets, earthquakes, thunder, lightning, &c. For instance, it may be that the sun (which is no bigger than it appears to the naked eye, so there is no need to be afraid of it or make a god of it), passes under the earth

[1] Diog. L. x 85 and 142, and other passages cited by Zeller, p. 382 foll.

[2] Paraphrased from Diog. x. 79, cf. § 93.

[3] Compare Diog. x 134, where he speaks of the blessedness of the man who has learnt that necessity is only a name for the effect of chance or of our own free will, and says that 'it were better to believe in the fables about the gods than in the Fate of the philosophers; the former at least allows us some hope of propitiation, but fate is inexorable.'

on setting, and comes above it again on rising; but it may be, and it is just as probable, that the fiery particles collect anew every day to form a fresh sun. We cannot bring the matter to the direct test of sense, and therefore we can only argue from our general experience of what happens on earth, which shows that the one view is as admissible as the other, spite of all that our system-mongers may say[1]. Nay, even supposing that a certain class of phenomena, such as eclipses, are always caused in the same way in our world, it is still probable, indeed almost certain, that they must be caused in different ways in the countless worlds contained in the universe[2].

As regards the Logic of the Epicureans we are told that they rejected as useless almost all that was known under that name, Definition, Generalization, Classification, the Syllogism, and that they had a special objection to the Law of the Excluded Middle (A either is or is not B, _aut vivet cras Hermarchus aut non vivet_), as involving the principle of Necessity[3]. But in that age of the world, it was no longer possible to fall back upon the master's _Ipse dixit_ with the implicit confidence of the old Pythagoreans: some reason for their faith had to be given. This ground of certainty Epicurus found in the senses and feelings. What our sense or feeling tells us,

---

[1] Cf. Diog. L. x 113 τὸ δὲ μίαν αἰτίαν τούτων ἀποδιδόναι, πλεονα-χῶς τῶν φαινομένων ἐκκαλουμένων, μανικόν. See examples of these alternative hypotheses in Diog. x 84 foll., Lucr. v 510—770.

[2] Compare Munro on Lucr. v. 532. In Diog. x. 78, Epicurus seems to be applying Aristotle's contrast between the disorderly and capricious movements of the sublunary sphere and the perfect order of the higher spheres, to his own κόσμοι and μετακόσμια, and to find in this a justification for the variety of causation in the former.

[3] See Cic. _Fin._ I 22, and _N. D._ I 70 and 89 with my notes.

we receive as certain. Even the supposed sensations of sleep or of insanity are in a way true. They have a real cause, viz. the influx of those images of which Democritus spoke. 'The error,' said Epicurus following Aristotle[1], 'lies not in the sensation, but in our interpretation of the sensation, in the inference we draw from it. If we once abandon this ground of certainty, all is gone. Whatever reasoning is not founded on the clear evidence (ἐνάργεια, *perspicuitas*) of sense, is mere words. It is true that the image which comes to us does not always correspond with the actual object (στερέμνιον). An image coming from a square tower at a distance, will perhaps be round by the time it reaches us, its edges having been rubbed away in its passage through the air: but the sensation has given the image correctly; error arises when we add to the sensation the opinion that the image is an exact representation of the object[2].' Opinions (ὑπολήψεις) are only true, if testified to by a distinct sensation, or, supposing such direct evidence unattainable, if there is no contrary sensation; they are false, in all other cases[3]. Repeated sensations produce a permanent image, πρό-ληψις, so called because it exists in the mind as an anticipation of the name, which would be unmeaning if it could not be referred to a known type. General terms can only be safely used for the purpose of argument when they rest upon and represent a πρόληψις. Otherwise

[1] See *De Anima* III 3, ἡ μὲν αἴσθησις τῶν ἰδίων ἀεὶ ἀληθής, διανοεῖσθαι δ' ἐνδέχεται καὶ ψευδῶς, and my note on *N. D.* I 70.

[2] Sext. Emp. *Adv. Math.* VII 203, foll.

[3] An instance given is the existence of void, of which there can be no distinct evidence, but it is in accordance with the fact of motion, which itself rests upon the evidence of our senses, Sext. Emp. *l. c.* 213.

their use only engenders strifes of words. Epicurus himself does not seem to have carried his logical investigations further than this; but among the Herculanean
papyri we have an interesting treatise by Philodemus in
which he deals with Analogical and Inductive Arguments[1].

It has been already stated that the only reason allowed
by the Epicureans for studying Physics was to free the
soul from superstitious fears, and with this view to prove
that the constitution of the universe might be explained
from mechanical causes. There is something very remarkable, and not altogether easy to account for, in the
extreme earnestness with which the Epicureans deprecated
the oppressive influence of superstition, at a time when
other philosophers, and writers in general, treated it as
too unimportant to deserve the slightest attention. Thus
Cicero asks 'where is the old woman so far gone in
dotage as to believe in a three-headed Cerberus and
those other bugbears which your sect tells us you have
only ceased to fear because of your knowledge of physical
science[2],' and in arguing against the fear of death, he
assumes as an undoubted point that death is either
annihilation or the admission to a higher state of
happiness[3]. Friedländer however in his *Sittengeschichte
Roms*[4] has shown that this only expresses the opinion of

---

[1] See Bahnsch on the περὶ σημείων καὶ σημειώσεων of Philodemus,
1879.

[2] See *Tusc.* I 10 and 48, and compare *N. D. I* 86, *quibus
mediocres homines non ita valde moventur, his ille clamat omnium
mortalium mentes esse perterritas.*

[3] Tusc. I 25.

[4] Bk. XI on the Immortality of the Soul.

a small educated class, and that the mass still clung to the old beliefs about Charon and Cocytus. Even Cicero himself elsewhere speaks of the spread of superstition in terms not unlike those employed by Lucretius[1]. The fact seems to be that while, on the one side, the spread of enlightenment made it more and more impossible for any educated man to accept the absurdities and immoralities of paganism; and while the prevalence of this educated scepticism cannot but have shaken the popular hold on the old superstitions, so far as this partook in any degree of the nature of belief rather than of unreasoning custom; on the other hand that deepening of the individual consciousness which accompanied the extinction of the public life of Greece, and which was fostered by the growing influence of philosophy and its more subjective tone, must have intensified the sense of moral and religious responsibility, and given rise to an increased anxiety as to a possible retribution to follow this life. This appears partly in the rapid growth of the Orphic and other mysteries, partly in philosophic or poetic imaginations of the unseen world, such as we read in the *Republic* and the *Aeneid*. And thus 'the general conviction of a judgment to come, where the deeds done in this life would receive their reward and punishment, seems to have been widely felt, and to have been, for priests and prophets, a fruitful soil. Indulgences for sin, propitiation of impiety, sacramental atonement, not to

---

[1] *De Divin.* II 148, *Nam, ut vere loquamur, superstitio fusa per gentes oppressit omnium fere animos atque hominum imbecillitatem occupavit*; compare Lucretius I 62, *Humana ante oculos foede cum vita jaceret in terris oppressa gravi sub religione, quae caput a caeli regionibus ostendebat horribili super aspectu mortalibus instans, &c.*

mention magic and baser forms of superstition, flourished alongside of Epicureanism all through its career, and probably reached their maximum in the first and second centuries of the Christian era[1].' The fault of Epicurus was that he only saw the bad side of this state of things. He saw, as Plato had done, that 'a corrupt religion gives birth to impious and unholy deeds;' he saw the paralyzing influence of a real belief in the never-ending punishment of sin[2]. Plato's remedy was to train the young in the belief of the perfect goodness and justice of God, that so they might learn to trust in His Providence, and receive with meekness His chastisements, knowing that He harms none and punishes only to reform. Epicurus thought there could be no security from superstitious terror unless men could be persuaded that death ended all, and that the Gods took no heed of our actions. Plutarch has well pointed out how little this accords with the experience of life[3]. 'It is far better,' says he, 'that there should be a blended fear and reverence in our feelings towards the Deity, than that, to avoid this, we should leave ourselves neither hope nor gratitude in the enjoyment of our good things, nor any recourse to the Divine aid in our adversity. Epicurus takes credit to himself for delivering us from the misery of fear, but in the case of the bad this fear is the

---

[1] Wallace *Epicureanism*, p. 123, Theophrastus *Characters* XVI. Plutarch *De Superstitione.*

[2] See Lucr. I 101, *tantum religio potuit suadere malorum*, and 107, *nam si certam finem esse viderent aerumnarum homines, aliqua ratione valerent religionibus atque minis obsistere vatum: nunc ratio nulla est restandi, nulla facultas, aeternas quoniam poenas in morte timendumst.*

[3] The quotation which follows is a paraphrase from the treatise *Non posse suaviter vivi secundum Epicurum*, p. 1101 foll.

one thing which enables them to resist temptation to vice, and in all other cases the thought of God and of a future life is a source of joy and consolation, in proportion as a man has come to know God as the Friend of man and the Father of all beautiful things.'

We will now see what was the talisman by which Epicurus endeavoured to arm the soul against the religion which he so much dreaded. The two main principles on which he built his physical system were that nothing could be produced out of nothing, and that what exists cannot become non-existent. From these principles he deduced the truth of the atomic doctrine, differing however from Democritus in one important point, viz. in his explanation of the manner in which the atoms were brought together. Democritus had asserted that the heavier atoms overtook the lighter in their downward course, and thus initiated the collision which finally resulted in a general vortical movement. Epicurus retaining the same crude view of 'up' and 'down' held that each atom moved with equal speed, and that they could only meet by an inherent power of self-movement which enabled them to swerve to the slightest possible extent from the rigid vertical line; and he found a confirmation of this indeterminate movement of the atoms in the free will of man[1]. In other respects there is little difference between the physical views of Democritus and Epicurus. Both held that there were innumerable worlds[2] continually coming into being and

[1] On the deviation of atoms (παρέγκλισις, *clinamen*), see Cic. *N. D.* 1 69 with my note.

[2] Epicurus defined a world as 'a section of the infinite, embracing in itself an earth and stars and all the phenomena of the heavens,'

passing out of being in the infinitude of space. Our own world is already showing signs of decay, and is no longer prolific of fresh life as in its beginning. As to subordinate arrangements Epicurus thought it unnecessary and indeed impossible to assign any one theory as certain. It was enough if we could imagine theories which were not palpably inadmissible, and which enabled us to dispense with any supernatural cause. The existence of the present race of animals was explained, as it had been by Empedocles, on a rude Darwinian hypothesis[1]. Out of the innumerable combinations of atoms which had been tried throughout the infinite ages of the past, those only survived which were found to be suited to their environment. The eye was not made to see with, but being made by the fortuitous concourse of atoms it was found on trial to have the property of seeing[2].

On the nature of the soul and the manner in which it receives its impressions by images from without, Epicurus, in the main, follows Democritus, adding a few unimportant modifications suggested by the subsequent course of speculation. Thus the soul is still made to consist of smooth round atoms, but it is no longer a simple substance: it is partly the irrational principle of life (*anima*) dispersed throughout the body, partly the rational principle (*mens, animus,*) concentered in the heart: and the atoms of which both of these are made up, though we must suppose not in the same proportions, have

---

(περιοχή τις οὐρανοῦ ἄστρα τε καὶ γῆν καὶ πάντα τὰ φαινόμενα περιέχουσα) ; such worlds are of every variety of form, Diog. L. x 88. (Hübner and other editors omit γῆν without reason.)

[1] Lucr. v 783 foll.
[2] Lucr. iv 823 foll.

already coalesced into four distinct elements, one resembling wind (πνεῦμα, *ventus* or *aura*), which predominates in the timid soul of the swift deer, one fire, which shows itself in the fury of the lion, the third air, which gives to the oxen their character of calm repose, midway between burning passion and chill fear; the last element (evidently suggested by the *Quinta Essentia* of Aristotle) is nameless, composed of the very finest atoms; sensation, thought and will, are transmitted from it to the other elements. Death ensues on the severing of the link which binds the soul to the body: the etherial atoms of soul are immediately dispersed into the outer air, the earthy atoms of body gradually fall apart and rejoin their parent earth. Every mental impression is a modification of touch. The images thrown off from the surface of solid objects (στερέμνια) are perceptible by the soul-atoms located in the bodily organs; but there are more delicate images which are only perceptible by the mind itself: such are the images presented to the mind in slumber, or in thinking of the absent or the unreal. These images are sometimes produced by the coalescence of two or more images as in the case of the centaur, sometimes by a chance concatenation of fine atoms. Often, as in recollection, it requires an effort of mind (ἐπιβολή, *injectus animi,*) to bring the fleeting image steadily before us. It is for the wise man to determine in the case of each image, whether it has a real object corresponding to it.

One class of images deserves especial attention. They are those which have led men to believe in the Gods. Shapes of superhuman size and beauty and strength appear to us both in our waking moments and

still more in sleep[1]. These recurring appearances have
given rise to an anticipation, πρόληψις, of Divinity, of which
the essential characteristics are immortality and blessedness. The truth of this πρόληψις is testified to by the
universal consent of mankind. Taking it as our starting
point we may go on to assign to the Gods such qualities
as are agreeable to these essential attributes. If, in doing
so, we run counter to the vulgar opinion and the many idle
imaginations (ὑπολήψεις) which have been added to the
πρόληψις, it is not we who are guilty of impiety, but
those who impute to the Gods what is inconsistent with
their true character. The idea of blessedness involves
not only happiness but absolute perfection. It forbids
us to suppose that the Gods can be troubled with the
creation or government of a world; and this conclusion
is confirmed by our experience of what our own world is,
the greatest portion of it uninhabitable from excess of
cold or heat, much of the remainder barren and unfruitful, even the best land requiring constant toil to make it
produce what is of use to man. Then think of the
various miseries of life, to which the good are exposed
no less than the bad,—all this shows

> *nequaquam nobis divinitus esse paratam*
> *naturam rerum; tanta stat praedita culpa*[2].

[1] The fact of these 'epiphanies' was generally accepted. For
recorded instances see my note on Cic. *N. D.* i 46. It is not very
clear why the appearances of Gods were considered to stand on
a different footing from those of departed spirits, which were
equally vouched for by experience. See Lucr. IV 32 foll. of
the shapes of the dead, which 'frighten our minds when they present
themselves to us awake as well as in sleep;' and compare 722 foll.
and I 132. Aristotle also referred to dreams as one cause of our
belief in Divine beings.

[2] Lucr. V 198.

There are other more general considerations which point to the same conclusion : for what sudden motive can we conceive which should make the Gods abandon their state of eternal repose, and set to the work of creation, and how, with no model before them, could they know what to make or how to make it; again, how can we possibly believe that any being should be powerful enough to administer, not to say to create, the infinity of nature ? It is equally impossible to ascribe to the Gods such weakness and pettiness of mind as to feel anger or be propitiated with gifts, or to take a fussy interest in the affairs of men. They enjoy undisturbed tranquillity in some region far removed from our troubled world.

This tranquil region Epicurus found in the *inter-mundia*, the spaces between his countless worlds. He seems to have borrowed the suggestion from Aristotle, who transformed the heaven of the poets into the supra-celestial region where space and time are not, but 'where the things outside enjoy through all eternity a perfect life of absolute joy and peace[1].' But the unchangeableness which belongs naturally to Aristotle's solitary world is altogether out of place in the countless perishable worlds of Epicurus. For successive worlds need not occupy the same point in space nor be made up of the same materials; new worlds are formed καὶ ἐν κόσμῳ καὶ ἐν μετακοσμίῳ, and their materials may have been either already made use of for the formation of a world or they may be floating loose in an *intermundium*[2]. Moreover, during the existence of each world, it is constantly either

---

[1] Arist. *De Caelo* I 9.
[2] Diog. x 89.

receiving an accession of atoms from the *intermundia* or, in its later stages, giving them back again. It is plain therefore that Epicurus has failed to find a safe retreat for his Gods in the *intermundia* and that they are quite as much exposed to the *metus ruinarum* there as they would have been within the world[1].

Again, the Gods, like every other existing thing, are made up of atoms and void; but every compound is liable to dissolution; how is this compatible with immortality? One answer given was that the destructive and conservative forces in the universe balance one another, but in this world the destructive forces have the upper hand, therefore elsewhere, probably in the *intermundia*, the conservative forces must prevail[2]. Another reason was that the atoms of which the Gods are composed, were so fine and delicate as to evade the blows of the coarser atoms[3]. This idea of the extreme tenuity of the divine corporeity was doubtless suggested partly by the Homeric description of the Gods 'who are bloodless and immortal' (*Il.* v 340) and partly by the shadowy *idola* of the dead, which escape the grasp of their living friends. We find yet another reason assigned, not so much perhaps for the actual immortality of the Gods, as for our belief in it, in the alleged fact of an incessant stream of divine images (εἴδωλα), too subtle to impinge on the bodily senses, but

---

[1] Compare Cic. *Divin.* II 40, *N. D.* I 18, 53, 114, Diog. X 89, Lucr. II 1105—1174.

[2] Cic. *N. D.* I 50, with my note.

[3] See Cic. *N. D.* I 68—71, and the passage from *Herculanensia*, Vol. VI. pt. 2 p. 35, quoted in my note on § 71 'no object which is perceptible to the senses is immortal, for its density makes it liable to severe shocks.'

perceptible by the kindred atoms of mind[1]. Evidently this incessant never-ending influx of divine images is not a thing which can be directly vouched for by any human experience. We are not directly conscious even of the stream of images. All that an Epicurean could say is that we seem from time to time to behold the same glorified form, and that there is some ground for supposing similar appearances during past ages; that we can only account for such appearances by the supposition of an uninterrupted succession of images continued from a very remote period. But this of course is no proof of immortality : if it were so, we must *a fortiori* believe the immortality of the sun, or indeed, as the Ciceronian Cotta remarks (*N. D.* I 109), of any common object, since our ordinary perceptions are due to such an uninterrupted stream of images[2]. If it is said that we cannot help attributing in our thought a permanent unchanging existence to the divine nature, and that this law of thought is only explicable, on the Epicurean hypothesis, by the supposition of an endless stream of images actuating our mind, then the belief in the divine immortality is made the

---

[1] Lucretius (v 1161 foll.) describing how the belief in the gods originated in visions, tells us that they were thought to be immortal, partly because they seemed to be too mighty to be overcome by any force, and partly *quia semper eorum subpeditabatur facies et forma manebat,* one image constantly succeeded another giving the impression of a permanent form. There is a similar use of the verb *suppedito* in IV 776, (where he explains the apparent movements in dreams by the rapid succession of particles, *tanta est copia particularum ut possit suppeditare*) and in Cic. *N. D.* I 109 (referring to the divine images) *innumerabilitas suppeditat atomorum.* See for a general discussion on the subject my notes on *N. D.* I 49.

[2] See Lucr. IV 26 foll., Diog. X 48.

ground of our belief in the interminableness of images, not *vice versa.* When we further remember that these countless images are supposed to travel intact all the way from the *intermundia,* (see Cic. *N. D.* I 114 *ex ipso (deo) imagines semper affluant,* and Lucr. VI 76 *de corpore quae sancto simulacra feruntur in mentes hominum divinae nuntia formae,*) and to be incessantly thrown off from bodies which were themselves scarcely more than images, we shall not wonder that some of the Epicureans failed to rise to the height of the *credo quia impossibile* which their system demanded, and fell back on the easier doctrine of Democritus, asserting the divinity of the images themselves, and deriving them not from the deities of the *intermundia,* but from the combinations of etherial atoms floating in the surrounding air[1].

---

[1] This seems to me to be the easiest explanation of the much disputed words of Diogenes X 139, ἐν ἄλλοις δέ φησι τοὺς θεοὺς λόγῳ θεωρητούς, οὓς μὲν κατ' ἀριθμὸν ὑφεστῶτας, οὓς δὲ καθ' ὁμοειδίαν ἐκ τῆς συνεχοῦς ἐπιρρύσεως τῶν ὁμοίων εἰδώλων ἐπὶ τὸ αὐτὸ ἀποτετελεσμένων ἀνθρωποειδῶς. Hirzel in his *Untersuchungen zu Cicero's philosophischen schriften,* pp. 46—90, whom Zeller follows in his last edition, p. 431, has shown, in opposition to Schömann (*De Epicuri Theologia,* contained in the 4th vol. of his *Opuscula*), that there is no reason for altering the text, and that we must accept it as a fact that there were two classes of gods recognized in the Epicurean school, one possessed of a separate individuality and having their abode in the *intermundia,* the other existing only in virtue of a continuous stream of undistinguishable images which in their combination produce on our minds the impression of a human form. Zeller thinks that the latter are meant for the unreal gods of the popular mythology, which, like the centaur and every other human imagination, must have their origin in some corresponding image; but the words of Diogenes seem to me to be less appropriate to the very concrete deities of the Greek pantheon than to some vague feeling of a divine presence such

Leaving the question of immortality, we pass on to speak of the Epicurean belief as to the shape of the Gods. They derided the spherical mundane God of the Stoics, and held that the direct evidence of visions, no less than the general belief of mankind, testified that the Gods were in the likeness of men. But this might also be proved by reasoning, for experience showed that rationality was only found in human form; and besides, the human, being the most perfect form, must be that of the most perfect being. Some of the later Epicureans went on to describe in detail the manner of life of their *Intermundian* Gods. They lived in houses, ate and drank celestial food, needed no sleep, for they were never weary; their chief enjoyment was conversation, which probably went on in Greek or something very like it: in fact they were in heaven what the Epicurean brotherhood was, or strove to be, on earth[1]. Such Gods were worthy of our reverence and imitation, but they were not objects of fear, as they neither could nor would do us harm[2].

While Epicurus agrees with Aristippus in making pleasure the sole natural end of life, the standard of good, as sensation is of truth, he differs from him in attaching more value to permanent tranquillity than to

as might be caused by the *idola* of Democritus. Compare also the parallel passage in Cic. *N. D.* I 49.

[1] See Philodemus, quoted by Zeller, p. 434 foll.

[2] Some of the Epicureans seem to have allowed to their Gods a certain influence over the happiness of men; see the passages quoted from Philodemus περὶ εὐσεβείας in my note on Cic. *N. D.* I 45, especially pp. 86—89 (Gompertz) 'the Stoics deny that the Gods are the authors of evil to men and thus take away all restraint on iniquity, while we say that punishment comes to some from the gods and the greatest of good to others.' See too Lucr. VI 70.

momentary gratification, and also in preferring mental
pleasures to bodily, as involving memory and hope, and
therefore both more enduring and more under our control.
Still bodily pleasure is the groundwork and foundation of
all other pleasure, as Epicurus says (Diog. x 6) 'I know
not what good means if you deny me the pleasures of the
senses;' and Metrodorus 'all good is concerned with
the belly' or, as it might be expressed in our own
day, 'the *summum bonum* is a healthy digestion' (Cic.
N. D. I 113). Virtue is not desirable for itself,
as an end, but only as the means to attain pleasure.
The wise man, i.e. the virtuous man, is happy because he is
free from the fear of the Gods and of death, because he
has learnt to moderate his passions and desires, because
he knows how to estimate and compare pleasures and
pains, so as to secure the largest amount of the former
with the least of the latter. The distinction between
right and wrong rests merely on utility and has nothing
mysterious about it. Thus Epicurus says 'Injustice is
not in itself evil, but it is rightly shunned because it is
always accompanied by the fear of detection and punishment[1].' 'Justice is nothing in itself; it is simply an
agreement neither to injure or be injured[2].' One chief
means of attaining pleasure is the society of friends. To

---

[1] Diog. X 151. ἡ ἀδικία οὐ καθ' ἑαυτὴν κακόν, ἀλλ' ἐν τῷ κατὰ τὴν
ὑποψίαν φόβῳ, εἰ μὴ λήσει τοὺς ὑπὲρ τῶν τοιούτων ἐφεστηκότας
κολαστάς.

[2] Diog. X 150. τὸ τῆς φύσεως δίκαιόν ἐστι σύμβολον τοῦ συμφέ-
ροντος εἰς τὸ μὴ βλάπτειν ἀλλήλους μηδὲ βλάπτεσθαι. 'There is no
justice or injustice for animals or for those tribes which have not
been able, or have not chosen to make such compacts : οὐκ ἦν τι
καθ' ἑαυτὸ δικαιοσύνη, but a kind of compact in regard to mutual
association extending over certain localities.'

enjoy this we should cultivate the feelings of kindness and benevolence. Epicurus does not recognize any claims of a wider society. He considers it folly to take part in public life, and Metrodorus dissuaded his brother from such a course in the words 'it is not our business to seek for crowns by saving the Greeks, but to enjoy ourselves in good eating and drinking' (Plut. *Adv. Col.* 1125 D.).

What has been said will sufficiently account for the dislike entertained by Cicero and others towards the 'swinish doctrines' of Epicurus. I subjoin a few other quotations from his writings, some of which may help to give a more favourable impression of the man and explain Seneca's admiration for him. 'We think contentment (αὐτάρκεια, self-sufficingness) a great good, not with a view to stint ourselves to a little in all cases, but in order that, if we have not got much, we may content ourselves with little, being fully persuaded that those enjoy luxury most who need it least, and that whatever is natural is easily procured, and only what is matter of vain ostentation is hard to win. Plain dishes give as much pleasure as expensive ones, provided there is enough to remove the pain of hunger; and bread and water are productive of the highest pleasure to one who is really in want. The regular use of a simple inexpensive diet not only keeps a man in perfect health, but it gives him promptness and energy to meet all the requirements of life, while it makes him more capable of enjoying an occasional feast and also renders him fearless of fortune. When we speak then of pleasure as the end, we do not mean the pleasure of the sensualist, as some accuse us of doing : we mean the absence of bodily pain and of mental anxiety[1].'

[1] From the Epistle of Epicurus to Menoeceus in Diog. x 130.

'Man cannot live pleasantly without living wisely and nobly and justly, nor can he live wisely and nobly and justly without living pleasantly[1].'

'The wealth of nature is limited and easily procured, the wealth of vain imagination knows no limit[2].'

'Fleshly pleasure, when once the pain of want is removed, admits of no increase, but only of variation[3].'

'Great pain cannot last long, lasting pain is never violent. In chronic diseases the bodily state is on the whole more pleasurable than painful[4].'

So far we may recognize a genuine Epicurean sentiment. In the two quotations which follow there is an imitation of Stoic bravado.

Epistle to Idomeneus. 'I write this to you on the last day of my life, a happy day in spite of the agonizing pain of my disease, for I oppose to all my pain the mental pleasure arising from the memory of our former discussions. My last request is that you will befriend the children of Metrodorus in a manner worthy of your life-long devotion to me and to philosophy[5].'

'Even in the bull of Phalaris the wise man would retain his happiness[6].'

'Courage does not come by nature, but by calculation of expediency[7].'

'Friendship exists for the sake of advantage. But we

---

[1] From the κύριαι δόξαι Diog. X 140.

[2] *Ib.* § 144. [3] *Ibid.*

[4] Diog. X 140, Plut. *Aud. Poet.* 36 B.; Cic. *Fin.* II 22, *si gravis brevis, si longus levis.*

[5] Diog. X 22, Cic. *Fin.* II 96.

[6] Cic. *Tusc.* II 17, Diog. X 118.

[7] Diog. X 120.

must be willing to take the initiative, just as we must begin by sowing, in order to reap afterwards[1].'

'The wise man will dogmatize and not raise sceptical objections (ἀπορήσειν)[2].'

'The wise man will not fall in love, nor will he marry or beget children except under special circumstances, for many are the inconveniences of marriage[3].'

'I add one more quotation to illustrate not so much the doctrines of Epicurus, as the grandeur and the gloom of one who was a Roman and a poet before he was an Epicurean.

'"Now no more shall thy home receive thee with glad welcome, nor wife and children run to be the first to snatch kisses and touch thy heart with a silent joy. One disastrous day has taken from thee, luckless man, all the many prizes of life." This do men say, but add not thereto "and now no longer does any craving for these things beset thee withal." For thus they ought rather to think "Thou, even as now thou art, sunk in the sleep of death, shalt continue so for ever, freed from all distress; but we with a sorrow that would not be sated, wept for thee, when close by, thou didst turn to an ashen hue on the appalling funeral pile, and no length of days shall pluck from our hearts our ever-

---

[1] Diog. X 121. Seneca *Ep.* 9, draws the contrast between the Epicurean view which recommended friendship in order that one might have a friend's help and succour, *ut habeat qui sibi aegro assideat, succurrat in vincula conjecto vel inopi,* and the Stoic view that he might be useful to others, *ut habeat aliquem cui ipse aegro assideat, quem ipse circumventum hostili custodia liberet.* But Epicurus allows there may be occasions on which the wise man would die for his friend, ὑπὲρ φίλου ποτὲ τεθνήξεσθαι. Diog. 121.

[2] Diog. X 121.

[3] Diog. X 119. The last clause is added by Seneca, see Zeller, p. 459, n.

during grief."...Once more, if Nature could suddenly
utter a voice and rally any one of us in such words as
these, "what reason hast thou, O mortal, for all this exceeding sorrow? why bemoan and bewail death? For,
if thy life past and gone has been welcome to thee, why
not take thy departure like a guest filled with life, and
enter with resignation on untroubled rest? But if all
thou hast enjoyed has been squandered and lost and life
is a grievance, why seek to add more, to be wasted in
its turn and utterly lost without avail? Why not rather
make an end of life and travail? for there is nothing
more which I can contrive to give thee pleasure: all
things are ever the same."...With good reason, methinks,
Nature would bring her charge; for old things give way
and are supplanted by new,...one thing never ceases to
rise out of another, and life is granted to none in fee-
simple, to all in usufruct...And those things sure enough,
which are fabled to be in the deep of Acheron, do all
exist for us in this life...Cerberus and the Furies and
Tartarus belching forth hideous fires from his throat,
these are things which nowhere are, nor sooth to say can
be. But there is in life a dread of punishment for evil
deeds, signal as the deeds are signal; there is the prison
and the hurling from the rock, the scourging and the
executioner, the dungeon of the doomed; or should
these be wanting, yet the conscience-stricken mind through
boding fears applies to itself whips and goads, and sees
not what end there can be of evils or what limit at last is
set to punishments, and fears lest these very evils be
aggravated after death, so that the life of fools becomes
at length a hell on earth. Remember too that even
worthy Ancus has closed his eyes in darkness, who was

far, far better than thou, unconscionable man. And since
then, many kings and potentates have been laid low, who
lorded it over mighty nations. He too, even he who erst
made a path for his legions to march over the deep, and
set at naught the roarings of the seas, trampling on them
with his horses, had the light taken from him and shed
forth his soul from his dying body. The son of the
Scipios, thunderbolt of war, terror of Carthage, yielded
his bones to earth, just as if he were the lowest menial.
Think too of the inventors of all sciences and graceful
arts, think of the companions of the Heliconian maids;
among whom Homer bore the sceptre without a peer,
and he now sleeps the same sleep as others...Even
Epicurus passed away, when his light of life had run its
course, he who surpassed in intellect the race of man
and quenched the light of all, as the etherial sun arisen
quenches the stars. Wilt thou then hesitate and think it
a hardship to die? thou for whom life is well nigh dead
whilst yet thou livest and seest the light, who wastest the
greater part of thy time in sleep and snorest wide awake
and ceasest not to see visions and hast a mind troubled
with groundless terror and canst not discover often what
it is that ails thee, when, besotted man, thou art sore
pressed on all sides with a multitude of cares and goest
astray still floundering in the maze of error[1].'

In tracing the history of the post-Aristotelian philosophy we have seen that, underneath the antagonisms of
the different schools of this period, there was, in the first
place, much which they held in common, in opposition

[1] Lucr. III 894—1052. The translation is Munro's, slightly
altered and abbreviated.

to the earlier schools; and secondly that there was a constant tendency, especially noticeable in the Academic and Stoic schools, to approximate to each other and to modify or suppress their own distinctive characteristics. Partly owing to better acquaintance and improved understanding of each other's doctrines, and partly as a result of criticism bringing to light the weak points of each, there was a double movement going on, towards eclecticism on the one side, as it began to be surmised that the different schools presented different aspects of truth, and towards scepticism on the other side, as it was felt that no school could boast to have attained to absolute truth. This natural tendency of speculative thought was further assisted by the circumstances of the time, especially by the rise of the Roman power and the growing intercourse between Greece and Rome. To estimate the nature and extent of this influence on the ulterior development of philosophy, there are four points to be considered; (1) what new factors were supplied by Rome? or, to express it differently, what were the distinguishing features of the Roman intellect and character before it underwent the process of Hellenizing? (2) through what channels was this process carried on ? (3) what was the result as regards the Romans? (4) how did Rome react on Greece?

As regards (1), if we compare a Roman or a Sabine at the beginning of the 3rd century B.C. with an Athenian, we shall probably find the latter to be a townsman, vain, flighty, impressible, excitable; tolerant and liberal in opinion, and lax, not to say loose, in morality; of ready and versatile talent, with a taste for literature and art, and a natural fondness for discussion, ever seeking for novelty and amusement; democratic in politics, so far as, under the altered circumstances of Athens, he still retains any interest in politics; half sceptical, half superstitious and wholly inquisitive in matters of religion. The former is the contrary of all this, a dweller in the country, fond of home, proud, stubborn, earnest, narrowly conservative, a stern moralist and strict disciplinarian, scorning luxury and refinement, and content to be guided in all things by the wisdom of his ancestors, suspicious of ideas and rhetoric, indifferent to all but practical considerations, aristocratic in politics, with a deep-rooted belief in his traditional religion, as the only foundation and safeguard of the fortune and the greatness of the city, for which he is at all times ready to sacrifice his life[1]. The contrast was often commented on both by Greeks and Romans. Thus Polybius in the middle of the 2nd century B.C. writes as follows, 'the great superiority of the Romans lies in their religious belief: what is blamed among other men is the foundation of their power, I mean, superstition. They endeavour in every way to heighten the imposing aspect of their religion (ἐπὶ τοσοῦτον ἐκτετραγῴδηται) and to extend its influence over the whole of life, both public and private. And this seems to be done especially with a view to the common people, for in a state consisting of wise men alone, perhaps such a course would be less necessary. But as the multitude is always frivolous, full of lawless passions and senseless anger, nothing remains but to restrain them by giving form and shape to the terrors of an unseen world (τοῖς ἀδήλοις φόβοις καὶ τῇ τοιαύτῃ τραγῳδίᾳ). Hence it appears to me that the ancients had good reason for in-

---

[1] See the account of Cato the elder in Mommsen, Bk. III. ch. 13.

troducing the beliefs in the gods and in the infernal regions, and that it is a far less rational course to attempt to get rid of these beliefs as some are now doing. This is shown by the difficulty of securing honesty in public men among the sceptical Greeks, in spite of every possible precaution, while a Roman on his oath may safely be entrusted with any amount of money[1].' The next passage is from Dionysius of Halicarnassus, a younger contemporary of Cicero. After enumerating the causes of national prosperity, viz. 1st the blessing of heaven, and 2ndly the moral qualities of the citizens, their temperance, justice and courage, and the habit of making honour, not pleasure, the distinguishing mark of happiness, he praises the wisdom of the founder of Rome in omitting from his religious system all that was immoral, useless or unseemly in the mythology of Greece; 'from whence,' he says, 'it comes that in all their actions and words, which have a reference to religious matters, the Romans show a devoutness not found among Greeks or barbarians[2].' Compare with these passages Cicero's words, 'however highly we may think of ourselves, we must confess that in many points we are inferior to other nations, in bodily strength to the Gauls, in art to the Greeks, &c, but in piety and religion and the wisdom to see that all things are directed by Divine Providence, we are unquestionably the first.' 'I allow to the Greeks literature, artistic training, genius, elegance, fluency; I make no objection to other claims which they may put forward; but they have not, they never have had, any feeling of the sanctity of an oath, any scruple in regard

[1] In the above, I give the substance of Polyb. VI 56.
[2] Dion. II 18, foll.

to the giving of evidence.' 'It is a nation made to de
ceive: I am utterly weary of their frivolity, their flattery,
their time-serving and unconscientious character.' 'It is
wonderful how they are delighted with trifles which we
despise[1].'

Our next business is to trace the growth of the
connexion between Rome and Greece, for which the
following dates will supply the most important land-
marks; but it must not be forgotten that the ground-work
of this connexion is to be found in the intercourse which
subsisted from a very early period between Rome and
the Greek cities of Southern Italy, such as Cumae, Nea-
polis, and Tarentum.

B.C. 281.   War with Pyrrhus.

250—150.   Rise of a Hellenized literature in Rome
represented by such names as Livius Andronicus (first
play 240 B.C.), Plautus d. 184, Ennius d. 169, Terence d.
159.

228.   First Roman embassy to Greece. Ambassadors admitted to the Isthmian games and the Eleusinian
mysteries.

213.   War between Rome and Philip of Macedon.

196.   Overthrow of Macedon at Cynoscephalae.
Declaration of the independence of Greece at the
Isthmian games in the following year by the philhellene
Flamininus.

191.   War with Antiochus.

168.   Final conquest of Macedon by Paullus Aemi-

---

[1] See Cic. *Harusp. Resp.* § 19, *Pro Flacco* 9, 11, *ad Q. Fr.* I. 2, § 2,
and compare the well-known lines in Hor. *Od.* III. 6, beginning *Dis
te minorem quod geris imperas*, and the still more famous lines from
the 6th *Aeneid* 848, foll. *excudent alii spirantia mollius aera*, also Juvenal *Sat.* III. 60—80. *non possum ferre, Quirites, Graecam urbem*, &c.

lius. One thousand Achaeans carried to Rome in the following year: among them the historian Polybius.

146. Fall of Carthage. Corinth taken by Mummius. Greece made into the Roman province of Achaia.

For an account of the social and literary influence of Greece on Rome, the reader is referred to Mommsen's *History of Rome* Bk. III. chapters 13 and 14. I must content myself here with a few remarks on the special influence of Greek philosophy[1]. This is first seen in the poet Ennius, who appears to have rationalized the national religion in two directions, 1st, by physical and allegorical explanations in his *Epicharmus*, and 2ndly by a so-called 'pragmatical' or historical explanation, in his translation of the *Sacred History* of Euhemerus, in which Jupiter and the rest of the Gods were represented as ancient kings or other historical personages, who had been deified by their descendants. His free-thinking is also shown in the lines quoted from one of his tragedies :

> *Ego deum genus esse semper dixi et dicam caelitum,*
> *Sed eos non curare opinor quid agat humanum genus;*
> *Nam, si curent, bene bonis sit, male malis, quod nunc abest.*

In 181 B.C. an attempt was made to add to what may be called the canonical books of Rome, certain spurious writings, said to have been discovered in the tomb of Numa, containing a sort of Pythagorean philosophy of religion. These were burnt by order of the Senate as likely to disturb the faith of their readers. Further evidence of the growing influence of philosophy may

---

[1] For what follows, see Marquardt *Römische Staatsverwaltung*, vol. VI. pp. 1—80; Preller *Römische Mythologie*; Benjamin Constant *Du Polythéisme Romain*; Havet *Le Christianisme et ses Origines*, Vol. II.

be seen in the decree of the senate made in 161 B.C. by which philosophers and rhetoricians were forbidden to reside in Rome, and still more in the interest excited by the Athenian embassy in the year 156 B.C. The object of the embassy was to induce the Romans to remit or reduce a fine which had been imposed upon the Athenians for plundering Oropus; and the fact that the leaders of the three schools which stood highest in public estimation, the Academic Carneades, the Peripatetic Critolaus and the Stoic Diogenes, were selected as ambassadors, not only shows the confidence which their fellow-citizens had in their powers of oratory, but also implies a belief, as Cicero has remarked, that their philosophy would not be unacceptable in Rome[1]. Accordingly we are told that the envoys found there numerous patrons and admirers, and that, while their cause was pending in the senate, each of them, but especially Carneades, drew crowds of the young nobility to their private exhibitions of philosophical rhetoric. Cato was deeply displeased and alarmed by the reports he heard of the fascination they were exerting on the Roman youth : and censured the magistrates for allowing men, who had the power of making the worst doctrines seem probable, to wait so long for the dispatch of their business. It seems that Carneades had shocked the moral sense of Rome by arguing on one day in favour of justice, and the next day taking the opposite side and citing the greatness of Rome itself as a proof that justice was impracticable, since it would necessitate the Romans giving back their conquests and returning to their primitive huts. Cicero tells another anecdote of the embassy on the authority of

---

[1] *Tusc.* IV. 5.

Clitomachus, the pupil of Carneades. The praetor Albinus having asked, 'Is it true, Carneades, that you hold me to be no praetor, because I am not wise, and this city to be no city?' 'It is not I, who thinks so,' replied Carneades, 'but this Stoic here,' pointing to Diogenes[1]. Cicero dates the commencement of the study of philosophy in Rome from this embassy, and there is no doubt that from this time forward we constantly find Greek philosophers resident in Rome, either as tutors of youth or as inmates of great houses, domestic chaplains, as they have been called, and on the other hand that it became the practice for Romans who were ambitious of literary or oratorical distinction to attend lectures at Athens and the other seats of Greek philosophy. The earliest and most famous philosophical coterie in Rome was that of which Panaetius was the centre, including such names as the younger Africanus, with whom he resided, Laelius, Tubero, Q. Mucius Scaevola, and many others[2].

We have next to consider what was the effect on the Romans of this influx of Greek philosophy. We may probably say that, in the first instance, it was not unlike the effect of the Sophistic rhetoric on the Athenians in the days of Socrates. It was welcomed as promising new light when people were beginning to feel that there was great need for light, and as providing new powers just at the time when the field for the use of those powers was immensely widened. The old religion, which had stood the Romans in good stead, as we have seen, while they were still a struggling Italian tribe, was after all little better than a mere ceremonial drill, which fostered religious awe and deepened the sense of duty, but supplied no food for

[1] Cic. *Acad.* II. 137, *Tusc.* IV. 5.   [2] See Zeller, pp. 535, 548, 571.

thought or imagination; the Gods whom it taught them
to worship were objects of fear, not of veneration or love,
and the worship which it inculcated was not Socrates'
prayer of mingled trust and resignation, not the spontaneous expression of gratitude or repentance, but the use
of certain rites and formulas, now generally felt to be
irrational or unintelligible, by the mechanical repetition
of which it was asserted that the will of the Gods might be
ascertained, their wrath averted, or their favour secured.
Already the faith in the old religion had been seriously
undermined[1]. It was no longer a secret that it was employed as a political engine by the magistrates ; and the
introduction of various foreign deities, of Cybele, of
Bacchus, of Isis, showed that even among the multitude
a more full-blooded religion was wanted, that the religious
instinct could no longer be satisfied with the old dreary
round of lifeless ceremonial. In this state of things the
first effect of philosophy was to open men's eyes to that
of which they had been dimly conscious before ; and hence
it was, as Cicero tells us, that the common opinion identified philosophy with unbelief[2].

But, however it might be with the other sects, it was
never the aim of Stoicism to overthrow a traditional
religion, but rather to purify and strengthen it. And so
we find the *Pontifex*, Mucius Scaevola, in accordance
with the principles of his master Panaetius, distinguishing
between three different theologies, that of the poets, that
of the philosophers, and that of the magistrates: the first

---

[1] It was Cato, the great opponent of philosophy, who wondered
how one soothsayer (*haruspex*) could meet another without laughing,
Cic. *Divin.* II. 51.

[2] Cic. *De Invent.* § 46.

he said was altogether unworthy of belief, the second was true, but not suited to the multitude,—for instance it was not expedient to proclaim openly that the images did not really resemble the Gods after whom they were named, since the true God was without sex or age and had no resemblance to the form of man,—the third ought to be such an approach to the truth as the magistrates thought the people were capable of receiving. The same idea was developed with more fulness by Cicero's friend the antiquarian Varro, in his famous work on the religious antiquities of Rome, where he distinctly states that his object in writing it was to revive a decaying worship[1]. He classifies the almost countless deities of the Roman pantheon, as different manifestations or functions of the one self-existent God, whom he even compares with the God of the Jews[2]. He regrets that the use of images, unknown for 170 years after the founding of the city, had ever been introduced, and says that, if he had had to do with the first establishment of religion in Rome he would have kept more closely to the religion of nature as understood by the philosophers.

It may be doubted however whether the well-meant efforts of Varro and others were really successful in their object. Granting that the effect of philosophy was on the whole to elevate and improve the moral and religious ideal of the few who were capable of receiving it, we have to set against this the demoralizing tendency of Epicureanism, as vulgarly understood, and the general

[1] August. *C. D.* IV. 31, *ad eum finem illa scribere se dicit Varro ut potius deos magis colere quam despicere vulgus velit.*

[2] Aug. *de Cons. Evang.* I. 22, 41, cited by Döllinger, and *de Civ. Dei* IV. 31.

unsettling of belief which was encouraged by the negative criticism of the Academy. Even the teaching of the
Stoics, though it set before the more educated classes an
object which they could feel to be worthy of their veneration and worship, and thus effected for them a recon-
ciliation between reason and religion; and though it
confirmed the old Roman ideas as to the essential connexion between national prosperity and religion; yet, so
far as it affected in any way the mass of the people, it
can only have acted as a solvent of the popular belief.
Religion is in danger of being degraded into a matter of
political expediency, when it is left to the magistrates to
determine what the people are to believe: indeed we
find Cicero, when he writes as an Academic, appealing
more than once to expediency as the sole or the chief
ground for religious belief; and this was also, according
to Dion Cassius, the avowed principle of the religious
reforms carried out by Augustus and dutifully hymned by
the Augustan poets[1]. But all experience, from the time of
Augustus to that of Napoleon, shows that the attempt to
retain religion simply as an instrument of police can never
succeed; without belief it is too weak to be of service;
with belief it is too powerful; and the mere suspicion
that it is so used deprives it of its natural force, and arms
against it the honesty and the conscience of the nation.

Passing out of the religious sphere we find two main
applications of philosophy among the Romans, two
advantages which they expected to gain from the study of

[1] See Cic. *Divin.* II. 70 *retinetur et ad opinionem vulgi et ad
magnas utilitates reipublicae mos, religio, disciplina, jus augurium,
collegii auctoritas*, and Dion. Cass. LII. 36, where Maecenas recom-
mends the maintenance of the national religion and the prohibition
of strange rites as the best protection against political revolution or
conspiracy.

philosophy. The one is subordinate and superficial, the training in oratory to which Cicero so often refers. The youthful aspirant to the honours of the forum and the senate may learn from the philosopher how to arrange the topics of his speech, how to marshal his arguments, how to work on the passions of his audience, and to give colour and elevation to his style by the purple patches borrowed from the great masters of Athenian eloquence and wisdom. Above all, the Academic school will teach him to see both sides of a question, to find arguments *pro* and *con* in regard to any subject which may be brought before him[1]. But the chief use of philosophy is to be the school of virtue, the guide of life, both the common life of the State and the private life of the individual, and to afford the only consolations in the hour of weakness and sorrow[2]. How it was to answer this purpose, is shown by Cicero in his various practical treatises on

---

[1] Cic. *De Orat.* I. 53, 60, 87, *Tusc.* II. 9, *Orator*, § 12, *Paradox.* pref., *De Fato* 3.

[2] Cicero often speaks of the benefits conferred by philosophy as a Christian might speak of the benefits conferred by religion: compare *Tusc.* V. 5, *vitiorum peccatorumque nostrorum omnis a philosophia petenda correctio est,...O vitae philosophia dux! O virtutis indagatrix, expultrixque vitiorum! quid non modo nos, sed omnino vita hominum sine te esse potuisset!...Ad te confugimus; a te opem petimus...Est autem unus dies bene ex praeceptis tuis actus peccanti immortalitati anteponendus.* See also Horace *Ep.* I. 1. 36, *laudis amore tumes? sunt certa piacula quae te ter pure lecto poterunt recreare libello, &c.;* Varro *ap.* Gell. XV. 19, 'if you had bestowed on philosophy a tenth part of the pains that you have taken to get good bread, you would long ago have been a good man.' On the other hand Nepos (*ap. Lact.* III. 15 § 10) is so far from ascribing such good effects to philosophy, that he says none need to be reformed more than the philosophers themselves. See *Juv.* III. 116 *Stoicus occidit Baream, &c.*

Duty, on Friendship, on Old age, on Law, on the State, as well as, no doubt, in the lost Hortensius, which first inflamed St Augustine with the love of heavenly wisdom[1], and in the Consolatio, by the composition of which he vainly endeavoured to soothe the bitter sorrow caused by the death of his beloved Tullia.

To turn now from the taught to the teacher, it is easy to understand that the change from a class of keen-witted but somewhat frivolous Greeks,—who looked upon philosophy as an intellectual amusement, and thought of eloquence merely as an exhibition of skill in the use of the technicalities of rhetoric, by means of which to win the applause of the theatre or the lecture-room,—to the proud and serious Roman, who sought for eloquence as a mighty engine by which to mould the destinies of Rome and of the nations which she held in subjection, and listened eagerly to the words of the professor in the expectation of hearing something which would make him a wiser and a better man, show him what his duty was and give him strength to do it,—it is easy to see that this could not but react upon the teacher himself, and, if it did not awaken a corresponding earnestness in his own mind, yet would at least make it clear to him that speculative subtleties and controversial minutiae[2] would be thrown away,

[1] *Confess.* III. 4, *ille liber mutavit affectum meum, et ad te ipsum, Domine, mutavit preces meas. Viluit repente mihi omnis vana spes, et immortalitatem sapientiae concupiscebam aestu cordis incredibili; et surgere cœperam ut ad te redirem.*

[2] Compare the amusing story told of the proconsul Gellius (Cic. *Leg.* I. 53). On his arrival in Athens he called together the philosophers and urged them at last to put an end to their disputes, offering his assistance as umpire, if they were unable to settle matters peaceably without him.

and that the plainer his teaching was, and the less he
deviated from common sense and common morality, the
more likely he was to recommend himself to the pupils,
from he had most to gain in the shape of honours and
emoluments.

We have seen that the Stoic Panaetius was the first
teacher who obtained any influence over the Romans:
can we find in him any trace of the re-action of which we
have spoken? If the Romans had made their acquaintance with Stoicism through Cleanthes, who was so
genuinely Roman in character, they might have been
satisfied to accept his doctrine in its integrity; but since
then the system had undergone the manipulation of that
subtle doctor of the Schools, the learned and ingenious
Chrysippus, inventor of those thorny syllogisms of which
Cicero so often complains. Comparing him with Panaetius,
we find the latter softening down the severity of the Stoics
in many particulars. Thus he adopted a more easy and
natural style of writing, and spoke with warm admiration
of philosophers belonging to other schools, especially of
Plato, whom he called the Homer of philosophers[1]. He
abandoned the Stoic belief in a cyclical conflagration, for
the Aristotelian doctrine of the eternity of the world,
and mitigated the austerity of the old view on the ἀδιάφορα and the necessity of ἀπάθεια. In his treatise on
Duty, which formed the model of Cicero's *De officiis*,

---

[1] Cic. *Tusc.* I. 79, cf. *Fin.* IV. 79 (*Stoicorum*) *tristitiam atque
asperitatem fugiens Panaetius nec acerbitatem sententiarum nec
disserendi spinas probavit, fuitque in altero genere mitior, in altero
illustrior, semperque habuit in ore Platonem, Aristotelem, Xenocratem,
Theophrastum, Dicaearchum, ut ipsius scripta declarant;* also *Off.*
II. 35 and *Acad.* II. 135.

he addressed himself not to the wise, but to those who were seeking wisdom; and spoke not of perfect duties (κατορθώματα) but of the *officia media* (καθήκοντα) which ordinary people need not despair of fulfilling. Lastly in respect to Divination he forsook the tradition of his school, which had always been disposed to regard this as an important evidence of divine agency, and followed the sceptical line of the Academy.

The eclectic character imprinted on the Porch by Panaetius was never obliterated, but rather became more marked in later writers such as Seneca and Marcus Aurelius. Our limits however do not permit us to speak of more than his immediate pupil Posidonius the Syrian, a man of great and varied learning, much esteemed by the Romans, many of whom attended his lectures at Rhodes. Among the number were Pompeius and Cicero, who calls him the greatest of the Stoics[1]. In regard to divination and the eternity of the world Posidonius went back to the old Stoic view, but in his unsectarian tone he is a faithful follower of Panaetius. He endeavoured to show that the opposition between the different systems of philosophy, far from justifying the sceptical conclusion, was not inconsistent with a real harmony upon the most important points. In regard to psychology his views were more in accordance with Plato and Aristotle than with Chrysippus. Finding it impossible to explain the passions as morbid conditions of the reason, he fell back on the old division into the rational and irrational parts of the soul, and was followed in this by the later Stoics.

[1] *Hortens. Frag.* 36 (Orelli); so Seneca *Ep.* XC. 20 *Posidonius, ut mea fert opinio, ex his qui plurimum philosophiae contulerunt.*

Among the Roman contemporaries of Cicero we need only mention Cato, as typical both of the weakness and the strength of the school, which in after years beheld in him the truest pattern of the sage, standing on the same level with Hercules or Ulysses[1]. Yet for him, as for all these later Stoics, it was Plato rather than Zeno, or at any rate not less than Zeno, who was the *deus philosophorum*, the fountain of inspiration to the Porch as much as to the Academy, of which we have next to speak[2].

Philo of Larissa, the disciple and successor of Clitomachus, took refuge in Rome during the Mithridatic war (B.C. 88) and lectured there with great applause. While maintaining the position of Carneades against the Stoics, he declared that it was a mistake to suppose that the Academy denied the possibility of arriving at truth. Concealed underneath their negative polemic, the teaching of Plato had always survived as an esoteric doctrine; there was no ground therefore for the distinction between the New and Old Academy; they were really the same, though the exigencies of controversy had for a while tended to obscure the positive side of their teaching, and thus led to a change of name. It was true, as against the Stoics, that irresistible evidence could not be derived from sensible perception, but the soul itself contains clear ideas on which we may safely act[3].

The most important representative of Eclecticism is Antiochus of Ascalon, who studied under Mnesarchus, a scholar of Panaetius, as well as under Philo, whom he

---

[1] Seneca *De Const.* II. I.

[2] Cic. *N. D.* II. 32, *Ad Att.* IV. 16.

[3] This account of Philo is taken from Zeller III. I, pp. 588—596[3].

succeeded as head of the Academy. Cicero who attended his lectures at Athens 79 B. C. calls him the most polished and acute of the philosophers of his time, and professes that he had ever loved him[1]. Antiochus was not satisfied with reverting to Plato, as Philo had done; he declared that the so-called New Academy of Arcesilaus and Carneades had not simply allowed the Platonic doctrines to fall into the background, but had altogether departed from them; and the object which he set before himself was to show that scepticism was self-contradictory and impossible. If it is impossible to know what is true, it must be impossible to know what is like the truth: thus the natural instinct of curiosity is stultified, and action becomes irrational. How can the Sceptics themselves learn the certainty of their first principle *nil percipi?* how assert the falsehood of this or that proposition, while they maintain that it is impossible to distinguish between truth and falsehood? how pretend to arrive at truth by argument, while they deny the principle on which all argument is based? Like Posidonius, Antiochus affirmed the real agreement of the orthodox schools: the difference between Plato, Aristotle and Zeno was in the main a difference in the mode of expressing a common truth. Thus in regard to the theory of knowledge, all hold that sensation is the first element in knowledge, but that it is only by the exercise of reason that it is changed into knowledge. So in Physics, all are agreed that there are two natures, active and passive, force and matter, which are always found in combination[2]. Not to dwell on the vague and confused statements ascribed by Cicero to Antiochus under this head, I pass on to his ethical doctrines. Starting with the Stoic *prima naturae,*

---

[1] *Acad.* II. 113. 　　　　　　　　[2] *Acad.* I. 23.

but enlarging their scope so as to take in not only all that belongs to self-preservation, but the rudiments of virtue and knowledge also, and defining the *Summum Bonum* as a life in accordance with the perfect nature of man, Antiochus includes under this, not only the perfection of reason, but all bodily and external good. Virtue in itself suffices for happiness, as the Stoics said, but not for the highest happiness : here we must borrow a little from the Peripatetics ; though they err in allowing too much weight to external good, as the Stoics err in the opposite direction. The Stoics are right in their high estimate of the Sage as being alone free and rich and beautiful, all others being slaves and fools : they are right in esteeming apathy, the absolute suppression of emotion, as essential to virtue; but they have gone wrong in affirming the equality of sins.

It is difficult to form any clear systematic conception of Antiochus' teaching from the existing evidence ; if it was really as loose and inconsistent as it would seem from Zeller's account, it only adds greater significance to the fact that from that time forward the Academy entirely loses its old sceptical character. The spirit of the age must evidently have been working strongly in favour of eclecticism, when Antiochus became the most influential of teachers, and the Fifth Academy could count among its members such names as those of Varro and Brutus and to a certain extent even Cicero himself. We shall be able to understand this better, if we realize to ourselves the position of the small band of philosophical enthusiasts in Rome. They were conscious that their own lives had gained in largeness of view, in dignity and in strength, from the study of philosophy ; but all around them were the rude mass, the *hircosa gens centurionum* with their *quod sapio satis est mihi*, jeering at the endless disputes of the schools; and thus the natural instinct of self-preservation impelled them to strengthen themselves by the re-union of philosophy, just as in our own days the same motive may be seen in aspirations after the re-union of Christendom.

Before speaking in detail of the Romans, we must say a word as to the signs of eclecticism in the two remaining schools. It has been mentioned that the activity of the later Peripatetics was mainly of the commentatorial kind, but, in the spurious treatise *De Mundo*, which is included in the works of Aristotle, but was probably written in the middle of the 1st century B.C., we find a decided admixture of Stoic elements, especially where it treats of the action of the Deity on the world. Again, even among the Epicureans, in spite of their hostility to the other schools and their own proverbial conservatism, we have already noticed a departure from the teaching of their founder, in the writings of Philodemus and others, 1st as regards the greater importance attributed to art and science and literature[1], 2ndly in the recognition, to a greater or less extent, of a Divine government of the world[2], 3rdly in the abandonment of the old cynical repudiation of higher motives. Cicero tells us that this was especially the case in regard to the relation between bodily and mental pleasure, and to the selfish theory of friendship[3].

[1] See above, p. 184, n. 3.   [2] See above, p. 199, n. 2.

[3] Cic. *Fin.* I. 55 'there are many Epicureans who think erroneously that mental pleasure need not be dependent on bodily pleasure;' § 69 'there are some weak brethren among the Epicureans who are ashamed to confess that our own pleasure is the sole ground of friendship;' compare Hirzel *l. c.* p. 168 foll. and my note on *N. D.* I. 111.

The four last mentioned schools, *i.e.* the Academy, the Lyceum, the Porch and the Garden were, and had long been, the only recognized schools at the time when Cicero was growing up to manhood. Cicero was personally acquainted with the most distinguished living representatives of each. In his 19th year, B. C. 88, he had studied under Phaedrus the Epicurean and Philo the Academic at Rome; in his 28th year, B. C. 79, he attended the lectures of the Epicureans Phaedrus and Zeno, as well as of Antiochus, the eclectic Academic, at Athens, and in the following year those of Posidonius, the eclectic Stoic, at Rhodes. Diodotus the Stoic was for many years the honoured inmate of his house. He had also a high esteem for the Peripatetic Cratippus, whom he selected as the tutor for his son at, what we may call, the University of Athens. Nor did he only attend lectures: his letters show that he was a great reader of philosophical books, and he left behind him translations or adaptations of various dialogues and treatises of Plato, Aristotle, Theophrastus, Crantor, Carneades, Panaetius, Antiochus, Posidonius and others[1]. In a word he was

---

[1] He translated the *Oeconomicus* of Xenophon and the *Protagoras* and *Timaeus* of Plato, whom he also imitates in the *Leges* and *Respublica*. The last is in part borrowed from Aristotle's *Politics*. Other treatises in which he follows Aristotle are the *Hortensius*, probably written on the model of Aristotle's προτρεπτικός, and the *Topica*, professedly a reminiscence of Aristotle's treatise bearing the same name. The *Laelius* is said to be founded on the περὶ φιλίας of Theophrastus; the *Consolatio* was mainly taken from Crantor's περὶ πένθους; but the materials for the great majority of his books are derived from Panaetius, Posidonius, Clitomachus and Antiochus, when he is treating of the orthodox schools, and probably from Zeno, Phaedrus or Philodemus, where he gives the Epicurean doctrines.

confessed to be by far the most accomplished of the philosophical amateurs of his time.

As to the nature of his own views, we shall be better able to form a judgment, if we look first at the man and his position. Cicero was much more of a modern Italian than of an ancient Roman. A *novus homo*, sprung from the Volscian *municipium* of Arpinum, he had none of that proud, self-centred hardness and toughness of character which marked the Senator of Rome. Nature had gifted him with the sensitive, idealistic temperament of the artist and the orator, and this had been trained to its highest pitch by the excellent education he had received. If he had been less open to ideas, less many-sided, less sympathetic, less conscientious, in a word, if he had been less human, he would have been a worse man, he would have exercised a less potent influence on the future of Western civilization, but he would have been a stronger and more consistent politician, more respected no doubt by the blood-and-iron school of his own day, as of ours. While his imagination pictured to him the glories of old Rome and inflamed him with the ambition of himself acting a Roman part, as in the matter of Catiline, and in his judgment of Caesar, and while therefore he on the whole espoused the cause of the Senate, as representing the historic greatness of Rome, yet he is never fully convinced in his own mind, never satisfied either with himself or with the party or the persons with whom he is most closely allied.

And this indecision of his political views is reflected in his philosophy. Epicureanism indeed he condemns, as heartily as he condemns Clodius or Antony: its want of idealism, its prosaic regard for matter of fact, or rather its exclusive regard for the lower fact to the neglect of the higher, its aversion to public life, above all, perhaps, its contempt for literature, as such, were odious in his eyes. But neither is its rival quite to his taste. While attracted by the lofty tone of its moral and religious teaching, he is repelled by its dogmatism, its extravagance and its technicalities. Of the two remaining schools, the Peripatetic had forgotten the more distinctive portion of the teaching of its founder, until his writings were re-edited by Andronicus of Rhodes (who strangely enough is never mentioned by Cicero, though he must have been lecturing about the time of his consulship), and it had dwindled accordingly into a colourless doctrine of common sense, of which Cicero speaks with respect, indeed, but without enthusiasm. The Academy on the other hand was endeared to him as being lineally descended from Plato, for whose sublime idealism and consummate beauty of style he cherished an admiration little short of idolatry, and also as being the least dogmatic of systems, and the most helpful to the orator from the importance it attached to the use of negative dialectic.

In the *Academica* Cicero declares himself to be an adherent of the New Academy, as opposed to the reformed 'Old Academy' of Antiochus; but though he makes use of the ordinary sceptical arguments, he is scarcely more serious in his profession of agnosticism, than his professed pattern, the Platonic Socrates, is in his irony. All that he is anxious for is to defend himself from being tied down too definitely to any one system, and to protest against the overbearing dogmatism of the Stoics, or of such Old Academics as the strong-willed Brutus. He is fond of boasting of the freedom of his school, which permits him to advocate whatever doctrine takes his fancy at the time; and, like Dr Johnson, he refuses to be bound by any reference to previous inconsistent utterances[1]. He even tries to make out that the sceptical arguments of Carneades were only meant to rouse men from the slumber of thoughtless acquiescence, and to lead them to judge of the truth of doctrines by reason and not by authority[2]. Even in the *Academica*, the scepticism which he professes is hardly more than verbal. Let Antiochus consent to use the term *probare* instead of *percipere* or *assentiri*, let him adopt the courteous 'perhaps' (σχεδόν or ἴσως) of Aristotle, and there seems no reason why the discussion should continue any longer[3]. Cicero has himself no real doubt as to the trustworthiness of the evidence of the bodily senses; and, beyond this sensible evidence, he recognizes a higher source of knowledge in the mind itself. Accepting, as he does, the Platonic and Stoic doctrine of the divine origin of the soul, he believes that it has in itself the seeds of virtue and knowledge, which would grow up to maturity of themselves, if it were not for the corrupting influences of society. We may see the unsophisticated working of nature in children; we may hear the voice of nature in the general consent of mankind, in the judgment of the wise and good, and above all in the teaching of old tradition handed down from our ancestors . It is this natural

---

[1] *Tusc.* v. 33, *Off.* III. 20, *N. D.* I. 47.

[2] *N. D.* I. 4, 10.

[3] *Acad.* II. 99, 112, *Fin.* v. 76.

[4] *Tusc.* III. 2 *sunt enim ingeniis nostris semina innata virtutum; quae si adolescere liceret, ipsa nos ad beatam vitam natura perduceret;*

revelation (*naturae lumen*) which shows us the excellency of virtue, the dignity and freedom of man, and the existence of a Divine Being[1].

But though nature gives us light, so far as is needed for action and for life, it does not satisfy our curiosity on speculative matters : it does not tell us, for instance, what is the form or the abode of the Deity, or whether the soul is material or immaterial[2]. Cicero however believes, in common with all but the Epicureans, that God is eternal, all-wise, all-powerful and all-good ; he believes with Plato and the Stoics that the world was formed and is providentially governed by Him for the good of man ; he believes, in accordance with Plato but in opposition to the Stoics, that God is pure Spirit[3]; and he thinks that

Fin. V. 59 (*natura homini*) *dedit talem mentem quae omnem virtutem accipere posset, ingenuitque sine doctrina notitias parvas rerum maximarum et quasi instituit docere et induxit in ea quae inerant tanquam elementa virtutis ;* ib. V. 61 *indicant pueri, in quibus, ut in speculis, natura cernitur ; Leg.* I. 24 *animum esse ingeneratum a deo...ex quo efficitur illud, ut is agnoscat deum, qui unde ortus sit quasi recordetur ac noscat ; Tusc.* I. 35 *omnium consensus naturae vox est; ib.* I. 65, 70, V. 70, *Consol.* fr. 6, *De Fato* 23 foll., *Tusc.* IV. 65, 79.

[1] *Tusc.* I. 27, 30, 66, *Rep.* VI. 13, *Leg.* I. 59 *qui se ipse norit, primum aliquid se habere sentiet divinum, ingeniumque in se suum sicut simulacrum aliquod dicatum putabit, tantoque munere deorum semper dignum aliquid et faciet et sentiet ei intelliget quem ad modum a natura subornatus in vitam venerit, quantaque instrumenta habeat ad obtinendam adipiscendamque sapientiam, quoniam principio rerum omnium quasi adumbratas intellegentias animo ac mente conceperit, quibus illustratis sapientia duce bonum virum et ob eam ipsam causam cernat se beatum fore.*

[2] *Tusc.* I. 70, *N. D.* I. 60.

[3] *Tusc.* I. 66 *nec vero deus ipse qui intellegitur a nobis alio modo intellegi potest, nisi mens soluta quaedam et libera, segregata ab omni concretione mortali, omnia sentiens et movens ipsaque praedita motu*

the same is true also of the soul, which is an emanation
from Him and which, 'as we have been taught by
our ancestors, and as Plato and Xenophon have shown
by many excellent arguments,' is destined to enjoy
a blissful immortality in the case of the wise and good[1].
Perhaps that which has most weight with Cicero is
the practical consideration, 'if we give up our faith in an
over-ruling Providence, we cannot hope to retain any
genuine piety or religion; and if these go, justice and
faith and all that binds together human society, must go
too[2].' He is also fully convinced that reverence is due
to what is old and long established, and that it is the
duty of a good citizen to conform to the established
church, to accept the tenets of the national religion and
observe its customs, except so far as they might be inconsistent with the plain rules of morality, or so flagrantly
opposed to reason as to come under the head of superstition. Thus, while he is himself a disbeliever in divination, and argues convincingly against it in his book on the
subject, yet, as a statesman, he approves the punishment
of certain consuls who had disregarded the auspices.
'They ought,' he says, 'to have submitted to the rule of
the established religion.'[3] He cannot approve of the in-

sempiterno; Rep. VI. 26 foll. Yet he does not altogether deny the
possibility of the Stoic view, that God is of a fiery or ethereal
nature, *Tusc.* I. 65.

[1] *Tusc.* I. 70, *Lael.* 13, *Cato* 77 foll.

[2] See *N. D.* I. 4 with the passages cited in my note, II. 153, *Leg.*
II. 16.

[3] *Divin.* II. 71 *parendum fuit religioni, nec patrius mos tam
contumaciter repudiandus,* and just before, *retinetur et ad opinionem
vulgi et ad magnas utilitates reipublicae mos, religio, disciplina, jus,
augurium, collegii auctoritas.*

genious defence of divination by the Stoics, any more than he does of their elastic allegorical method, which might be stretched to cover the worst absurdities of mythology. Religion is to be upheld, in so far as it is in accordance with the teaching of nature; but superstition is to be torn up by the root. Unfortunately Cicero gives no precise definition of the latter opprobrious word, nor does he distinctly say how the existing religion is to be cleared of its superstitious elements.

In regard to ethics Cicero openly disclaims the negative view of Carneades[1], and only wavers between a more or less thorough acceptance of the Stoic doctrine. In general, it may be said that he has a higher admiration for the Stoic system of ethics and theology than he has for any other. Thus he calls it the most generous and masculine of systems, and is even inclined to deny the name of philosopher to all but the Stoics[2]. He defends their famous paradoxes as being absolutely true and genuinely Socratic[3], and finds fault with Antiochus and the Peripatetics for hesitating to admit that the wise man will retain his happiness in the bull of Phalaris[4]. Similarly he blames the latter for justifying a moderate indulgence of the various emotions instead of eradicating

---

[1] *Leg.* I. 39 *perturbatricem harum omnium rerum Academiam, hanc ab Arcesila et Carneade recentem exoremus, ut sileat; nam si invaserit in haec quae satis scite nobis instructa et composita videntur, nimias edet ruinas.*

[2] *Tusc.* III. 22, IV. 53.

[3] *Paradoxa* § 4 *mihi ista* παράδοξα *maxime videntur esse Socratica longeque verissima, Acad.* II. 135. Arguing as a Peripatetic in the *De Finibus* IV. 74, Cicero takes the opposite side.

[4] *Tusc.* V. 75.

them altogether[1]. At the same time he confesses that Stoicism is hardly adapted for this work-a-day world; it would be more in place in Plato's Utopia[2]; when it is attempted to apply it to practice, common sense speedily reduces it to something not very different from the Academy or the Lyceum. Indeed we often find Cicero arguing that the difference is merely nominal, and that Zeno changed the terms, but not the doctrines of the original Socratic school of which these were offshoots[3].

I proceed to give a very brief survey of Cicero's philosophical works, all composed, with the exception of the *De Oratore*, the *De Republica* and *De Legibus*, within the last two years of his life. His object in writing them was to give his countrymen a general view of Greek philosophy, particularly of its practical side; and he claimed that in doing this he was labouring for the good of his country no less than, when he had been most active as a speaker in the Senate-House and the Forum[4].

---

[1] *Tusc.* IV. 38, *mollis et enervata putanda est Peripateticorum ratio et oratio, qui perturbari animos necesse dicunt esse, sed adhibent modum quendam, quem ultra progredi non oporteat. Modum tu adhibes vitio?* and § 42 *nihil interest utrum moderatas perturbationes approbent an moderatam injustitiam &c;* compare III. 22 and *Off.* I. 89. On the other hand in the *Academica* II. 135, where Cicero represents the New Academy, he defends, though in a somewhat perfunctory way, the moderate use of the emotions.

[2] *Fin.* IV. 21, *Tusc.* V. 3, *ad Att.* II. 1.

[3] *Fin.* V. 22, *restant Stoici, qui cum a Peripateticis et Academicis omnia transtulissent, nominibus aliis easdem res secuti sunt, Leg.* I. 54, 55.

[4] *N. D.* I. 7 foll. with my notes, *Divin.* II. 1, *quaerenti mihi multumque et diu cogitanti quanam re possem prodesse quam plurimis, ne quando intermitterem consulere rei publicae, nulla major occurrebat quam si optimarum artium vias traderem meis civibus.*

The earliest of this later group was the *Hortensius*, written in 46 B.C., but now lost. This was followed by several oratorical treatises. The *De Consolatione*, also lost, was written on the death of his daughter in 45. Then came the *Academica*, of which only a portion has come down to us. In this, as has been already mentioned, Cicero defends the doctrine of Probability, as enunciated by Philo, which may be regarded as a softened form of the scepticism of Carneades, against the 'Certitude' of Antiochus, the champion of the Eclectics. The *Academica* would be reckoned with the *Topica* and the rhetorical treatises, as coming under the head of Logic[1]. Under the head of Ethics we have (1) the *De Finibus*[2], a treatise on the *Summum Bonum*. In the 1st book the Epicurean doctrine is expounded by Torquatus; in the 2nd it is controverted with Stoic arguments by Cicero; the 3rd book contains an account of the Stoic doctrine by Cato, to whom Cicero replies with an argument taken from Antiochus in the 4th book, in which he endeavours to show, first, that all that is of value in Zeno's teaching is really Socratic, being derived from his master Polemo, and secondly, that the innovations of Zeno, where they are not confined to the use of an unnatural and paradoxical terminology, involve a contradiction between the *prima naturae* with which he starts, and his final conclusion that virtue is the only good; in the 5th book the doctrine of Antiochus himself—it will be remembered that this is an amalgam of the three anti-Epicurean systems—is expounded by the Peripatetic Piso.

[1] *Divin.* II. 4, *Acad.* I. 32.

[2] On the plural, see Madvig's ed. *Praef.* p. lxi n. It is uncertain who introduced the idea of a *Summum Malum* to correspond with the *Summum Bonum*.

After dealing with the theory of morals in the *De Finibus*, Cicero goes on to treat of practical morality in the *De Officiis* (2) addressed to his son, then studying under Cratippus at Athens. In a work intended for direct instruction, Cicero abandons the form of dialogue, which he was accustomed to employ in order to exhibit the views of others without necessarily indicating his own; and lays down in plain terms the principles and rules which he held to be of most importance for the guidance of conduct. It is therefore significant that here, where he is speaking in his own person and not acting a character in a dialogue, he shows himself most distinctively Stoic in doctrine[1], though he still only claims to be giving utterance to probabilities not to certainties[2]. The treatise is further of special interest as being the earliest we possess on Duty, and on that conflict between different kinds of Duty or between Duty and Expediency, which forms the subject of Casuistry. In the 1st book Cicero treats of the *honestum* (τὸ καλόν) subdividing it into the four cardinal virtues, and gives directions for action in cases where one duty seems to conflict with another. In the 2nd he does the same for the *utile* (τὸ ὠφελιμόν). Up to this point he had been able to make use of the περὶ καθήκοντος of Panaetius as his guide; but in the 3rd book he broaches a question to which Panaetius had given no answer, viz. how we are to act, when the *honestum* conflicts with the *utile*. For this he finds his authorities in Posidonius and Hecato, and shows, with abundant illustrations from Roman history, that there can be no real expediency apart from duty.

[1] See Holden's Introduction pp. xxxiv foll.   [2] *Off.* II. 7.

In the *Tusculanae Disputationes* (3) Cicero discusses at length particular questions of practical philosophy. Though the form of dialogue is preserved, there is no pretence of real disputation; Cicero simply gives his opinion on the points on which it is solicited by the anonymous questioner, and shows why he has adopted it in preference to others. Here too he is distinctly Stoic, except on the single question of Immortality, where he prefers to share the error of Plato, if it be an error, rather than assent to the depressing doctrines of the other schools. The general subject is to prove that man has in his own power all that is necessary for happiness, and to teach us how to guard against the usual causes of unhappiness. Thus in the 1st book we are armed against the fear of death, in the 2nd against pain, in the 3rd against sorrow, in the 4th against all other passions, while the 5th shows the sufficiency of virtue in itself for happiness, independently of all that is circumstantial and external.

In addition to these larger works we possess the following ethical tracts by Cicero, the *Cato Major* or *De Senectute* (4), showing how to spend old age happily; a good deal of this is borrowed from Plato and Xenophon; the *Laelius* or *De Amicitia* (5), on the benefits and duties of friendship, chiefly taken from the treatise by Theophrastus on the same subject, but with additions from Plato and Xenophon; there is nothing sectarian in the tone of either of these. The *Paradoxa* (6) is a defence of the Stoic paradoxes, viz. that the *honestum* is the only good, that virtue is sufficient for happiness, that good and evil admit of no degrees, that every fool is mad, that the wise man alone is free, that the wise man alone is rich. In his dedication Cicero tells Brutus that he has composed this for his amusement, but there is no reason for speaking of it as a mere *jeu d'esprit*[1]. He writes in a tone of conviction, and most of the propositions which he maintains here, if attacked, are also defended, by him in other passages.

Under the same head of Ethics we should arrange the political treatises, *De Republica* (7) and *De Legibus* (8). The former, of which about one third is still extant, was composed in six books, on the best form of government and the grounds of national prosperity. The writers chiefly followed are Plato, Aristotle, Theophrastus and Polybius; but, both in this and in the treatise on Law, Cicero is more independent than he is in discussing questions of a more strictly philosophic character. The book ends, like the Republic of Plato, with an account of the rewards awaiting the righteous in a future life: it is noticeable however that, in the 'Dream of Scipio,' the highest rewards are reserved for the patriotic statesman, and that no mention is made of the punishments of the guilty, which fill so large a space in the story of Er.

In imitation of Plato, Cicero followed up his treatise on the State by one on the Laws. There seems good reason for believing that the *De Legibus* was never completed. We only possess three books, but Macrobius quotes from a fifth book, and the latest editor conjectures that eight books were contemplated by the author[2]. The work is in the form of a monologue by Cicero, inter-

---

[1] As is done by the writer of the article on Cicero in Smith's *Dictionary of Biography.*

[2] See editions by Du Meslin pp. 5, 6, and Bake pp. xv foll.

spersed with a few remarks from his brother Quintus and Atticus. The 1st book, on the origin and nature of Justice and Law, is taken from Stoic sources; the 2nd, on the laws relating to Religion, and the 3rd, on the powers and duties of Magistrates, though modelled after Plato's Νόμοι, as far as their form goes, derive their contents mainly from the institutions of Rome, as idealized by Cicero. Besides Plato and the Stoics, Cicero mentions particularly Theophrastus and other Peripatetics, as authorities on the subject of which he treats. He distinctly abjures the New Academy of Arcesilaus and Carneades, and upholds the Antiochian view of the fundamental agreement of the Socratic, i.e. of the anti-Epicurean schools.

The third great division of philosophy is Physics. Under this head would come the *De Natura Deorum* (1) *De Divinatione* (2) and the fragmentary *De Fato* (3) and *Timaeus* (4). The first is composed much on the same principle as the *De Finibus*. It begins with an exposition of the Epicurean view, which is then controverted with Stoic arguments by Cotta representing the New Academy. In the 2nd book Balbus expounds the Stoic view, which again is severely criticized in the 3rd and final book by Cotta, who thus seems to remain in possession of the field[1]. And as Cicero, in the introductory chapters, avows himself a disciple of the Agnostic school of Arcesilaus and Carneades[2], we might be tempted

[1] On the question whether the Epicurean argument is taken from Zeno or Philodemus or Phaedrus, see my edition pp. xlii to liv. The opposite argument is in all probability taken from Posidonius, who is also the authority used in the 2nd book. The 3rd book is taken from Clitomachus.

[2] *N. D.* I. 11 and 17.

to say that the conclusion arrived at must represent his own view. That this however was not the case is apparent from the assertion repeated in two passages, that, for his own part, he regarded the view of Balbus as more probable than that of Cotta[1]. Nor does there seem any reason to suppose that this is said merely as a salve to popular prejudice. He had begun the discussion by laying down that the existence of a Divine Being was highly probable, and that we were by nature drawn to believe in it; that the denial of a superintending Providence must lead to the overthrow of all that binds together society; and that the object of Carneades was, not to make men unbelievers, but to stimulate thought by stating the arguments on both sides with clearness and fairness, and then leaving his hearers to make up their minds for themselves[2].

In the *De Divinatione* Quintus Cicero gives the Stoic argument, probably taken from Posidonius, for the truth of Divination in the first book; Marcus replies with unusual earnestness in the 2nd book, proving after Clitomachus and Panaetius that all Divination is deceptive and superstitious. Of the *De Fato* and *Timaeus* only fragments are extant. In the former Cicero reproduces for the benefit of his pupil Hirtius, the consul elect, the subtle arguments by which Carneades endeavoured to disprove the Stoic doctrine of Necessity. The latter is a paraphrase of a portion of the Timaeus of Plato, intended apparently to have been inserted in a dialogue on the origin of the Universe, in which Nigidius the Pythagorean would have appeared as one of the interlocu-

---

[1] *N. D.* III. 95, *Divin.* I. 8.
[2] *N. D.* I. 2, 3, 4, 13, *Divin.* I. 8.

tors. Probably the design was cut short by the author's death[1].

Having thus briefly analysed the philosophical writings of Cicero, it remains for us to endeavour to form some estimate of their value to readers of the present day. There can be no doubt that on their first appearance they supplied to the Romans all that Cicero had promised, a philosophical vocabulary of their own, together with an agreeable introduction to the study of Greek philosophy. But it is a different question how far they are of value to those who can read for themselves the actual works of the greatest of the Greeks. We may consider this question from two points of view, according as we regard Cicero as being himself a philosopher or as merely supplying materials to the historian of philosophy. It is in the latter point of view undoubtedly that he is of most importance to us now. Yet, if we divide Greek philosophy into three periods, that of its youth, its maturity, its old age, it cannot be said that we gain much from Cicero for the knowledge of the two earlier periods. He had probably not read for himself a single treatise by any pre-Socratic philosopher[2]; and the occasional second-hand references to them, which occur in his works, convey very little information beyond what is known from other sources[3]. Sometimes also they are full of mistakes; as we

---

[1] See K. F. Hermann *De Interpretatione Timaei*. Göttingen 1842.

[2] Perhaps an exception should be made in the case of Democritus whom he repeatedly praises for his style, see *De Oratore* I. 49, *Orator* 67, *Divin.* II. 133.

[3] That the references are second-hand is shown in a crucial instance by a comparison between the περὶ εὐσεβείας of Philodemus and the Epicurean sketch of early philosophers contained in the first book of the *De Natura Deorum*. See my notes on §§ 25—41.

find to be the case in the Epicurean sketch of the early philosophers contained in the 1st book of *De Natura Deorum*.
No doubt it may be said that Cicero was not bound to
correct all the errors of his Epicurean authority, that he
might in fact have intentionally introduced them as
characteristic of the school; but in any case he was
hardly justified in adding to them, as he has done; and
if he had had any familiar knowledge of the philosophers
mentioned, it seems scarcely likely that he would have
lost the opportunity of pointing out these errors in the
speech of Cotta which follows[1].

He had considerably more acquaintance with the
writers of the 2nd period. He had translated portions
of Plato and Xenophon and had probably read the
greater part of their works. But when we talk of
'reading,' we must remember who and what the
reader was. He was an extremely busy man, a
leading statesman, the most popular of orators, a con-
noisseur and virtuoso, fond of society and evidently
much sought after for his social qualities, and besides all
this he was an unwearied correspondent. Under these
circumstances it was plainly impossible for him to devote
to Plato and Aristotle that patient and continuous study
which alone could have enabled him thoroughly to understand their teaching. Even if he had had leisure for
this, it may be questioned whether there is not something
in the temperament of the orator which is inconsistent
with a profound study of philosophy. The aim of the
philosopher is an ever closer approach to perfect truth;
the aim of the orator is to persuade the multitude to
adopt a certain course of action. While the philosopher

[1] See my edition with the notes on §§ 25—29.

is always on the watch for difficulties or exceptions, which
may lead to an extension or modification of his theory;
the orator prefers to select topics which admit of broad
and simple statements and are calculated to excite
emotion both in himself and his audience. So with
Cicero: perhaps no man was ever more sensitive to the
loftiness and beauty of Plato's idealism; but he had
neither leisure nor taste for a prolonged piece of close
technical argumentation, such as we find in the *Parmenides* or in Aristotle's metaphysical works. Nor
again did he ever take the pains to trace out the inner
connexion of a philosophical system, so as to see its
several parts combined into a consistent whole. In
spite therefore of his delight in Plato, he has not, as far
as I am aware, contributed anything to our present
understanding of Plato, very little even to our knowledge
of Plato's surroundings, which we should not have learnt
from other sources. On the contrary any reader who
derived his notion of Plato's, and still more of Aristotle's
system, exclusively from Cicero, would undoubtedly form
a very erroneous notion of what Plato and Aristotle really
were. Notwithstanding his protest against the theoretical
positiveness of Antiochus, Cicero seems to have had no
scruple in accepting his utterly uncritical view of the
previous history of philosophy. He usually speaks of
Aristotle and Plato as if their differences were scarcely
more than those of style and manner of expression, and
attributes to them doctrines which belong to later
schools, such as the triple division of philosophy, and
even the Stoic cosmopolitanism and humanitarianism,
the distinction between perfect and imperfect duties, and
the definition of the *summum bonum* as a life in accor-

dance with nature[1]. It is a little remarkable that though Cicero knew much less of Aristotle than he did of Plato, yet he has really added to our knowledge of the former by preserving to us some interesting fragments of his lost dialogues[2].

But it is in the 3rd or post-Aristotelian period that Cicero becomes an authority of first-rate importance. The original writers for this period have all disappeared, leaving only a few fragments behind them; but their best thoughts still survive in a nobler form in the pages of Cicero. Even here, it may be doubted whether Cicero himself had read several of the earlier treatises, such as those of Zeno and Cleanthes, to which we find references in his works. But these post-Aristotelian schools were still flourishing when he wrote: he had heard their doctrines discussed by living expositors; he was personally acquainted with the authors of the most popular manuals, and he was himself a sincere believer in that common basis of practical philosophy to which all were more or less rapidly gravitating, in proportion as they were influenced by the eclectic spirit of their age.

We may therefore in the main accept Cicero as a

---

[1] See *Acad.* I. 19 foll. with Reid's notes. Though Antiochus is responsible for much of Cicero's inaccuracy, yet the latter's translation of the *Timaeus* shows that it was possible for him occasionally to go wrong through misinterpretation of the Greek, see Gedike *Ciceronis historia philosophiae antiquae* pp. 164, 171 foll. and K. F. Hermann *De Interpretatione Timaei*. Again he often loses the point of an argument through carelessness and over-haste, see the notes on the *N. D.* I. 25 *si di possunt &c.* § 26 *Anaximenes*, § 31 *Xenophon*, § 33 *replicatione*, and especially § 87 *quid? solus &c.* also Madvig's note and *excursus* on *Fin.* II. 34.

[2] See the quotation given above, p. 142.

trustworthy witness of the doctrines taught in the schools of his time; and, if we make allowance for the growth of eclecticism, we may further accept these as representing fairly the views of the same schools during the earlier part of this period, except where they have been confused by the harmonizing treatment of Antiochus. One instance of this confusion has been already noticed, where Cicero identifies the Stoic *prima naturae* i.e. the objects of the instinctive, prae-moral impulses of childhood, with the *prima constitutio*, the rudimentary constitution of Antiochus, involving the seeds of all virtues, and makes this a part of the *Summum Bonum*, a dogma which he also ascribes to Aristotle and the early Academics[1]. But the larger part of Cicero's philosophical works is, as he modestly confesses, merely paraphrased from the Greek[2]; and when he is reproducing a treatise of Panaetius or Posidonius or Clitomachus or the Epicurean Zeno, we are tolerably safe from the disturbing influence of Antiochus. And I venture to think there are few remains of antiquity which are more worthy the attention of one who is interested in the development of human thought in its relation to the highest subjects, than the treatise of Panaetius on Duty, and the arguments and counter-arguments of Posidonius and Clitomachus on Natural Theology and Divination, preserved to us in the *De Natura Deorum* and *De Divinatione*; or perhaps, above all, than the exposition of the Stoic conception of Law in the 1st book of the *De Legibus*. Yet even in these we have to pay something for the beautiful form

---

[1] See Madvig *Excursus* IV. on the *De Finibus*.

[2] *Ad Att.* XII. 52 ἀπόγραφα *sunt; minore labore fiunt; verba tantum affero, quibus abundo.*

which Cicero has given to the clumsy Greek of the
1st century B.C. The argument has not always been
understood; the connexion is often broken; sometimes
different treatises will have been somewhat carelessly
pieced together; scarcely ever do we find a rounded
whole dominated by a single conception with all the parts
in due subordination and harmony.

It remains still to ask what Cicero himself has contributed to philosophy, independently of translations and
paraphrases in which he has embalmed for us the
thoughts of others. And the first thing to be said is, that
he has not only given a new form, but he has breathed a
new spirit into the dry bones of this later philosophy.
The same wide experience of practical life which made
him indifferent to subtle distinctions of thought, brought
its compensation by enabling him to give life and reality
to the bare abstractions of the schools. We feel that he
is animated by a genuine enthusiasm when, amid the
furious party-strife and the self-seeking lawlessness which
marked the close of the Republic, he comes forward to
preach of that supreme Law by which all Nature is
governed, and which is written in the heart and conscience
of each individual of our race, thus forming a common
bond of brotherhood, which knits all mankind together
and engages those who own that bond to love each other
as they love themselves[1]. Whether he was actually the
first to give prominence to this conception of an original
revelation written on the heart of man, is not absolutely
certain: he is at any rate the first writer in whom we find
it distinctly expressed. Even Plato only spoke of our
having beheld the ideas in a previous state of existence;

[1] *Leg.* I. 28 foll., *N. D.* I. 121.

Cicero supposes them to be implanted in us at our birth, and to grow with our growth, when they are not blighted by ungenial influences[1]. Another characteristic which adds a charm to the works of Cicero is his fondness for tracing in the ancient worthies of Rome the unconscious operation of those principles of generosity and fairness, which had been brought out into the distinct light of consciousness by Plato and the Stoics. Thus his moral treatises, even when they are most defective in logical arrangement, form a treasure-house in which the best sayings and doings of the best men of antiquity are set forth in the noblest language for the delight and instruction of posterity. However it may please some writers of our time to vaunt their ingratitude to Cicero, it cannot be denied that to none of those great writers and thinkers, who 'like runners in the torch-race have passed from hand to hand the light of civilisation,' is the world more indebted than it is to him; that it was he who first made the thoughts of the mighty masters of old the common property of mankind; that he, beyond all others, raised the general standard of sentiment and morality in his own age; and that his writings kept alive through the Dark Ages, to be rekindled with a fresh glow in the Humanists of the Renaissance, the recollection of a glorious past, and a tradition of sound thinking and judging unfettered by the terrors of church authority.

---

[1] See *Fin.* v. 59 (*natura homini*) *dedit talem mentem, quae omnem virtutem accipere posset, ingenuitque sine doctrina notitias parvas rerum maximarum, et quasi instituit docere et induxit in ea quae inerant tanquam elementa virtutis. Sed virtutem ipsam inchoavit, nihil amplius;* also *Leg.* I. 33, *Tusc.* III. 2 quoted by Zeller p. 659.

M. Terentius Varro, the most learned and most voluminous of Roman writers was born B.C. 116. He took an active part in public affairs and served under Pompeius in the Civil War. After the battle of Pharsalia he submitted to Cæsar, who employed him to superintend the collection and arrangement of books for a public library. He escaped from the proscription under the second triumvirate, and continued his literary labours without interruption till his death in B.C. 28. In philosophy he followed his master, Antiochus, with perhaps even a more decided leaning to Stoicism. Thus he holds that that which distinguishes the different schools is their view as to the *Summum Bonum*, on which he reckoned up 288 possible theories. He himself makes it consist in virtue combined with the *prima naturae*, which he identifies with the lower 'goods' (external and corporeal) of the Peripatetics. Probability is not sufficient for the guidance of life: a man cannot act resolutely unless he has full conviction. His religious opinions have been already referred to: the supreme God is the soul of the world, whose varied manifestations constitute the deities of the common worship, some belong to the higher spheres, others, such as the heroes and demigods, to the sublunary sphere: in man the Divine Spirit manifests himself as the genius or soul, which Varro identified with the warm breath which pervades and vivifies the body.

Another contemporary of Cicero is of interest to us as the first sign of a revival which was to be of increasing importance in the following age, I mean Nigidius Figulus, the restorer of the extinct philosophy of Pytha-

goras[1]. With him we may connect the short-lived school
of the Sextii, in which Seneca received his philosophical
training. The founder Q. Sextius was born B.C. 70.
He combined certain Pythagorean elements with Stoicism.
Thus he held that the soul was incorporeal, and urged
on his pupils abstinence from meat, and the practice of
daily self-examination. He spoke of man's life as a
continuous struggle against folly, and said that constant
vigilance is needed if we would contend victoriously
against the foes by whom we are surrounded. A saying
of his disciple Fabianus may be noted here as prophetic
of the new spirit of the coming age: 'Reason is not
sufficient to overcome passion: we must take to us the
power of a noble enthusiasm[2].'

[1] So Cicero calls him in the introduction to his translation of the
Timaeus, *sic judico post illos nobiles Pythagoreos, quorum disciplina
extincta est quodammodo, hunc exstitisse qui illam renovaret.*

[2] See passages cited in R. and P. §§ 469—472, and Zeller p. 680
foll. The last quotation is from Seneca *De Brevit.* x. *contra affectus
impetu, non subtilitate pugnandum, nec minutis vulneribus, sed
incursu avertendam aciem.*

WE have thus reached the limit which I proposed for my sketch of Ancient Philosophy. We have watched the growth of philosophy from the small seed, possibly a single Homeric line[1], dropped in the fruitful soil of Miletus, to the mighty tree overshadowing the earth, whose branches we distinguish by such names as Socrates and Plato and Aristotle and Zeno. We have seen it throwing out offshoots in the shape of the various sciences, arithmetic, geometry, mechanics, astronomy, grammar, rhetoric, logic, and even zoology and botany. We have seen it withdrawing more and more from those vague speculations on the nature and origin of the universe, which first attracted the dawning intelligence of Greece, and concentrating its energies on the nature, the duty and the destiny of man. We have seen how it revolutionized men's thoughts in regard to religion, how, as early as the 6th century B.C.[2], it had risen to the conception of One eternal all-wise and all-righteous God, how it gradually came to see in Him the object, not of fear alone, but of reverence and trust and love; how sternly it denounced the follies and impurities of paganism, and taught men that the only acceptable worship was that

[1] *Il.* XIV. 201.
[2] See above on Xenophanes, p. 14.

which was offered in a spirit of purity and truth[1]. As to
men's relations towards each other, we have seen the
change from the old narrowing and dividing principle
'thou shalt love thy neighbour and hate thine enemy,' to
the recognition of the brotherhood which unites together
all nations and all conditions of men, all alike sharing
in one common humanity and being members of that
great body of which God Himself is the head and which
includes within it all rational existences whatsoever,
whether human, angelic or divine[2]. We have seen too
how the human consciousness was deepened and elevated
as well as widened by philosophy. Instead of the old
superficial conception of truth as that which is commonly
believed, the investigation of the grounds of belief led
many to doubt altogether of the possibility of the attainment of truth, and convinced all of their need of further
light to dispel the shadows which obscured the subjects
of highest and deepest interest. Happiness was no
longer the simple indulgence of the natural impulses.
The schools which began with the loudest profession of
eudaemonism ended by acknowledging that the mis-
fortune of the wise was better than the prosperity of the
fool[3], that if happiness was to be attained by man, it
could only be through imperturbability and self-mastery,
which would enable him to conquer pain and force
pleasure out of whatever circumstances; while we find

---

[1] Cic. *N. D.* II. 71 *cultus autem deorum est optimus idemque
castissimus atque sanctissimus plenissimusque pietatis, ut eos semper
pura integra incorrupta et mente et voce veneremur.*

[2] See above, p. 159 and compare Cic. *Fin.* III. 64.

[3] Diog. L. X. 135 κρεῖττον εὐλογίστως ἀτυχεῖν ἢ ἀλογίστως
εὐτυχεῖν.

writers of other schools maintaining that happiness is merely the accompaniment of virtuous energy, and can never be regarded as in itself constituting the end of action, or repudiating it altogether as something unworthy of our attention and likely to distract us from the one thing needful, or in fine despairing of its attainment in a world like this. Thus the life beyond the grave, that shadowy realm to which the Homeric Achilles preferred the meanest lot on earth, became to Plato and his followers the only real existence; death was the enfranchisement from the prison of the body[1], the harbour of rest from the storms of life[2], the re-union of long-parted friends[3], the admission into the society of the wise and good of former ages, the attainment of that perfect goodness and wisdom and beauty, which had been the yearning of the embodied spirit during the weary years of its mortal pilgrimage[4]. So also in regard to virtue. This was no longer limited to the performing well the duties of a citizen, obeying the laws of the State and fighting its battles. It was the inner righteousness of the soul, the fixed habit of subordinating the individual

---

[1] Cic. *Tusc.* I. 118 'if we are called to depart from this life,' *laeti et agentes gratias pareamus emittique nos e custodia et levari vinclis arbitremur, ut in aeternam et plane in nostram domum remigremus; Somn. Scip.* 14, 25.

[2] *Tusc.* I. 118 *profecto fuit quaedam vis quae generi consuleret humano, nec id gigneret aut aleret, quod, cum exanclavisset omnes labores, tum incideret in mortis malum sempiternum: portum potius paratum nobis et perfugium putemus.*

[3] Cic. *Cato* 84 *O praeclarum diem cum in illud divinum animorum concilium proficiscar,* foll., Plato *Phaedo* 63.

[4] Plat. *Phaed.* 67 πολλὴ ἂν ἀλογία εἴη, εἰ μὴ ἀσμένοι ἐκεῖσε ἴοιεν, οἱ ἀφικομένοις ἐλπίς ἐστιν οὗ διὰ βίου ἤρων τυχεῖν.

will to the Divine will, of acting not for private interest but for the good of all. And just as deeper thoughts about the nature of knowledge forced on men the conviction of their own ignorance, so deeper thoughts about virtue made men conscious of their own deficiency in virtue, and produced in them the new conviction of sin. The one conviction taught them their need of a revelation, the other conviction taught them their need of a purifying and sanctifying power[1]. And one step more philosophy could take : it chose out for its ideal of humanity, the Zeus-sprung son of Alcmena, whose life was spent in labours for the good of others, and who, after a death of agony on the burning pyre, was received up into heaven, thenceforth to be worshipped with divine honours by the gratitude of mankind[2].

---

[1] See above, p. 160 foll. The prevalence of this feeling of guilt and need of atonement is shown by the rapid growth of Jewish proselytism about the time of Augustus, by the new forms of ablution and sacrifice introduced in connexion with the worship of strange deities such as Isis, Serapis, Cybele, Bellona, especially the blood-bath, *taurobolium*, which came into vogue in the 2nd century A. D. Virgil in his Messianic eclogue makes the power of cleansing from sin one of the attributes of the new-born King.

[2] Cicero and the Stoics continually appeal to the example of Hercules, see *Off.* III. 25 'It is more in accordance with nature to undergo the greatest labours and pains in order to save or help mankind, as Hercules did, whom the gratitude of men has placed among the company of the immortals, than to live alone in the highest enjoyment,' also *Fin.* II. 118, III. 66, *Tusc.* I, 32 'That man is of the noblest character who believes himself born for the assistance, the preservation, the salvation, of his fellows. Hercules would never have ranked among the Gods, if he had not paved his own way to heaven, while still on earth,' Hor. *Od.* III. 3, 9, IV. 5, 35, 8, 29, *Epist.* II. I, 10.

Thus far the light of nature had carried men. Here, when it had reached its climax, in the fulness of time, as we believe, the light of revelation was vouchsafed, to confirm its hesitating utterances, to answer its questions, to supply its deficiencies, to manifest before the eyes of men the power of a new life in the Word made flesh. In Christianity we reach the true goal of the ethical and religious philosophy of the Ancients. Christ fulfilled the hopes and longings of the Stoic and the Platonist, as He fulfilled the law of Moses and the prophecies of Isaiah.

Here therefore, it seems to me, is the natural place to pause in our sketch of the development of ancient thought and see what was the highest attainment of the human mind, uninfluenced by Christianity. It is true there is one phase of that development, the mysticism of the Neo-Pythagorean and the Neo-Platonist schools, which we shall have to exclude, as it lies still in the future which we forbid ourselves to enter. But Neo-Platonism can, no more than Christianity, be regarded as a simple development of Hellenic or Western thought; it is a hybrid between East and West. Among its chief precursors we find the Alexandrian Jew Philo, born shortly after the death of Cicero, the object of whose teaching was to harmonize Judaism and Platonism, and Plutarch of Chaeronea, born about 50 A.D., who believed that a divine revelation was contained in the mysterious rites of Egypt no less than in the oracles of Delphi. The mixture of Orientalism is even more marked in the marvellous history of the Neo-Pythagorean Apollonius of Tyana, born about the time of the Christian era, which was afterwards utilized by the opponents of Christianity as a rival to the Gospel history. If then we are to

admit these into a history of Western philosophy, on
what principle are we to exclude genuine Greeks and
Romans who added to a training in the old systems
of philosophy, ideas borrowed, not from Judaism or
Zoroastrianism or the religion of Egypt, but from Christianity? For instance, on what grounds are we to
exclude Justin Martyr, himself a philosopher by profession, who tells us that he had tried every sect, and at
last found in Christianity what he had been vainly
seeking in them? or Pantaenus the Stoic, or his pupil
Clement of Alexandria, who saw in Christianity the
perfect wisdom which united all the broken lights which
had been divided in the several schools of the earlier
philosophy? Why admit Apuleius, and exclude his
fellow-countrymen Tertullian and Augustine, men not
only of far greater natural ability, but of keener philosophical interest, and probably even better acquainted
with the past history of philosophy? Why admit Plotinus
and exclude his fellow-disciple Origen? The difficulty is
increased when we remember the mutual influence of the
Pagan and Christian philosophy. While some of the
Pagan philosophers, such as Julian and Porphyry, owe
their significance mainly to the fact that they endeavoured
to remodel the old paganism into something which might
hold its own against the rising religion; on the other
hand many of the heresies were attempts to perpetuate
some special doctrine of pagan philosophy within the
pale of the Christian Church.

Or we may state the question in another way,
as follows: up to the date of the Christian era the
history of philosophy has been the history of thought
in its most general sense, whether materialistic or

idealistic, whether sceptical or religious. It includes the allegorical mythology of the Stoics and the mysticism of Pythagoras, no less than the logic of Aristotle and the physics of Epicurus. Why then, after this era, are we to confine our attention to a portion, and that the less important portion, of the mental activity of the time? Why are we to turn our eyes exclusively to the philosophy of the Decline, and refuse to see the new life which is springing up by its side? By so doing, we lose, as it seems to me, one of the most interesting and instructive of spectacles; we spoil our view of history, and do injustice to both sides, while we insist on keeping them separate from each other. It is a partial but, so far as it goes, a true account of Christianity that it is the meeting-point of Judaism and Hellenism. We get a very wrong impression of the early Christian writers, if we disregard the Hellenic element in them. We should be able to judge more fairly of many of the Fathers, if we regarded them as successors of the philosophers, especially of practical teachers such as Epictetus and Dio Chrysostom, instead of treating them as channels of a sort of supernatural tradition. Superstitious reverence for their supposed authority makes it impossible to appreciate their real greatness as men. I think therefore that, after the rise of Christianity, Christian and Pagan philosophy should be treated of together, until the time when the West was again separated from the East, and Western thought was crushed under the invasion of the barbarians.

To give an accurate picture of the religious thought of the first four centuries after Christ, (and all thought was then more or less religious), to exhibit it in its relation not only to the earlier philosophical ideas, but to the contemporary religious systems of Egypt and the East, is a work which still remains to be done, and one which would require a variety of the highest qualities for its adequate performance. I have been merely occupied here with the preliminary inquiry as to the manner in which the philosophy of Greece prepared the way for that great central epoch of all human history; to show how, in the words of Clement of Alexandria, 'philosophy was to the Greek, what the Law was to the Jew, the schoolmaster to bring him to Christ[1].' It has therefore been my endeavour, while tracing the general development of philosophy in accordance with the lines laid down by Zeller, to note particularly the interaction of religion and philosophy, and show how the early hostility gave place to sympathy, as out of the old corrupt religion the form of a purer religion gradually disclosed itself to the mind of the philosopher, and philosophy itself learnt from fuller experience to distrust its own power whether of attaining to absolute truth or of moulding the character to virtue.

[1] Clem. Al. *Strom.* I. 5 p. 122.

For EU product safety concerns, contact us at Calle de José Abascal, 56–1°, 28003 Madrid, Spain or eugpsr@cambridge.org.

www.ingramcontent.com/pod-product-compliance
Ingram Content Group UK Ltd.
Pitfield, Milton Keynes, MK11 3LW, UK
UKHW012328130625
459647UK00009B/148